CONTENTS

	PAGE
NOTES ON THE USE OF THIS BOOK	4
LOCOMOTIVE SHEDS AND SHED CODES	5
STEAM LOCOMOTIVES :	
Ex-G.W.R.	9
Ex-S.R.	37
Ex-L.M.S.	50
Ex-L.N.E.R.	83
B.R.	104
DIESEL LOCOMOTIVES	119
DIESEL MULTIPLE-UNITS	184
ELECTRIC LOCOMOTIVES	251
ELECTRIC MULTIPLE-UNITS	261
PRESERVED LOCOMOTIVES	312
PULLMAN CARS	318

NOTES ON THE USE OF THIS BOOK

THE following notes are a guide to the system of reference marks and other details given in the lists of dimensions shown for each class.

Many of the classes listed are sub-divided by reason of mechanical or constructional differences (on the Eastern and North Eastern Regions the sub-divisions are denoted in some cases by "Parts," shown thus: O4(1). At the head of each class will be found a list of such sub-divisions, if any, usually arranged in order of introduction. Each part is given there a reference mark by which its relevant dimensions, if differing from those of other parts, and the locomotives included in this sub-division, or part, may be identified. Any other differences between locomotives are also included, with reference marks, below the details of the class's introduction. The date on which the first locomotive of a class was built or modified is denoted by "Introduced."

The lists of dimensions at the head of each class show locomotives fitted with two inside cylinders, and slide valves, unless otherwise stated, e.g. (O) = two outside cylinders.

All engines of a class are superheated unless shown otherwise. "NS" indicates all locomotives unsuperheated; "SS" indicates some locomotives superheated.

The code shown in the headings to each class, e.g. "5MT," "7P6F," denotes the British Railways power classification.

S. denotes Service (Departmental) locomotive still carrying B.R. number. This reference letter is introduced only for the reader's guidance and is not borne by the locomotive concerned.

4

BRITISH RAILWAYS LOCOMOTIVE
SHEDS AND SHED CODES
AND PRINCIPAL SIGNING-ON POINTS

All B.R. steam locomotives carry the code of their home depot on a small plate affixed to the smokebox door.

Diesel and electric locomotives carry the plate on the cab side or have the depot name painted on the buffer beam.

LONDON MIDLAND REGION

LMW **Western A.C. Lines**

IA **Willesden**
IB Camden
IC Watford
ID Marylebone
IE Bletchley
IF Rugby
IG Woodford Halse
IH Northampton

2A **Tyseley**
    Stratford-on-Avon
2B Oxley (Wolverhampton)
2C Stourbridge
2D Banbury
2E Saltley
2F Bescot
2G Ryecroft (Walsall)
2H Monument Lane
2J Aston
2K Bushbury
2L Leamington Spa
2M Wellington
2P Kidderminster

5A **Crewe North**
5B Crewe South
5C Stafford
5D Stoke & Cockshute
5E Nuneaton
5F Uttoxeter

6A **Chester (Midland)**
6B Mold Junction
6C Croes Newydd
    Bala
    Penmaenpool
6D Shrewsbury
    Builth Road
6E Oswestry
    Llanidloes
    Moat Lane

6F Machynlleth
    Aberystwyth
    Aberystwyth (V. of R.)
    Portmadoc
    Pwllheli
6G Llandudno Junction
6H Bangor
6J Holyhead

8A **Edge Hill (Liverpool)**
8B Warrington (Dallam)
8C Speke Junction
8D Widnes
8E Northwich
8F Springs Branch (Wigan)
8G Sutton Oak
8H Birkenhead
8J Allerton
8K Bank Hall
8L Aintree
8M Southport

9A **Longsight (Manchester)**
9B Stockport (Edgeley)
9C Reddish
9D Newton Heath
9E Trafford Park
    Glazebrook
9F Heaton Mersey
    Gowhole
9G Gorton
    Dinting
    Guide Bridge
9H Patricroft
9J Agecroft
9K Bolton
9L Buxton
9M Bury

10A	**Carnforth**	15A	**Leicester (Midland)**
10B	Blackpool		Market Harborough
10C	Fleetwood	15B	Wellingborough
10D	Lostock Hall	15C	Kettering
10E	Accrington	15D	Leicester (Central)
10F	Rose Grove	15E	Coalville
10G	Skipton		
10H	Lower Darwen		
10J	Lancaster (Green Ayre)	16A	**Toton**
			(Stapleford & Sandiacre)
		16B	Annesley
12A	**Carlisle (Kingmoor)**	16C	Derby
12B	Carlisle (Upperby)		Cromford
12C	Barrow		Middleton
12D	Workington		Sheep Pasture
12E	Tebay	16D	Nottingham
		16E	Kirkby-in-Ashfield
		16F	Burton
14A	**Cricklewood East**		Overseal
14B	Cricklewood West	16G	Westhouses
14C	Bedford	16H	Hasland

EASTERN REGION

30A	**Stratford**	36A	**Doncaster**
30F	Parkeston	36C	Frodingham
		36E	Retford
31A	**Cambridge**		
	Ely	40A	**Lincoln**
31B	March	40B	Immingham
			Grimsby
32A	**Norwich (Thorpe)**		New Holland
	Cromer Beach	40E	Colwick
32B	Ipswich	40F	Boston
32C	Lowestoft Central		Sleaford
32D	Yarmouth South Town		
		41A	**Tinsley (Sheffield)**
33B	Tilbury	41B	Darnall (Sheffield)
33C	Shoeburyness	41C	Wath
		41D	Canklow
34B	Hornsey	41E	Staveley (Barrow Hill)
34D	Hitchin	41F	Mexborough
34E	New England	41H	Staveley (G.C.)
34G	Finsbury Park	41J	Langwith

NORTH EASTERN REGION

50A	**York**	51J	Northallerton
50B	Hull (Dairycoates)	51L	Thornaby
	Hull (Alexandra Dock)	52A	**Gateshead**
50C	Hull (Botanic Gardens)		Bowes Bridge
50D	Goole	52B	Heaton
		52C	Blaydon
			Alston
51A	**Darlington**	52D	Tweedmouth
51C	West Hartlepool		Alnmouth

52E	Percy Main	55F	Bradford (Manningham)
52F	North and South Blyth		Keighley
52G	Sunderland	55G	Huddersfield
52H	Tyne Dock	55H	Leeds (Neville Hill)
	Pelton Level		
52K	Consett	56A	**Wakefield**
			Knottingley
		56B	Ardsley
55A	**Leeds (Holbeck)**	56C	Copley Hill
55B	Stourton	56D	Mirfield
55C	Farnley	56E	Sowerby Bridge
55D	Royston	56F	Low Moor
55E	Normanton	56G	Bradford (Hammerton St.)

SCOTTISH REGION

60A	**Inverness (Lochgorm)**	64A	**St. Margarets (Edinburgh)**
	Dingwall		Dunbar
	Forres		Galashiels
	Kyle of Lochalsh		Granton
60B	Aviemore		Hardengreen
	Boat of Garten		Longniddry
60C	Helmsdale		North Berwick
	Tain		Seafield
60D	Wick		South Leith
	Thurso	64B	Haymarket
		64C	Dalry Road
		64F	Bathgate
61A	**Kittybrewster**	64G	Hawick
	Ballater	64H	Leith Central
	Fraserburgh		
	Inverurie		
	Peterhead	65A	**Eastfield (Glasgow)**
61B	Aberdeen (Ferryhill)		Arrochar
61C	Keith	65B	St. Rollox
	Banff	65C	Parkhead
	Elgin	65D	Dawsholm
			Dumbarton
		65E	Kipps
62A	**Thornton**	65F	Grangemouth
	Anstruther	65G	Yoker
	Burntisland	65H	Helensburgh
	Kirkcaldy	65I	Balloch
	Ladybank	65J	Stirling
	Methil		Killin
62B	Dundee		
	Arbroath		
	Montrose	66A	**Polmadie (Glasgow)**
	St. Andrews	66B	Motherwell
62C	Dunfermline	66C	Hamilton
	Alloa	66D	Greenock (Ladyburn)
	Kelty	66E	Carstairs
		66F	Beattock
63A	**Perth**	67A	**Corkerhill (Glasgow)**
	Aberfeldy	67B	Hurlford
	Crieff		Beith
	Forfar		Muirkirk
63B	Fort William	67C	Ayr
	Mallaig	67D	Ardrossan
63C	Oban	67E	Dumfries
	Ballachulish	67F	Stranraer

SOUTHERN REGION

70A	**Nine Elms**	70H	Ryde (I.O.W.)
70B	Feltham	70I	Southampton Docks
70C	Guildford		
	Reading South		
70D	Eastleigh	73C	Hither Green
	Andover Junction	73D	St. Leonards
	Southampton Terminus	73F	Ashford (Kent)
	Winchester		
70E	Salisbury		
70F	Bournemouth	75A	**Brighton**
	Branksome	75B	Redhill
70G	Weymouth	75C	Norwood Junction
	Bridport	75D	Stewarts Lane

WESTERN REGION

81A	**Old Oak Common**	85B	Gloucester (Horton Road)
81B	Slough	85D	Bromsgrove
81C	Southall		Redditch
81D	Reading		
81E	Didcot		
81F	Oxford	86A	**Canton (Cardiff)**
		86B	Newport (Ebbw Junction)
82A	**Bristol (Bath Road)**	86C	Hereford
	Marsh Junction		Craven Arms
82B	St. Phillip's Marsh	86E	Severn Tunnel Junction
82C	Swindon	86F	Aberbeeg
	Chippenham	86G	Pontypool Road
82E	Bristol (Barrow Road)		
82F	Bath (Green Park)		
	Highbridge	87A	**Neath**
	Radstock		Glyn Neath
			Neath (N. & B.)
83A	**Newton Abbot**	87B	Margam
83B	Taunton	87D	Swansea East Dock
	Tiverton Junction	87E	Landore
83C	Westbury	87F	Llanelly
83D	Exmouth Junction		Llandovery
	Bude		Pantyffynnon
	Callington	87H	Whitland
	Okehampton		
83E	Yeovil		
83F	Barnstaple Junction	88A	**Cardiff (East Dock)**
	Ilfracombe	88B	Radyr (Cardiff)
83G	Templecombe	88C	Barry
		88D	Merthyr
			Cae Harris (Dowlais)
84A	**Laira (Plymouth)**		Rhymney
84B	St. Blazey	88E	Abercynon
84C	Truro	88F	Treherbert
84D	Penzance		Ferndale
84E	Wadebridge	88G	Llantrisant
		88H	Tondu
85A	**Worcester**	88J	Aberdare
	Honeybourne	88M	Cathays (Cardiff)
	Ledbury		

Ex-G.W.R. STEAM LOCOMOTIVES
Nos. 7-9798

The numbers of locomotives in service have been checked in W.R. to July 20, 1964; S.R. to July 20, 1964; and L.M.R. to July 11, 1964

Unclass.	V. of R.	2-6-2T

Introduced 1902. Davies and Metcalfe design for Vale of Rheidol 1' 11½" gauge.
*Introduced 1923. G.W. development of Vale of Rheidol design.

Weight
25 tons

Gauge
1' 11½"

Boiler pressure
165 lb sq in NS

Cylinders
(O) 11" × 17"
(O) 11½" × 17" *

Driving wheel diameter
2' 6"

Tractive effort
9,615 lb
10,510 lb *

Valve gear
Walschaerts

7 *   Owain Glyndŵr
8 *   Llywelyn

9   Prince of Wales

TOTAL: 3

6MT	1000	4-6-0
	"County"	

Introduced 1945. Hawksworth design with 280 lb boiler pressure since reduced to 250 lb.
Fitted with double chimney.

Weight
Locomotive: 76 tons 17 cwt
Tender: 49 tons

Boiler pressure
250 lb sq in

Cylinders
(O) 18½" × 30"

Driving wheel diameter
6' 3"

Tractive effort
28,241 lb

Valve gear
Stephenson (piston valves)

1011   County of Chester

TOTAL: 1

1F   **1366**   **0-6-0PT**

Introduced 1934. Collett development of 1361 class, with pannier tanks.

Weight
Locomotive: 35 tons 15 cwt

Driving wheel diameter
3' 8"

Boiler pressure
165 lb sq in NS

Tractive effort
16,320 lb

Cylinders
(O) 16" × 20"

Valve gear
Stephenson

1367	1368	1369

TOTAL: 3

1P   **1400**   **0-4-2T**

Introduced 1932. Collett design for light branch work (originally designated 4800). Push-and-pull fitted.

Weight
Locomotive: 41 tons 6 cwt

Driving wheel diameter
5' 2"

Boiler pressure
165 lb sq in NS

Tractive effort
13,900 lb

Cylinders
16½" × 24"

Valve gear
Stephenson

1420	1444	1450	1453	1458	1472	1474
1442	1445					

TOTAL: 9

2F   **1600**   **0-6-0PT**

Introduced 1949. Hawksworth light branch line and shunting design.

Weight
Locomotive: 41 tons 12 cwt

Driving wheel diameter
4' 1½"

Boiler pressure
165 lb sq in NS

Tractive effort
18,515 lb

Cylinders
16½" × 24"

Valve gear
Stephenson

1607	1623	1638	1643	1657	1663	1667
1611	1628	1639	1651	1658	1664	1668
1612	1631	1641	1655	1660	1665	1669
1613	1632					

TOTAL: 23

Top: Class 1000
4-6-0 No. 1010
County of Caernarvon
(since withdrawn)
[*P. J. Sharpe*

Centre: Class 1366
0-6-0PT No. 1369

Right: Class 1400
0-4-2T No. 1472
[*P. J. Sharpe*

Top: Class 1600
0-6-0PT No. 1643
[J. C. Haydon

Centre: Class 2251
0-6-0 No. 3218
[G. H. Wheeler

Left: Class 2800
2-8-0 No. 3855 (with
side-window cab)
[P. H. Wells

3MT   2251   0-6-0

Introduced 1930. Collett design.

Weight
Locomotive: 43 tons 8 cwt
Tender: 36 tons 15 cwt
         47 tons 6 cwt
         (ex-R.O.D. tender from
         3000 Class 2-8-0)

Boiler pressure
200 lb sq in

Cylinders
17½″ × 24″

Driving wheel diameter
5′ 2″

Tractive effort
20,155 lb

Valve gear
Stephenson

2210	2217	2222	2236	2248	2257	2286
2211	2218	2231	2242	2249	2261	2287
2214	2221	2232	2244	2253	2268	2291

Class continued with 3200

8F   2800   2-8-0

Introduced 1903. Churchward design, earlier locomotives subsequently fitted with new boiler and superheater.
*Introduced 1938. Collett locomotives with side-window cab and detail alterations.

Weight
Locomotive: 75 tons 10 cwt
         76 tons 5 cwt*
Tender: 40 tons

Boiler pressure
225 lb sq in

Cylinders
(O) 18½″ × 30″

Driving wheel diameter
4′ 7½″

Tractive effort
35,380 lb

Valve gear
Stephenson (piston valves)

2822	2873	2879	2891*	2895*	2898*	2899*
2859	2876	2890*	2893*			

Class continued with 3800

3MT   2251   0-6-0

Class continued from 2291

3200	3201	3205	3208	3210	3217	3218

TOTAL: 28

Introduced 1947. Hawksworth taper boiler design for heavy shunting.

*Introduced 1949. Locomotives with non-superheated boiler.

Weight	**Driving wheel diameter**
Locomotive: 55 tons 7 cwt	4′ 7½″
Boiler pressure	**Tractive effort**
200 lb sq in SS	22,515 lb
Cylinders	**Valve gear**
17½″ × 24″	Stephenson

3400*	3401*	3402*	3403*	3405*	3406*	3409*

Class continued with 8400

*Introduced 1929. Collett design for shunting and light goods work developed from 2021 class.

†Introduced 1930. Locomotives with steam brake and no A.W.S. fittings, for shunting only.

‡Introduced 1933. Locomotives with condensing apparatus for working over L.T. Metropolitan line.

§Introduced 1933. Locomotives with detail alterations, modified cab and increased weight.

Weight	**Cylinders**
Locomotive: 47 tons 10 cwt*†	17½″ × 24″
50 tons 15 cwt‡	**Driving wheel diameter**
49 tons§	4′ 7½″
Boiler pressure	**Tractive effort**
200 lb sq in NS	25,515 lb
	Valve gear
	Stephenson

3601§	3622§	3661§	3690§	3725§	3749§	3776§
3605§	3625§	3662§	3691§	3728§	3751§	3782§
3607§	3631§	3669§	3696§	3730§	3753§	3784§
3608§	3635§	3671§	3699§	3735§	3754§	3788§
3610§	3642§	3675§	3700§	3737§	3758§	3789§
3612§	3643§	3677§	3705§	3738§	3759§	3790§
3615§	3644§	3681§	3707§	3739§	3763§	3792§
3616§	3647§	3682§	3708§	3742§	3767§	3794§
3617§	3654§	3683§	3709§	3744§	3770§	3796§
3619§	3658§	3686§	3715§	3745§	3772§	3797§
3620§	3659§	3687§	3717§	3747§	3775§	3798§
3621§						

Class continued with 4602

8F   2800   2-8-0

Class continued from 2899

3800*	3810*	3818*	3826*	3838*	3851*	3861*
3801*	3812*	3819*	3828*	3840*	3854*	3862*
3802*	3813*	3820*	3830*	3842*	3855*	3863*
3805*	3814*	3821*	3835*	3848*	3856*	3864*
3807*	3816*	3823*	3836*	3849*	3859*	3865*
3808*	3817*	3825*	3837*	3850*	3860*	3866*
3809*						

TOTAL: 54

7P   4073   4-6-0

"Castle"

Introduced 1923. Collett design, developed from "Star" (5089/91 converted from "Star").
†Introduced 1946. Fitted with 3-row superheater.
‡Introduced 1947. Fitted with 4-row superheater.
*Introduced 1956. Fitted with double chimney.

Weight
Locomotive: 79 tons 17 cwt
Tender: 46 tons 14 cwt

Boiler pressure
225 lb sq in

Cylinders
Four, 16″ × 26″

Driving wheel diameter
6′ 8½″

Tractive effort
31,625 lb

Valve gear
Inside Walschaerts (rocking shafts and piston valves)

4080‡*Powderham Castle
4082 Windsor Castle

4089 Donnington Castle
4093‡*Dunster Castle

Class continued with 5000

4MT   5101   2-6-2T

Introduced 1929. Modified design for new construction, with detail alterations and increased weight, of Collett rebuild of Churchward 3100 class (introduced 1903 and subsequently fitted with superheater).

Weight
Locomotive: 78 tons 9 cwt

Boiler pressure
200 lb sq in

Cylinders
(O) 18″ × 30

Driving wheel diameter
5′ 8″

Tractive effort
24,300 lb

Valve gear
Stephenson (piston valves)

4100	4115	4131	4144	4155	4165	4174
4103	4120	4132	4147	4156	4166	4175
4107	4121	4133	4148	4157	4168	4176
4108	4122	4135	4150	4158	4169	4177
4110	4124	4136	4151	4159	4171	4178
4111	4125	4137	4153	4160	4172	4179
4113	4128	4143	4154	4161	4173	

Class continued with 5153

7F   4200   2-8-0T

Introduced 1910. Churchward design.

Weight
Locomotive: 81 tons 12 cwt

Driving wheel diameter
4′ 7½″

Boiler pressure
200 lb sq in

Tractive effort
31,450 lb

Cylinders
(O) 18½″ × 30″

Valve gear
Stephenson (piston valves)

4222	4253	4273	4283	4285	4292	4295
4227	4254	4277	4284	4286	4294	4297
4233	4258					

Class continued with 5200

4MT   4500   2-6-2T

Introduced 1906. Churchward design for light branches, developed from 4400 class with larger wheels, earlier locomotives subsequently fitted with superheater.

Weight
Locomotive: 57 tons

Driving wheel diameter
4′ 7½″

Boiler pressure
200 lb sq in

Tractive effort
21,250 lb

Cylinders
(O) 17″ × 24″

Valve gear
Stephenson (piston valves)

| 4564 | 4569 |

TOTAL: 2

Above: Class 4073
4-6-0 No. 4082
Windsor Castle
[*R. A. Panting*

Right: Class 5101
2-6-2T No. 4107
[*J. White*

Below: Class 4200
2-8-0T No. 4292
[*P. J. Sharpe*

Class 4500 2-6-2T No. 4564   [N. E. Preedy

Class 5700 0-6-0PT No. 4662   [R. A. Panting

4MT   4575   2-6-2T

Introduced 1927. Development of Churchward 4500 class with detail alterations and increased weight.
*Introduced 1953. Push-and-pull fitted.

Weight
Locomotive: 61 tons

Boiler pressure
200 lb sq in

Cylinders
(O) 17″ × 24″

  4591   4593

Driving wheel diameter
4′ 7½″

Tractive effort
21,250 lb

Valve gear
Stephenson (piston valves)

Class continued with 5508

3F   5700   0-6-0PT

Class continued from 3798

4602§	4613§	4627§	4645§	4663§	4673§	4687§
4604§	4614§	4630§	4646§	4664§	4674§	4689§
4606§	4615§	4631§	4648§	4665§	4675§	4691§
4607§	4616§	4634§	4649§	4666§	4676§	4692§
4608§	4619§	4635§	4650§	4668§	4679§	4694§
4609§	4620§	4636§	4653§	4669§	4680§	4696§
4610§	4621§	4638§	4655§	4670§	4683§	4697§
4611§	4623§	4639§	4662§	4671§	4684§	4698§
4612§	4624§	4643§				

Class continued with 7782

5MT   4900   4-6-0
"Hall"

Introduced 1928. Modified design of Collett rebuild with 6′ 0″ driving wheels of "Saint" (built 1907) for new construction, with higher-pitched boiler, modified footplating and detail differences.

Weight
Locomotive: 75 tons
Tender: 46 tons 14 cwt

Boiler pressure
225 lb sq in

Cylinders
(O) 18½″ × 30″

Driving wheel diameter
6′ 0″

Tractive effort
27,275 lb

Valve gear
Stephenson (piston valves)

4903	Astley Hall	4958	Priory Hall
4916	Crumlin Hall	4959	Purley Hall
4919	Donnington Hall	4962	Ragley Hall
4920	Dumbleton Hall	4978	Westwood Hall
4929	Goytrey Hall	4985	Allesley Hall
4932	Hatherton Hall	4989	Cherwell Hall
4933	Himley Hall	4992	Crosby Hall
4949	Packwood Hall	4993	Dalton Hall
4954	Plaish Hall		

Class continued with 5927

7P   4073   4-6-0

"Castle"

Class continued from 4093

5000†	Launceston Castle	5055	Earl of Eldon
5002	Ludlow Castle	5056*	Earl of Powis
5014	Goodrich Castle	5063†	Earl Baldwin
5026‡*	Criccieth Castle	5076	Gladiator
5042	Winchester Castle	5089	Westminster Abbey
5054	Earl of Ducie	5091	Cleeve Abbey

Class continued with 7003

4MT   5101   2-6-2T

Class continued from 4179

5153   5184

TOTAL: 50

7F   4200   2-8-0T

Class continued from 4297

5200   5202

TOTAL: 19

8F   5205   2-8-0T

Introduced 1923. Development of Churchward 4200 class, with enlarged cylinders and detail alterations.

Weight
Locomotive: 82 tons 2 cwt

Boiler pressure
200 lb sq in

Cylinders
(O) 19″ × 30″

Driving wheel diameter
4′ 7½″

Tractive effort
33,170 lb

Valve gear
Stephenson

5206	5210	5218	5235	5242	5252	5261
5208	5213	5223	5237	5243	5256	5264
5209	5214	5226	5241	5245	5257	

TOTAL: 20

4MT   4300   2-6-0

Introduced 1911. Churchward design.

*Introduced 1925. Locomotives with detail alterations affecting weight.

†Introduced 1932. Locomotives with side-window cab and detail alterations.

Weight
Locomotive: 62 tons
64 tons*
65 tons 6 cwt†
Tender: 40 tons

Boiler pressure
200 lb sq in

Cylinders
(O) 18½″ × 30″

5336

Driving wheel diameter
5′ 8″

Tractive effort
25,670 lb

Valve gear
Stephenson (piston valves)

Class continued with 6309

4MT   4575   2-6-2T

Class continued from 4593

5508	5531	5545*	5563	5564	5569	5571

TOTAL: 9

5MT   **5600**   **0-6-2T**

Introduced 1924. Collett design for service in Welsh valleys.
*Introduced 1927. Locomotives with detail alterations.

Weight   **Driving wheel diameter**
Locomotive: 68 tons 12 cwt   4′ 7½″
            69 tons 7 cwt*
                                            Tractive effort
Boiler pressure   25,800 lb
200 lb sq in
                                            Valve gear
Cylinders   Stephenson (piston valves)
18″ × 26″

5601	5613	5641	5660	5670	5681	5691
5602	5618	5648	5662	5673	5684	5692
5603	5621	5651	5665	5675	5686	5694
5605	5632	5655	5667	5676	5688	5696
5606	5633	5658	5668	5677	5689	5699
5609	5634	5659	5669			

Class continued with 6602

5MT   **4900**   **4-6-0**

"Hall"

Class continued from 4993

5927	*Guild Hall*	5974	*Wallsworth Hall*
5932	*Haydon Hall*	5975	*Winslow Hall*
5933	*Kingsway Hall*	5979	*Cruckton Hall*
5936	*Oakley Hall*	5983	*Henley Hall*
5939	*Tangley Hall*	5984	*Linden Hall*
5955	*Garth Hall*	5988	*Bostock Hall*
5961	*Toynbee Hall*	5990	*Dorford Hall*
5962	*Wantage Hall*	5991	*Gresham Hall*
5971	*Merevale Hall*	5992	*Horton Hall*

Class continued with 6900

4MT   **6100**   **2-6-2T**

Introduced 1931. Development of Collett 5101 class. Locomotives
for London surburban area with increased boiler pressure.
*Introduced 1932 with smaller wheels.

Class 4575 2-6-2T No. 5508   [A. R. Carpenter

Class 4900 4-6-0 No. 5979 *Cruckton Hall*   [G. H. Wheeler

Class 6100 2-6-2T No. 6165   [G. H. Wheeler

Weight	**Driving wheel diameter**
Locomotive: 78 tons 9 cwt	5′ 8″
	5′ 3″*
Boiler pressure	**Tractive effort**
225 lb sq in	27,340 lb
Cylinders	**Valve gear**
(O) 18″ × 30″	Stephenson (piston valves)

6103	6112	6122	6132	6141	6150	6161
6106	6113	6125	6134	6142	6154	6163
6107	6114	6126	6135	6143	6155	6165
6108	6115	6128	6136	6145	6156	6167
6110	6116*	6129	6137	6147	6159	6169
6111	6117	6131	6139	6148	6160	

TOTAL: 41

4MT   4300   2-6-0

Class continued from 5336

6309	6345	6349	6363	6364	6367	6395
6326	6346	6361				

Class continued with 7303

2P   6400   0-6-0PT

Introduced 1932. Collett design for light passenger work, variation of 5400 class with smaller wheels, push-and-pull fitted.

Weight	**Driving wheel diameter**
Locomotive: 45 tons 12 cwt	4′ 7½″
Boiler pressure	**Tractive effort**
180 lb sq in NS	18,010 lb
Cylinders	**Valve gear**
16½″ × 24″	Stephenson

6412	6419	6424	6430	6434	6435

TOTAL: 6

5MT   5600   0-6-2T

Class continued from 5699

6602*	6606*	6612*	6614*	6622*	6626*	6633*
6604*	6611*	6613*	6621*	6625*	6628*	6643*

Above: Class 6400
0-6-0PT No. 6412
[*P. J. Sharpe*

Right: Class 5600
0-6-2T No. 6614
[*J. White*

Below: Class 6800
4-6-0 No. 6812
Chesford Grange
[*B. J. Ashworth*

6644*	6651*	6657*	6667*	6678*	6684*	6691*
6648*	6654*	6658*	6668*	6679*	6685*	6692*
6649*	6655*	6661*	6671*	6681*	6689*	6697*
6650*	6656*	6665*	6672*	6683*		

TOTAL: 79

5MT   6800   4-6-0

"Grange"

Introduced 1936. Collett design, variation of "Hall" with smaller wheels, incorporating certain parts of withdrawn 4300 class 2-6-0 locomotives.

Weight
Locomotive: 74 tons
Tender: 40 tons

Boiler pressure
225 lb sq in

Cylinders
(O) 18½″ × 30″

Driving wheel diameter
5′ 8″

Tractive effort
28,875 lb

Valve gear
Stephenson (piston valves)

6803	Bucklebury Grange	6838	Goodmoor Grange
6804	Brockington Grange	6840	Hazeley Grange
6806	Blackwell Grange	6841	Marlas Grange
6808	Beenham Grange	6842	Nunhold Grange
6810	Blakemere Grange	6845	Paviland Grange
6811	Cranbourne Grange	6846	Ruckley Grange
6812	Chesford Grange	6847	Tidmarsh Grange
6813	Eastbury Grange	6848	Toddington Grange
6815	Frilford Grange	6849	Walton Grange
6816	Frankton Grange	6850	Cleeve Grange
6817	Gwenddwr Grange	6851	Hurst Grange
6819	Highnam Grange	6853	Morehampton Grange
6820	Kingstone Grange	6854	Roundhill Grange
6821	Leaton Grange	6855	Saighton Grange
6822	Manton Grange	6856	Stowe Grange
6823	Oakley Grange	6857	Tudor Grange
6826	Nannerth Grange	6858	Woolston Grange
6827	Llanfrechfa Grange	6859	Yiewsley Grange
6829	Burmington Grange	6860	Aberporth Grange
6830	Buckenhill Grange	6861	Crynant Grange
6831	Bearley Grange	6862	Derwent Grange
6833	Calcot Grange	6863	Dolhywel Grange
6836	Estevarney Grange	6864	Dymock Grange
6837	Forthampton Grange	6866	Morfa Grange

6867	Peterston Grange	6874	Haughton Grange
6868	Penrhos Grange	6876	Kingsland Grange
6869	Resolven Grange	6877	Llanfair Grange
6870	Bodicote Grange	6878	Longford Grange
6871	Bourton Grange	6879	Overton Grange
6872	Crawley Grange		

TOTAL: 59

5MT   4900   4-6-0

"Hall"

Class continued from 5992

6900	Abney Hall	6931	Aldborough Hall
6903	Belmont Hall	6932	Burwarton Hall
6904	Charfield Hall	6933	Birtles Hall
6906	Chicheley Hall	6934	Beachamwell Hall
6907	Davenham Hall	6935	Browsholme Hall
6908	Downham Hall	6936	Breccles Hall
6910	Gossington Hall	6937	Conyngham Hall
6911	Holker Hall	6938	Corndean Hall
6915	Mursley Hall	6940	Didlington Hall
6916	Misterton Hall	6942	Eshton Hall
6917	Oldlands Hall	6944	Fledborough Hall
6918	Sandon Hall	6945	Glasfryn Hall
6921	Borwick Hall	6947	Helmingham Hall
6922	Burton Hall	6951	Impney Hall
6923	Croxteth Hall	6952	Kimberley Hall
6924	Grantley Hall	6953	Leighton Hall
6925	Hackness Hall	6954	Lotherton Hall
6926	Holkham Hall	6955	Lydcott Hall
6927	Lilford Hall	6956	Mottram Hall
6928	Underley Hall	6957	Norcliffe Hall
6930	Aldersey Hall	6958	Oxburgh Hall

TOTAL: 77

Class 6959 4-6-0 No. 6959 *Peatling Hall* [*P. H. Groom*

Class 4073 4-6-0 No. 7029 *Clun Castle* (fitted with double chimney) [*G. H. Wheeler*

Class 7200 2-8-2T No. 7250 [*J. White*

"Modified Hall"

Introduced 1944. Hawksworth development of "Hall", with larger superheater, "one-piece" main frames and plate-framed bogie.

Weight
Locomotive: 75 tons 16 cwt
Tender: 46 tons 14 cwt

Boiler pressure
225 lb sq in

Cylinders
(O) 18½" × 30"

Driving wheel diameter
6' 0"

Tractive effort
27,275 lb

Valve gear
Stephenson (piston valves

6959	Peatling Hall	6983	Otterington Hall
6960	Raveningham Hall	6984	Owsden Hall
6961	Stedham Hall	6985	Parwick Hall
6963	Throwley Hall	6986	Rydal Hall
6964	Thornbridge Hall	6987	Shervington Hall
6965	Thirlestaine Hall	6988	Swithland Hall
6966	Witchingham Hall	6989	Wightwick Hall
6967	Willesley Hall	6990	Witherslack Hall
6969	Wraysbury Hall	6991	Acton Burnell Hall
6971	Athelhampton Hall	6993	Arthog Hall
6973	Bricklehampton Hall	6994	Baggrave Hall
6974	Bryngwyn Hall	6995	Benthall Hall
6976	Graythwaite Hall	6996	Blackwell Hall
6978	Haroldstone Hall	6997	Bryn-Ivor Hall
6979	Helperly Hall	6998	Burton Agnes Hall
6980	Llanrumney Hall	6999	Capel Dewi Hall
6982	Melmerby Hall		

Class continued with 7900

"Castle"

Class continued from 5091

7003†*Elmley Castle	7022‡*Hereford Castle
7005† Sir Edward Elgar	7023†*Penrice Castle
7008†*Swansea Castle	7024‡*Powis Castle
7011† Banbury Castle	7025† Sudeley Castle
7012† Barry Castle	7026† Tenby Castle
7013‡*Bristol Castle	7029‡*Clun Castle
7014†*Caerhays Castle	7032†*Denbigh Castle
7019‡*Fowey Castle	7034‡*Ince Castle
7020†*Gloucester Castle	7035†*Ogmore Castle

TOTAL: 34

8F   7200   2-8-2T

Introduced 1934. Collett rebuild, with extended bunker and trailing wheels, of Churchward 4200 class 2-8-0T.

Weight	**Driving wheel diameter**
92 tons 2 cwt	4' 7½"

Boiler pressure	**Tractive effort**
200 lb sq in	33,170 lb

Cylinders	**Valve gear**
(O) 19" × 30"	Stephenson (piston valves)

7201	7210	7221	7229	7240	7245	7250
7205	7213	7222	7231	7243	7248	7252
7207	7218	7223	7232	7244	7249	7253
7209	7220	7226	7233			

TOTAL: 25

4MT   4300   2-6-0

Class continued from 6395

7303*	7306	7318	7319	7320	7327†	7337†

TOTAL: 18

2F   7400   0-6-0PT

Introduced 1936. Development of Collett 6400 class. Non push-and-pull fitted locomotives.

Weight	**Driving wheel diameter**
Locomotive: 45 tons 9cwt	4' 7½"

Boiler pressure	**Tractive effort**
180 lb sq in NS	18,010 lb

Cylinders	**Valve gear**
16½" × 24"	Stephenson

7413	7418	7431	7435	7437	7439	7443
7414	7424	7432				

TOTAL: 10

3F   5700   0-6-0PT

Class continued from 4698

7782*

Class continued with 8718

Above: Class 4300
2-6-0 No. 7327 (with
side-window cab)
[*J. White*

Right: Class 7400
0-6-0PT No. 7414
[*R. H. G. Simpson*

Below: Class 7800
4-6-0 No. 7800
Torquay Manor
[*G. H. Wheeler*

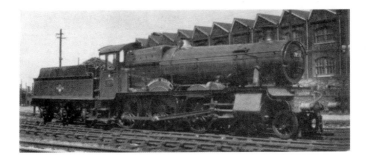

5MT   **7800**   **4-6-0**

"Manor"

Introduced 1938. Collett design for secondary lines, incorporating certain parts of withdrawn 4300 class 2-6-0 locomotives.

Weight
Locomotive: 68 tons 18 cwt
Tender: 40 tons

Boiler pressure
225 lb sq in

Cylinders
(O) 18″ × 30″

Driving wheel diameter
5′ 8″

Tractive effort
27,340 lb

Valve gear
Stephenson (piston valves)

7800	Torquay Manor	7815	Fritwell Manor
7801	Anthony Manor	7816	Frilsham Manor
7802	Bradley Manor	7818	Granville Manor
7803	Barcote Manor	7819	Hinton Manor
7804	Baydon Manor	7820	Dinmore Manor
7805	Broome Manor	7821	Ditcheat Manor
7806	Cockington Manor	7822	Foxcote Manor
7807	Compton Manor	7823	Hook Norton Manor
7808	Cookham Manor	7824	Iford Manor
7810	Draycott Manor	7825	Lechlade Manor
7811	Dunley Manor	7826	Longworth Manor
7812	Erlestoke Manor	7827	Lydham Manor
7813	Freshford Manor	7828	Odney Manor
7814	Fringford Manor	7829	Ramsbury Manor

TOTAL: 28

5MT   **6959**   **4-6-0**

"Modified Hall"

Class continued from 6999

7900	Saint Peter's Hall	7917	North Aston Hall
7904	Fountains Hall	7918	Rhose Wood Hall
7906	Fron Hall	7919	Runter Hall
7907	Hart Hall	7920	Coney Hall
7908	Henshall Hall	7922	Salford Hall
7909	Heveningham Hall	7923	Speke Hall
7910	Hown Hall	7924	Thornycroft Hall
7912	Little Linford Hall	7925	Westol Hall
7913	Little Wyrley Hall	7926	Willey Hall
7914	Lleweni Hall	7927	Willington Hall
7915	Mere Hall	7928	Wolf Hall
7916	Mobberley Hall	7929	Wyke Hall

TOTAL: 57

4MT   8100   2-6-2T

Introduced 1938. Collett rebuild, with higher pressure and smaller wheels, of Churchward locomotives in 5100 class.

Weight
Locomotive: 76 tons 11 cwt

Driving wheel diameter
5′ 6″

Boiler pressure
225 lb sq in

Tractive effort
28,165 lb

Cylinders
(O) 18″ × 30″

Valve gear
Stephenson (piston valves)

8104   8109

TOTAL: 2

4F   9400   0-6-0PT

Class continued from 3409

8400*	8405*	8420*	8437*	8471*	8481*	8493*
8401*	8409*	8431*	8446*	8474*	8484*	8495*
8402*	8415*	8433*	8459*	8475*	8486*	8498*
8403*	8418*	8436*	8469*	8479*	8488*	

Class continued with 9404

3F   5700   0-6-0PT

Class continued from 7782

8718*	8739*	8745*	8767§	8768§	8793§	8795§
8720*	8743*	8749*				

Class continued with 9600

4F   9400   0-6-0PT

Class continued from 8498

9404	9418*	9437*	9453*	9470*	9477*	9493*
9405	9426*	9446*	9461*	9471*	9480*	9494*
9406	9430*	9450*	9463*	9472*	9488*	9495*
9411*	9435*	9452*	9464*	9475*	9490*	9498*
9415*						

TOTAL: 63

Top: Class 8100
2-6-2T No. 8109
[*G. H. Wheeler*

Centre: Class 8400
0-6-0PT No. 8481
[*G. H. Wheeler*

Left: Class 5700
0-6-0PT No. 9710
(with condensing
apparatus) [*A. Swain*

Class continued from 8795

9600§	9616§	9632§	9653§	9669§	9706‡	9773§
9601§	9617§	9637§	9654§	9670§	9707‡	9774§
9602§	9619§	9639§	9656§	9671§	9710‡	9776§
9605§	9621§	9640§	9657§	9672§	9711§	9778§
9606§	9622§	9641§	9658§	9675§	9716§	9780§
9608§	9623§	9642§	9659§	9676§	9724§	9782§
9609§	9624§	9644§	9660§	9677§	9726§	9787§
9610§	9625§	9646§	9661§	9678§	9729§	9789§
9611§	9626§	9647§	9662§	9679§	9733§	9790§
9613§	9629§	9649§	9663§	9680§	9753§	9794§
9614§	9630§	9650§	9666§	9681§	9754§	9796§
9615§	9631§	9651§	9667§	9682§	9768§	9798§

TOTAL: 232

LOCOMOTIVE SUPERINTENDENTS AND CHIEF MECHANICAL ENGINEERS

G.W.R.

Sir Daniel Gooch	...	1837–1864	William Dean ...	...	1877–1902
Joseph Armstrong	...	{1854–1864* {1864–1877	G. J. Churchward	...	1902–1921
			Charles B. Collett	...	1922–1941
George Armstrong	...	1864–1896*	F. W. Hawksworth	...	1941–1949

*In charge of standard gauge locomotives at Stafford Road Works, Wolverhampton, with wide powers in design and construction.

POWER AND WEIGHT CLASSIFICATION

Since 1920 Western Region locomotives have been classified for power and weight by a letter on a coloured disc on the cab side. The letter represents the power of the locomotive and is approximately proportional to the tractive effort as under:

Power class	Tractive effort lb.	Power class	Tractive effort lb.
E	33,001–38,000	B	18,501–20,500
D	25,001–33,000	A	16,500–18,500
C	20,501–25,000	Ungrouped	Below 16,500

The colour of the circle represents the routes over which the engine may work. Red engines are limited to the main lines and lines capable of carrying the heaviest locomotives; blue engines are allowed over additional routes, yellow engines over nearly the whole system and uncoloured engines are more or less unrestricted.

Class	Power Class	Route Restriction Colour	Class	Power Class	Route Restriction Colour
4–6–0			**2–8–0T**		
1000	D	Red	4200	E	Red
4073	D	Red			
4900	D	Red			
6800	D	Red	**2–6–2T**		
6959	D	Red	4500	C	Yellow
7800	D	Blue	5101	D	Blue
			6100	D	Blue
			8100	D	Blue
2–8–0					
2800	E	Blue	**0–6–2T**		
			5600	D	Red
2–6–0					
4300	D	Blue	**0–6–0T**		
			1366	—	—
			1600	A	—
0–6–0			5700	C	Yellow
2251	B	Yellow	9700–10	C	Blue
			6400	A	Yellow
			7400	A	Yellow
			9400	C	Red
2–8–2T			**0–4–2T**		
7200	E	Red	1400	—	—

Ex-S.R. STEAM LOCOMOTIVES
Nos. 30064-35030
and Isle of Wight Locos 14-35

The numbers of locomotives in service have been checked in S.R. to July 20, 1964; and W.R. to July 20, 1964

NOTE: Certain Southern classes are not numbered in a continuous numerical sequence. For the sake of clarity therefore, some locomotives are shown out of numerical order.

3F	USA	0-6-0T

Introduced 1942. U.S. Army Transportation Corps design, purchased by S.R. 1946 and fitted with modified cab and bunker and other detail alterations.

Weight
Locomotive: 46 tons 10 cwt

Boiler pressure
210 lb sq in NS

Cylinders
(O) $16\frac{1}{2}'' \times 24''$

Driving wheel diameter
4' 6"

Tractive effort
21,600 lb

Valve gear
Walschaerts (piston valves)

30064	30067	30069	30071	30072	30073

See also Departmental Locomotives

TOTAL: 12

4F	Q	0-6-0

Introduced 1938. Maunsell design, later fitted with multiple-jet blastpipe and large-diameter chimney.
*Subsequently fitted with single chimney.

Weight
Locomotive: 49 tons 10 cwt

Boiler pressure
200 lb sq in

Cylinders
19" × 26"

Driving wheel diameter
5' 1"

Tractive effort
26,160 lb

Valve gear
Stephenson (piston valves)

30530*   30535   30541   30542   30543*   30545*   30548
30531

TOTAL: 8

6F   S15   4-6-0

*Introduced 1927. Maunsell development of Urie L.S.W. design, with higher boiler pressure. smaller grate, modified footplating and other detail differences. 30833-7 with 6-wheel tenders for Central Section.
†Introduced 1936. Later locomotives with detail differences and reduced weight.

Weight
Locomotive: 80 tons 14 cwt*
            79 tons 5 cwt†

Boiler pressure
200 lb sq in*†

Cylinders
(O) 20½" × 28"

Driving wheel diameter
5' 7"

Tractive effort
29,855 lb

Valve gear
Walschaerts (piston valves)

30823*	30830*	30834*	30837*	30839†	30842†	30843†
30824*	30833*	30835*	30838†	30840†		

TOTAL: 12

4P5F   N   2-6-0

Introduced 1917. Maunsell S.E.C. mixed traffic design.

Weight
Locomotive: 61 tons 4 cwt

Boiler pressure
200 lb sq in

Cylinders
(O) 19" × 28"

Driving wheel diameter
5' 6"

Tractive effort
26,035 lb

Valve gear
Walschaerts (piston valves)

31401	31411	31816	31835	31843	31855	31866
31405	31412	31828	31837	31845	31858	31869
31406	31811	31831	31840	31846	31859	31873
31408	31814	31834	31842	31853	31862	31875
31410						

TOTAL: 29

4P3F   U   2-6-0

Introduced 1928. Rebuild of Maunsell S.E.C. Class K ("River") 2-6-4T (introduced 1917).
*Introduced 1928. Locomotives built as Class U, with smaller splashers and detail alterations.

Right: Class USA
0-6-0T No. 30071
[*P. H. Wells*

Centre: Class Q
0-6-0 No. 30542
[*J. Scrace*

Bottom: Class Q
0-6-0 No. 30545
(with B.R. chimney)
[*W. G. Sumner*

Class S15 4-6-0 No. 30824   *[P. H. Wells*

Class S15 4-6-0 No. 30834 (with six-wheel tender)   *[A. Trickett*

Class N 2-6-0 No. 31873   *[J H. Aston*

Weight
Locomotive: 63 tons
           62 tons 6 cwt*

Boiler pressure
200 lb sq in

Cylinders
(O) 19″ × 28″

Driving wheel diameter
6′ 0″

Tractive effort
23,865 lb

Valve gear
Walschaerts (piston valves)

31619*	31627*	31639*	31791	31798	31800	31803
31620*	31632*	31790	31792	31799	31802	31809

TOTAL: 14

6F   W   2-6-4T

Introduced 1931. Maunsell design, developed from Class N1 2-6-0.

Weight
Locomotive: 90 tons 14 cwt

Boiler pressure
200 lb sq in

Cylinders
Three, 16½″ × 28″

Driving wheel diameter
5′ 6″

Tractive effort
29,450 lb

Valve gear
Walschaerts (piston valves)

31912   31914   31924

TOTAL: 3

5F   Q1   0-6-0

Introduced 1942. Bulleid "Austerity" design.

Weight
Locomotive: 51 tons 5 cwt

Boiler pressure
230 lb sq in

Cylinders
19″ × 26″

Driving wheel diameter
5′ 1″

Tractive effort
30,080 lb

Valve gear
Stephenson (piston valves)

33004	33009	33015	33018	33020	33026	33027
33006	33012					

TOTAL: 9

Class U 2-6-0 No. 31620 [*P. H. Wells*

Class W 2-6-4T No. 31912 [*J. Scrace*

Class Q1 0-6-0 No. 33018 [*F. Church*

†Introduced 1945. Bulleid "West Country" class, with Bulleid valve gear.
‡Introduced 1946. Bulleid "Battle of Britain" class, with Bulleid valve gear.
*Introduced 1957. Rebuilt with Walschaerts valve gear, modified details and air-smoothed casing removed.
§Introduced 1962. Fitted with Giesl oblong ejector.

Weight
Locomotive: 86 tons†‡
           90 tons I cwt*

Boiler pressure
250 lb sq in

Cylinders
Three, 16⅞" × 24"

Driving wheel diameter
6′ 2″

Tractive effort
27,715 lb

Valve gear
Bulleid (piston valves)†‡
Walschaerts (piston valves)*

34001†*Exeter	34037†*Clovelly
34002† Salisbury	34038‡ Lynton
34003†*Plymouth	34039†*Boscastle
34004†*Yeovil	34040†*Crewkerne
34005†*Barnstaple	34041† Wilton
34006† Bude	34042†*Dorchester
34007‡ Wadebridge	34044†*Woolacombe
34008†*Padstow	34046†*Braunton
34009†*Lyme Regis	34047†*Callington
34010†*Sidmouth	34048†*Crediton
34012†*Launceston	34050†*Royal Observer Corps
34013†*Okehampton	34051‡ Winston Churchill
34014†*Budleigh Salterton	34052‡*Lord Dowding
34015† Exmouth	34053‡*Sir Keith Park
34017†*Ilfracombe	34054‡ Lord Beaverbrook
34018†*Axminster	34056‡*Croydon
34019† Bideford	34057‡ Biggin Hill
34020† Seaton	34058‡*Sir Frederick Pile
34021†*Dartmoor	34059‡*Sir Archibald Sinclair
34022†*Exmoor	34060‡*25 Squadron
34023† Blackmore Vale	34061‡ 73 Squadron
34024†*Tamar Valley	34063‡ 229 Squadron
34025†*Whimple	34064‡ §Fighter Command
34026†*Yes Tor	34066‡ Spitfire
34027†*Taw Valley	34070‡ Manston
34029†*Lundy	34071‡*601 Squadron
34030† Watersmeet	34072‡ 257 Squadron
34031†*Torrington	34076‡ 41 Squadron
34032†*Camelford	34077‡*603 Squadron
34033† Chard	34078‡ 222 Squadron
34034†*Honiton	34079‡ 141 Squadron
34036†*Westward Ho	34080‡ 74 Squadron

Class WC 4-6-2 No. 34006 *Bude* (with extended smoke deflectors)

[R. A. Panting]

34081‡ 92 Squadron	34096†*Trevone
34082‡*615 Squadron	34097†*Holsworthy
34084‡ 253 Squadron	34098†*Templecombe
34085‡*501 Squadron	34099† Lynmouth
34086‡ 219 Squadron	34100†*Appledore
34087‡*145 Squadron	34101†*Hartland
34088‡*213 Squadron	34102† Lapford
34089‡*602 Squadron	34103† Calstock
34090‡*Sir Eustace Missenden, Southern Railway	34104†*Bere Alston
	34105† Swanage
34091† Weymouth	34106† Lydford
34092† City of Wells	34107† Blandford Forum
34093†*Saunton	34108†*Wincanton
34094† Mortehoe	34109‡*Sir Trafford
34095†*Brentor	Leigh-Mallory

TOTAL: 92

8P MN 4-6-2

Introduced 1941. Bulleid design originally with 280 lb. pressure multiple-jet blastpipe and Bulleid valve gear. Rebuilt since 1956 with Walschaerts valve gear and modified details; air-smoothed casing removed.

Weight
Locomotive: 97 tons 18 cwt

Driving wheel diameter
6′ 2″

Boiler pressure
250 lb sq in

Tractive effort
33,495 lb

Cylinders
Three, 18″ × 24″

Valve gear
Walschaerts (piston valves)

35001	Channel Packet	35017	Belgian Marine
35003	Royal Mail	35018	British India Line
35004	Cunard White Star	35019	French Line CGT
35005	Canadian Pacific	35020	Bibby Line
35006	Peninsular & Oriental S.N. Co.	35021	New Zealand Line
		35022	Holland-America Line
35007	Aberdeen Commonwealth	35023	Holland-Afrika Line
35008	Orient Line	35024	East Asiatic Company
35009	Shaw Savill	35025	Brocklebank Line
35010	Blue Star	35026	Lamport & Holt Line
35011	General Steam Navigation	35027	Port Line
35012	United States Lines	35028	Clan Line
35013	Blue Funnel	35029	Ellerman Lines
35014	Nederland Line	35030	Elder Dempster Lines
35016	Elders Fyffes		

TOTAL: 28

ISLE OF WIGHT LOCOMOTIVES

0P   O2   0-4-4T

Introduced 1889. Adams L.S.W. design. Fitted with Westinghouse brake for I.O.W. in 1923. Bunkers enlarged from 1932.

Weight
Locomotive: 48 tons 8 cwt

Boiler pressure
160 lb sq in NS

Cylinders
17½" × 24"

Driving wheel diameter
4' 10"

Tractive effort
17,235 lb

Valve gear
Stephenson

14	Fishbourne	27	Merstone
16	Ventnor	28	Ashey
17	Seaview	29	Alverstone
18	Ningwood	30	Shorwell
20	Shanklin	31	Chale
21	Sandown	32	Bonchurch
22	Brading	33	Bembridge
24	Calbourne	35	Freshwater
26	Whitwell		

TOTAL: 17

PRESERVED LOCOMOTIVE IN WORKING ORDER

3P   T9   4-4-0

Introduced 1899. Drummond L.S.W. design, fitted with superheater and larger cylinders by Urie from 1922. Withdrawn 1962 as B.R. No. 30120, and restored to pre-grouping condition. Later returned to service for special use.

Weight
Locomotive: 51 tons 18 cwt

Boiler pressure
175 lb sq in

Cylinders
19" × 26"

Driving wheel diameter
6' 7"

Tractive effort
17,675 lb

Valve gear
Stephenson

120

Rebuilt Class WC 4-6-2 No. 34040 *Crewkerne*

[G. H. Wheel

Class MN 4-6-2 No. 35029 *Ellerman Lines*

[G. H. Wheeler

Class 02 0-4-4T No. 21 *Sandown*

[M. Edwards

Above: Class T9 4-4-0 No. 120 (restored to L.S.W.R. livery)

[*R. A. Panting*

Left: Class USA 0-6-0T departmental locomotive No. DS238 *Wainwright*

[*J. Scrace*

Below: Class C 0-6-0 departmental locomotive No. 31271

[*J. Davenport*

DEPARTMENTAL LOCOMOTIVES

Former running number in brackets

3F   **USA**   **0-6-0T**

For details see 30064-73

DS233 (30061)   DS234 (30062)   DS235 (30066)   DS236 (30074)

DS237 *Maunsell* (30065)
DS238 *Wainwright* (30070)

2F   **C**   **0-6-0**

Introduced 1900. Wainwright S.E.C. design.

Weight Locomotive: 43 tons 16 cwt	**Driving wheel diameter** 5′ 2″
Boiler pressure 160 lb sq in NS	**Tractive effort** 19,520 lb
Cylinders 18½″ × 26″	**Valve gear** Stephenson

DS239 (31592)   31271   31280   **TOTAL: 3**

LOCOMOTIVE SUPERINTENDENTS AND CHIEF MECHANICAL ENGINEERS
S.R.

R. E. L. Maunsell   ...   1923–1937   O. V. Bulleid   1937–1949

LONDON & SOUTH WESTERN RAILWAY

J. Woods	... ...	1835–1841
J. V. Gooch	... ...	1841–1850
J. Beattie	... ...	1850–1871
W. G. Beattie	... ...	1871–1878
W. Adams	... ...	1878–1895
D. Drummond	... ...	1895–1912
R. W. Urie	... ...	1912–1922

LONDON, BRIGHTON AND SOUTH COAST RAILWAY

—. Statham	... ...	?–1845
J. Gray	... ...	1845–1847
S. Kirtley	... ...	1847
J. C. Craven	... ...	1847–1869
W. Stroudley	... ...	1870–1889
R. J. Billinton	... ...	1890–1904
D. Earle Marsh	... ...	1905–1911
L. B. Billinton	... ...	1911–1922

SOUTH EASTERN RAILWAY

B. Cubitt	... ...	1842–1845
J. Cudworth	... ...	1845–1876
A. M. Watkin	... ...	1876
R. Mansell	... ...	1877–1878
J. Stirling	... ...	1878–1898

LONDON, CHATHAM & DOVER RAILWAY

W. Cubitt	... ...	1853–1860
W. Martley	... ...	1860–1874
W. Kirtley	... ...	1874–1898

SOUTH EASTERN & CHATHAM RAILWAY

H. S. Wainwright	...	1899–1913
R. E. L. Maunsell	...	1913–1922

EX-L.M.S. STEAM LOCOMOTIVES
Nos. 41200-53807

The numbers of locomotives in service have been checked in L.M.R. to July 11, 1964; E.R. to July 25, 1964; to N.E.R. to July 25, 1964; Sc.R. to July 25, 1964; S.R. to July 20, 1964; and W.R. to July 20, 1964.

2MT   2-6-2T

Introduced 1946. Ivatt L.M.S. taper boiler design.

Weight
63 tons 5 cwt

Driving wheel diameter
5′ 0″

Boiler pressure
200 lb sq in

Tractive effort
17,410 lb
18,510 lb*

Cylinders
(O) 16″ × 24″
(O) 16½″ × 24″*

Valve gear
Walschaerts (piston valves)

41200	41215	41226	41243	41283	41297*	41312*
41201	41216	41227	41244	41284	41298*	41313*
41202	41217	41229	41248	41285	41299*	41314*
41204	41218	41230	41249	41286	41300*	41316*
41206	41219	41232	41251	41287	41301*	41317*
41207	41220	41233	41260	41290*	41303*	41319*
41208	41221	41234	41261	41291*	41304*	41320*
41209	41222	41237	41264	41293*	41305*	41321*
41211	41223	41238	41270	41294*	41307*	41324*
41212	41224	41241	41272	41295*	41308*	41325*
41214	41225	41242	41275	41296*	41310*	

TOTAL: 76

0F   0-4-0T

Introduced 1907. Deeley Midland design.

Weight
32 tons 16 cwt

Driving wheel diameter
3′ 9¾″

Boiler pressure
160 lb sq in NS

Tractive effort
14,635 lb

Cylinders
(O) 15″ × 22″

Valve gear
Walschaerts

41528	41533	41535

TOTAL: 3

Class 2MT 2-6-2T No. 41220   [J. White

Class 0F 0-4-0T No. 41528   [D. Smith

1F   0-6-0T

Introduced 1878. Johnson Midland design. Rebuilt with Belpaire firebox.

Weight
39 tons 11 cwt

Boiler pressure
140 lb sq in NS

Cylinders
17″ × 24″

Driving wheel diameter
4′ 7″

Tractive effort
15,005 lb

Valve gear
Stephenson

| 41708 | 41712 | 41734 | 41763 | 41804 | 41835 |

TOTAL: 6

4MT   2-6-4T

Introduced 1945. Fairburn development of Stanier design with shorter wheelbase and detail alterations.

Weight
85 tons 5 cwt

Boiler pressure
200 lb sq in

Cylinders
(O) 19⅝″ × 26″

Driving wheel diameter
5′ 9″

Tractive effort
24,670 lb

Valve gear
Walschaerts piston valves)

42050	42075	42103	42127	42154	42194	42224
42051	42076	42104	42128	42155	42195	42225
42052	42078	42105	42129	42156	42196	42230
42053	42079	42106	42131	42158	42197	42232
42055	42080	42107	42132	42159	42198	42233
42056	42081	42108	42133	42160	42199	42235
42058	42082	42109	42134	42161	42201	42236
42060	42083	42110	42138	42165	42202	42240
42061	42084	42112	42139	42169	42204	42241
42062	42085	42113	42141	42170	42208	42242
42064	42086	42114	42142	42174	42209	42243
42065	42087	42115	42143	42176	42210	42245
42066	42089	42116	42145	42177	42212	42247
42069	42092	42118	42147	42179	42213	42249
42070	42093	42119	42148	42181	42214	42250
42071	42095	42121	42149	42183	42216	42251
42072	42096	42124	42150	42184	42218	42252
42073	42099	42125	42152	42187	42221	42259
42074	42102	42126	42153	42189	42222	42260

Class IF 0-6-0T No. 41763   [A. W. Martin

Fairburn Class 4MT 2-6-4T No. 42082   [C. P. Boocock

Fowler Class 4MT 2-6-4T No. 42317   [J. C. Haydon

42262	42266	42273	42282	42285	42289	42296
42263	42267	42274	42283	42286	42291	42297
42264	42269	42277	42284	42287	42295	42299
42265	42271					

Class continued with **42673**

4MT   2-6-4T

Introduced 1927. Fowler L.M.S. parallel boiler design.
*Introduced 1933. Fitted with side window cab and doors.

Weight
86 tons 5 cwt

Driving wheel diameter
5′ 9″

Boiler pressure
200 lb sq in

Tractive effort
23,125 lb

Cylinders
(O) 19″ × 26″

Valve gear
Walschaerts (piston valves)

42309	42327	42350	42369	42381	42405*	42414*
42317	42334	42359	42374	42394	42406*	42421*
42322	42343	42368	42379	42400*	42410*	42424*

TOTAL: 21

4MT   2-6-4T

Introduced 1935. Stanier taper-boiler design.

Weight
87 tons 17 cwt

Driving wheel diameter
5′ 9″

Boiler pressure
200 lb sq in

Tractive effort
24,670 lb

Cylinders
(O) 19⅝″ × 26″

Valve gear
Walschaerts (piston valves)

42426	42459	42489	42566	42597	42620	42649
42430	42460	42492	42567	42601	42622	42650
42431	42462	42494	42573	42602	42625	42651
42432	42464	42542	42574	42604	42626	42654
42435	42465	42546	42577	42605	42629	42656
42436	42468	42548	42581	42606	42630	42657
42439	42474	42551	42583	42608	42631	42660
42442	42477	42554	42584	42609	42634	42662
42445	42478	42555	42586	42610	42639	42663
42447	42481	42558	42587	42611	42640	42664
42449	42482	42559	42588	42613	42644	42665
42451	42484	42564	42589	42616	42645	42667
42455	42488	42565	42590	42618	42647	42670
42456						

TOTAL: 92

4MT

Class continued from 42299

42673	42676	42682	42689	42691	42694	42697
42675	42680	42688	42690	42693	42696	42699

TOTAL: 170

5MT

2-6-0

Introduced 1926. Hughes L.M.S. design built under Fowler's direction.

Weight
Locomotive: 66 tons

Boiler pressure
180 lb sq in

Cylinders
(O) 21″ × 26″

Driving wheel diameter
5′ 6″

Tractive effort
26,580 lb

Valve gear
Walschaerts (piston valves)

42700	42732	42772	42803	42845	42892	42919
42701	42733	42777	42812	42846	42894	42920
42702	42734	42778	42814	42848	42896	42924
42703	42736	42780	42815	42849	42898	42925
42705	42737	42782	42816	42855	42900	42926
42707	42739	42783	42817	42856	42901	42931
42710	42740	42787	42819	42859	42904	42932
42712	42741	42788	42826	42860	42905	42934
42715	42748	42789	42827	42861	42907	42936
42716	42751	42791	42828	42863	42908	42937
42717	42753	42793	42831	42869	42909	42938
42722	42754	42795	42832	42878	42912	42940
42725	42755	42799	42840	42879	42913	42941
42727	42760	42800	42841	42880	42916	42942
42730	42765	42801	42844	42886	42917	

TOTAL: 104

5MT

2-6-0

Introduced 1933. Stanier L.M.S. taper boiler design, some with safety valves mounted on the top feed.

Weight
Locomotive: 69 tons 2 cwt

Boiler pressure
225 lb sq in

Cylinders
(O) 18″ × 28″

Driving wheel diameter
5′ 6″

Tractive effort
26,290 lb

Valve gear
Walschaerts (piston valves)

Left: Stanier Class 4MT 2-6-4T No. 42626 [*J. K. Morton*

Centre: Hughes-Fowler Class 5MT 2-6-0 No. 42880 [*P. Ransome-Wallis*

Bottom: Stanier Class 5MT 2-6-0 No. 42975 [*R. A. Panting*

42945	42951	42956	42961	42967	42972	42979
42946	42952	42957	42963	42968	42974	42980
42947	42953	42958	42964	42969	42975	42981
42948	42954	42959	42965	42970	42977	42982
42950	42955	42960	42966	42971	42978	42983

TOTAL: 35

4MT   2-6-0

Introduced 1947. Ivatt L.M.S. taper boiler design with double chimney. Later engines introduced with single chimney with which earlier engines have been rebuilt.

Weight
Locomotive: 59 tons 2 cwt

Boiler pressure
225 lb sq in

Cylinders
(O) 17½″ × 26″

Driving wheel diameter
5′ 3″

Tractive effort
24,170 lb

Valve gear
Walschaerts (piston valves)

43000	43022	43044	43067	43090	43116	43139
43001	43023	43045	43069	43091	43117	43140
43002	43024	43046	43070	43092	43118	43141
43003	43025	43047	43071	43093	43119	43143
43004	43026	43048	43072	43095	43120	43144
43005	43027	43049	43073	43096	43121	43145
43006	43028	43050	43074	43097	43122	43146
43007	43029	43051	43075	43098	43123	43147
43008	43030	43052	43076	43099	43124	43148
43009	43031	43054	43077	43100	43125	43149
43010	43032	43055	43078	43101	43126	43150
43011	43033	43056	43079	43102	43127	43151
43012	43034	43057	43080	43103	43128	43153
43013	43035	43058	43081	43105	43129	43154
43014	43036	43059	43082	43106	43130	43155
43015	43037	43060	43084	43108	43132	43156
43016	43039	43062	43085	43109	43133	43157
43017	43040	43063	43086	43111	43134	43158
43018	43041	43064	43087	43112	43135	43159
43019	43042	43065	43088	43113	43137	43160
43020	43043	43066	43089	43115	43138	43161
43021						

TOTAL: 148

4F   0-6-0

Introduced 1911. Fowler superheated Midland design.

Weight
Locomotive: 48 tons 15 cwt

Boiler pressure
175 lb sq in

Cylinders
20″ × 26″

Driving wheel diameter
5′ 3″

Tractive effort
24,555 lb

Valve gear
Stephenson (piston valves)

43850	43893	43924	43949	43958	43975	43991
43856	43906	43928	43950	43960	43979	43994
43865	43908	43929	43951	43963	43981	43999
43871	43913	43931	43952	43964	43982	44003
43887	43917	43940	43953	43967	43983	44023
43888	43918	43947	43954	43968	43988	44025

TOTAL: 42

4F   0-6-0

Introduced 1924. Post-grouping development of Midland design with reduced boiler mountings.
*Introduced 1922. Locomotives built for S. & D.J. to Midland design (taken into L.M.S. stock 1930).

Weight
Locomotive: 48 tons 15 cwt

Boiler pressure
175 lb sq in

Cylinders
20″ × 26″

Driving wheel diameter
5′ 3″

Tractive effort
24,555 lb

Valve gear
Stephenson (piston valves)

44027	44081	44149	44211	44264	44349	44402
44028	44086	44155	44214	44266	44350	44405S
44035	44092	44157	44215	44269	44353	44408
44040	44096	44160	44218	44271	44355	44414
44042	44099	44165	44220	44275	44356	44420
44043	44102	44169	44222	44276	44358	44421
44044	44113	44170	44226	44277	44362	44422
44045	44115	44177	44229	44278	44367	44425
44048	44117	44178	44233	44284	44373S	44429
44049	44118	44179	44235	44294	44376	44431
44051	44121	44181	44236	44300	44377	44433
44054	44123	44182	44240	44305	44379	44441
44056	44125	44185	44243	44310	44380	44443
44057	44127	44188	44244	44311	44381	44446
44059	44130	44191	44246	44332	44384	44449
44061	44131	44192	44247	44334	44386	44450
44063	44134	44195	44248	44339	44389	44451
44065	44135	44197	44250	44344	44390	44456
44075	44137	44200	44259	44346	44394	44458
44076	44139	44203	44260	44347	44400	44460
44079	44146	44210	44263	44348	44401	44461

Class 4MT 2-6-0 No. 43138

Ex-Midland Class 4F 0-6-0 No. 43893 (with tender cab)   [R. J. Buckley

Class 4F 0-6-0 No. 44581   [D. Kingston

44462	44489	44516	44544	44566	44581	44593S
44463	44490	44522	44548	44570	44583S	44597
44466	44497	44525	44552	44571	44586	44599
44468	44499	44527	44554	44572	44587	44601
44478	44500	44528	44558*	44575	44588	44602
44481	44501	44529	44560*	44577	44589	44603
44484	44505	44534	44564	44580	44591	44605
44486	44514	44536	44565			

TOTAL: 200

5MT

4-6-0

Introduced 1934. Stanier L.M.S. taper boiler design.

Experimental locomotives:
Introduced 1947[1]. Stephenson link motion (outside), Timken roller bearings.
Introduced 1948[2]. Caprotti valve gear.
Introduced 1948[3]. Caprotti valve gear, Timken roller bearings.
Introduced 1948[4]. Caprotti valve gear, Timken roller bearings, double chimney.
Introduced 1947[5]. Timken roller bearings.
Introduced 1947[6]. Timken roller bearings, double chimney.
Introduced 1949[7]. Fitted with steel firebox.
Introduced 1950[8]. Skefko roller bearings.
Introduced 1950[9]. Timken roller bearings on driving coupled axle only.
Introduced 1950[10]. Skefko roller bearings on driving coupled axle only.
Introduced 1951[11]. Caprotti valve gear, Skefko roller bearings, double chimney.

Weight
Locomotive: 72 tons 2 cwt
75 tons 6 cwt ([1,5,6,8,9,10])
74 tons ([2,3,4,11])
72 tons 2 cwt ([7])

Boiler pressure
225 lb sq in

Cylinders
(O) $18\frac{1}{2}$" × 28"

Driving wheel diameter
6' 0"

Tractive effort
25,455 lb

Valve gear
Walschaerts (piston valves) except where otherwise shown

44658	44663	44668[10]	44673[10]	44679[8]	44684[8]	44689[9]
44659	44664	44669[10]	44674[10]	44680[8]	44685[8]	44690[9]
44660	44665	44670[10]	44675[10]	44681[8]	44686[11]	44691[9]
44661	44666	44671[10]	44677[10]	44682[8]	44687[11]	44692[9]
44662	44667	44672[10]	44678[8]	44683[8]	44688[9]	44693[9]

44694[9]	44751[3]	44806	44854	44903	44953	45012
44695[9]	44753[3]	44807	44855	44904	44954	45013
44696[9]	44756[4]	44808	44856	44905	44955	45014
44697[9]	44757[4]	44809	44857	44906	44956	45015
44698	44758[5]	44810	44858	44907	44958	45016
44699	44759[5]	44811	44859	44908	44959	45017
44700	44760[5]	44812	44860	44909	44960	45018
44702	44761[5]	44813	44861	44910	44962	45019
44703	44762[5]	44814	44862	44911	44963	45020
44704	44763[5]	44815	44863	44912	44964	45021
44705	44764[5]	44816	44864	44913	44965	45024
44707	44765[6]	44817	44865	44914	44966	45025
44708	44766[6]	44818	44866	44915	44970	45026
44709	44767[1]	44819	44867	44916	44971	45027
44710	44768	44820	44868	44917	44972	45028
44711	44769	44821	44869	44918	44973	45029
44712	44770	44822	44870	44919	44974	45031
44713	44771	44823	44871	44920	44975	45033
44714	44772	44824	44872	44921	44977	45034
44715	44773	44825	44873	44924	44978	45035
44716	44774	44826	44874	44925	44979	45037
44717	44775	44827	44875	44926	44980	45038
44718[7]	44776	44828	44876	44927	44981	45039
44719[7]	44777	44829	44877	44928	44982	45040
44720[7]	44778	44830	44878	44929	44983	45041
44721[7]	44779	44831	44879	44930	44984	45042
44722[7]	44780	44832	44880	44931	44985	45043
44723[7]	44781	44833	44881	44932	44986	45044
44724[7]	44782	44834	44882	44933	44987	45045
44725[7]	44786	44835	44883	44934	44988	45046
44726[7]	44787	44836	44884	44935	44989	45047
44727[7]	44788	44837	44886	44936	44990	45048
44728	44789	44838	44887	44937	44991	45050
44729	44790	44839	44888	44938	44992	45051
44730	44791	44840	44889	44939	44993	45052
44731	44792	44841	44890	44940	44995	45053
44732	44793	44842	44891	44941	44997	45054
44733	44794	44843	44892	44942	44998	45055
44734	44795	44844	44893	44943	44999	45056
44735	44796	44845	44894	44944	45000	45057
44736	44797	44846	44895	44945	45001	45058
44737	44798	44847	44896	44946	45002	45059
44739[2]	44799	44848	44897	44947	45003	45060
44741[2]	44800	44849	44898	44948	45004	45061
44743[2]	44802	44850	44899	44949	45005	45062
44745[2]	44803	44851	44900	44950	45006	45063
44748[3]	44804	44852	44901	44951	45009	45064
44749[3]	44805	44853	44902	44952	45011	45065

Class 5MT 4-6-0 No. 44686 (with Caprotti valve gear, Skefko roller bearings and double chimney)
[A. W. Martin

Class 5MT 4-6-0 No. 44753 (with Caprotti valve gear and Timken roller bearings)
[D. C. Smith

Class 5MT 4-6-0 No. 45421
[J. B. Bucknall

45067	45078	45092	45105	45115	45130	45140
45068	45079	45093	45106	45116	45131	45141
45069	45080	45094	45107	45117	45132	45142
45070	45081	45095	45108	45118	45133	45143
45071	45082	45096	45109	45120	45134	45145
45072	45083	45097	45110	45124	45135	45146
45073	45084	45101	45111	45126	45136	45147
45074	45088	45102	45112	45127	45137	45148
45075	45089	45103	45113	45128	45138	45149
45076	45090	45104	45114	45129	45139	45150
45077	45091					

45154 *Lanarkshire Yeomanry*   45156 *Ayrshire Yeomanry*
45155   45160

45161	45206	45240	45278	45312	45349	45390
45162	45207	45241	45279	45313	45350	45391
45163	45208	45242	45280	45314	45351	45392
45164	45209	45243	45281	45316	45352	45393
45167	45210	45245	45282	45318	45353	45394
45168	45211	45246	45283	45319	45354	45395
45171	45212	45247	45284	45321	45357	45396
45176	45213	45248	45285	45322	45359	45397
45177	45214	45249	45286	45323	45360	45398
45178	45215	45250	45287	45324	45362	45399
45180	45216	45252	45288	45325	45363	45402
45181	45217	45253	45289	45326	45364	45403
45182	45218	45254	45290	45327	45365	45404
45183	45219	45255	45291	45328	45368	45405
45184	45220	45256	45292	45329	45369	45406
45185	45221	45257	45293	45330	45370	45407
45186	45222	45258	45294	45331	45371	45408
45187	45223	45259	45295	45332	45372	45409
45188	45224	45260	45296	45333	45373	45410
45190	45225	45261	45297	45334	45374	45411
45191	45226	45262	45298	45335	45375	45412
45192	45227	45263	45299	45336	45376	45413
45193	45228	45264	45300	45337	45377	45414
45194	45229	45267	45301	45338	45378	45415
45195	45230	45268	45302	45339	45379	45416
45196	45231	45269	45303	45340	45380	45417
45197	45232	45270	45304	45341	45381	45418
45198	45233	45271	45305	45342	45382	45419
45200	45234	45272	45306	45343	45383	45420
45201	45235	45273	45307	45344	45385	45421
45202	45236	45274	45308	45345	45386	45422
45203	45237	45275	45309	45346	45387	45423
45204	45238	45276	45310	45347	45388	45424
45205	45239	45277	45311	45348	45389	45425

45426	45435	45444	45455	45469	45477	45490
45427	45436	45445	45456	45470	45478	45491
45428	45437	45446	45460	45471	45480	45492
45429	45438	45447	45461	45472	45481	45493
45430	45439	45448	45463	45473	45483	45494
45431	45440	45449	45464	45474	45486	45495
45432	45441	45450	45466	45475	45488	45498
45433	45442	45451	45467	45476	45489	45499
45434	45443	45454				

TOTAL: 744

7P   "Patriot"   4-6-0

Introduced 1946. Ivatt rebuild of Fowler parallel boiler locomotives introduced 1933, with larger taper boiler, new cylinders and double chimney. (Fowler locomotives numbered 45502–41 were officially considered as rebuilds of L.N.W. "Claughton" class, introduced 1912).

Weight
Locomotive: 82 tons

Driving wheel diameter
6' 9"

Boiler pressure
250 lb sq in

Tractive effort
29,570 lb

Cylinders
Three, 17" × 26"

Valve gear
Walschaerts (piston valves)

45512	Bunsen	45527	Southport
45522	Prestatyn	45530	Sir Frank Ree
45526	Morecambe and Heysham	45531	Sir Frederick Harrison

TOTAL: 6

6P5F, 7P*   "Jubilee"   4-6-0

6P5F, introduced 1934. Stanier L.M.S. taper boiler development of the "Patriot" class.

†Fitted with double chimney.

***7P**, introduced 1942. Rebuilt with larger boiler and double chimney.

Weight
Locomotive: 79 tons 11 cwt
               82 tons*

Driving wheel diameter
6' 9"

Boiler pressure
225 lb sq in
250 lb sq in*

Tractive effort
26,610 lb
29,570 lb*

Cylinders
Three, 17" × 26"

Valve gear
Walschaerts (piston valves)

45552	Silver Jubilee	45556	Nova Scotia
45553	Canada	45557	New Brunswick
45554	Ontario	45558	Manitoba

45561	Saskatchewan	45635	Tobago
45562	Alberta	45641	Sandwich
45563	Australia	45642	Boscawen
45564	New South Wales	45643	Rodney
45565	Victoria	45647	Sturdee
45567	South Australia	45652	Hawke
45573	Newfoundland	45653	Barham
45574	India	45654	Hood
45577	Bengal	45655	Keith
45579	Punjab	45657	Tyrwhitt
45580	Burma	45658	Keyes
45581	Bihar and Orissa	45660	Rooke
45583	Assam	45661	Vernon
45584	North West Frontier	45663	Jervis
45586	Mysore	45664	Nelson
45588	Kashmir	45666	Cornwallis
45589	Gwalior	45667	Jellicoe
45590	Travancore	45670	Howard of Effingham
45592	Indore	45672	Anson
45593	Kholapur	45674	Duncan
45595	Southern Rhodesia	45675	Hardy
45596†	Bahamas	45676	Codrington
45597	Barbados	45681	Aboukir
45598	Basutoland	45684	Jutland
45599	Bechuanaland	45689	Ajax
45600	Bermuda	45694	Bellerophon
45601	British Guiana	45696	Arethusa
45602	British Honduras	45697	Achilles
45604	Ceylon	45698	Mars
45608	Gibraltar	45699	Galatea
45611	Hong Kong	45703	Thunderer
45613	Kenya	45704	Leviathan
45617	Mauritius	45705	Seahorse
45620	North Borneo	45716	Swiftsure
45622	Nyasaland	45721	Impregnable
45623	Palestine	45723	Fearless
45626	Seychelles	45726	Vindictive
45627	Sierra Leone	45733 *	Novelty
45629	Straits Settlements	45735*	Comet
45631	Tanganyika	45736*	Phoenix
45632	Tonga	45739	Ulster
45633	Aden	45742	Connaught

TOTAL: 90

Class 7P 4-6-0 No. 45522 *Prestatyn*   [*G. W. Morrison*

Class 6P5F 4-6-0 No. 45592 *Indore*   [*G. H. Wheeler*

Class 7P 4-6-0 No. 46128 *The Lovat Scouts*   [*G. H. Wheeler*

7P   "Royal Scot"   4-6-0

Introduced 1943. Stanier rebuild of Fowler L.M.S. locomotives (introduced 1927) with taper boiler, new cylinders and double chimney.

Weight
Locomotive: 83 tons

Boiler pressure
250 lb sq in

Cylinders
Three, 18″ × 26″

Driving wheel diameter
6′ 9″

Tractive effort
33,150 lb

Valve gear
Walschaerts (piston valves)

46115	Scots Guardsman	46155	The Lancer
46122	Royal Ulster Rifleman	46156	The South Wales Borderer
46125	3rd Carabinier		
46128	The Lovat Scouts	46160	Queen Victoria's Rifleman
46140	The King's Royal Rifle Corps	46163	Civil Service Rifleman
46148	The Manchester Regiment	46165	The Ranger (12th London Regiment)
46152	The King's Dragoon Guardsman	46166	London Rifle Brigade

TOTAL: 13

8P   "Coronation"   4-6-2

Introduced 1937. Stanier L.M.S. enlargement of "Princess Royal" class. 46225–29/35–48 originally streamlined. (Streamlined casing removed from 1946.)

*Introduced 1947. Ivatt development with roller bearings and detail alterations.

Weight
Locomotive: 105 tons 5 cwt
106 tons 8 cwt*

Boiler pressure
250 lb sq in

Cylinders
Four, 16½″ × 28″

Driving wheel diameter
6′ 9″

Tractive effort
40,000 lb

Valve gear
Walschaerts (rocking shafts and piston valves)

46225	Duchess of Gloucester	46239	City of Chester
46226	Duchess of Norfolk	46240	City of Coventry
46228	Duchess of Rutland	46241	City of Edinburgh
46235	City of Birmingham	46243	City of Lancaster
46237	City of Bristol	46244	King George VI
46238	City of Carlisle	46245	City of London

Class 8P 4-6-2 No. 46250 *City of Lichfield*

[R. A. Panting

46248 City of Leeds	46255 City of Hereford
46250 City of Lichfield	46256* Sir William A. Stanier,
46251 City of Nottingham	F.R.S.
46254 City of Stoke-on-Trent	46257* City of Salford

TOTAL: 19

2MT   2-6-0

Introduced 1946. Ivatt L.M.S. taper boiler design.

Weight
Locomotive: 47 tons 2 cwt

Boiler pressure
200 lb sq in

Cylinders
(O) 16″ × 24″
(O) 16½″ × 24″*

Driving wheel diameter
5′ 0″

Tractive effort
17,410 lb
18,510 lb*

Valve gear
Walschaerts (piston valves)

46400	46421	46437	46454	46475*	46498*	46513*
46401	46422	46439	46455	46479*	46499*	46514*
46402	46423	46440	46456	46480*	46500*	46515*
46404	46424	46441	46457	46482*	46501*	46516*
46405	46425	46442	46458	46484*	46502*	46517*
46406	46426	46443	46459	46485*	46503*	46518*
46410	46427	46444	46460	46486*	46504*	46519*
46411	46428	46445	46461	46487*	46505*	46520*
46412	46429	46446	46462	46488*	46506*	46521*
46413	46430	46447	46463	46490*	46507*	46522*
46414	46431	46448	46464	46491*	46508*	46523*
46416	46432	46449	46465*	46492*	46509*	46524*
46417	46433	46450	46468*	46495*	46510*	46525*
46418	46434	46451	46470*	46496*	46511*	46526*
46419	46436	46452	46472*	46497*	46512*	46527*
46420						

TOTAL: 106

Class 8P 4-6-2 No. 46256 *Sir William Stanier F.R.S.* (with detail differences)
[*G. H. Wheeler*

Class 2MT 2-6-0 No. 46479   [*R. A. Panting*

Class 0F 0-4-0ST No. 47002

0F   0-4-0ST

Introduced 1932. Kitson design prepared to Stanier's requirements for L.M.S.

*Introduced 1953. Extended side tanks and coal space.

Weight
33 tons
34 tons*

Boiler pressure
160 lb sq in NS

Cylinders
(O) 15½" × 20"

Driving wheel diameter
3' 10"

Tractive effort
14,205 lb

Valve gear
Stephenson

| 47000 | 47001 | 47002 | 47005* | 47006* | 47008* | 47009* |

TOTAL: 7

2F   0-6-0T

Introduced 1928. Fowler L.M.S. short-wheelbase dock tanks.

Weight
43 tons 12 cwt

Boiler pressure
160 lb sq in NS

Cylinders
(O) 17" × 22"

Driving wheel diameter
3' 11"

Tractive effort
18,400 lb

Valve gear
Walschaerts

| 47164S | 47165S |

TOTAL: 2

3F   0-6-0T

Introduced 1899. Johnson large Midland design, rebuilt with Belpaire firebox from 1919; fitted with condensing apparatus for London area.

*Non-condensing locomotives.

Weight
48 tons 15 cwt

Boiler pressure
160 lb sq in

Cylinders
18" × 26"

Driving wheel diameter
4' 7"

Tractive effort
20,835 lb

Valve gear
Stephenson

| 47201* | 47211 | 47230* | 47231* | 47236* | 47250* | 47257*S |
| 47202 |

TOTAL: 8

Class 0F 0-4-0ST No. 47009 (with extended side-tanks and coal space) [*C. Symes*

Class 2F 0-6-0T No. 47165 [*I. G. Holt*

Introduced 1924. Post-grouping development of Midland design with detail alterations.

*Introduced 1929. Locomotives built for S. & D.J. (taken into L.M.S. stock 1930).

†Push-and-pull fitted.

Weight
49 tons 10 cwt

Driving wheel diameter
4′ 7″

Boiler pressure
160 lb sq in NS

Tractive effort
20,835 lb

Cylinders
18″ × 26″

Valve gear
Stephenson

47266	47326	47378	47439	47500	47587	47647
47272	47327	47383	47442	47501	47590	47649
47273	47330S	47384S	47444	47505S	47592S	47653
47276	47333	47388	47445	47506	47596	47655†
47279	47336	47389	47447	47507	47597S	47656
47280	47338	47390	47450	47512	47598	47658S
47284	47341S	47391	47451S	47519	47599	47659
47285	47343	47393	47452	47520	47602	47660
47286	47344	47395	47453	47521	47603	47661S
47288	47345	47396S	47454	47524	47606	47662
47289	47349	47397	47461	47530	47611	47664
47293	47350	47399	47464	47531	47612	47665
47295	47354	47400S	47467	47533	47614	47666
47298	47355	47406	47468	47534	47615S	47667
47305	47357	47408	47471	47535	47616	47668
47306	47359	47410	47472	47543	47627	47669
47307	47361	47415	47480†	47544	47628	47671
47308	47362	47416	47482	47549S	47629	47673
47313*	47365	47423	47485	47564	47631	47674
47314*	47367	47427	47487	47565	47640	47675
47317	47371	47428	47492	47566	47641	47676
47318S	47372	47429S	47493	47577	47643	47677
47321	47373	47432	47494	47578	47645	47680
47324	47375	47435	47495	47584	47646S	47681†
47325	47377	47437	47499			

TOTAL: 172

Introduced 1935. Stanier L.M.S. taper boiler design.

Weight	Driving wheel diameter
Locomotive: 72 tons 2 cwt	4' 8½"

Boiler pressure	Tractive effort
225 lb sq in	32,440 lb

Cylinders	Valve gear
(O) 18½" × 28"	Walschaerts (piston valves)

48000	48069	48113	48155	48196	48258	48297
48001	48070	48114	48156	48197	48259	48301
48002	48073	48115	48157	48198	48260	48302
48003	48074	48116	48158	48199	48261	48303
48004	48075	48117	48159	48200	48262	48304
48005	48076	48118	48160	48201	48263	48305
48006	48077	48119	48161	48202	48264	48307
48007	48078	48120	48162	48203	48265	48308
48010	48079	48121	48163	48204	48266	48309
48011	48080	48122	48164	48205	48267	48310
48012	48081	48123	48165	48206	48268	48311
48016	48082	48124	48166	48207	48269	48312
48017	48083	48125	48167	48208	48270	48313
48018	48084	48126	48168	48211	48271	48314
48020	48085	48127	48169	48212	48272	48315
48024	48088	48128	48170	48213	48273	48316
48026	48089	48129	48171	48214	48274	48317
48027	48090	48130	48173	48215	48275	48318
48029	48092	48131	48174	48217	48276	48319
48033	48093	48132	48175	48218	48277	48320
48035	48094	48133	48176	48219	48278	48321
48036	48095	48134	48177	48220	48279	48322
48037	48096	48135	48178	48221	48280	48323
48039	48097	48136	48180	48222	48281	48324
48045	48098	48137	48181	48223	48282	48325
48046	48099	48138	48182	48224	48283	48326
48050	48100	48139	48183	48225	48284	48327
48053	48101	48141	48184	48246	48285	48328
48054	48102	48142	48185	48247	48286	48329
48055	48103	48143	48186	48248	48287	48330
48056	48104	48145	48187	48249	48288	48331
48057	48105	48146	48188	48250	48289	48332
48060	48106	48147	48189	48251	48290	48333
48061	48107	48148	48190	48252	48291	48334
48062	48108	48149	48191	48253	48292	48335
48063	48109	48151	48192	48254	48293	48336
48064	48110	48152	48193	48255	48294	48337
48065	48111	48153	48194	48256	48295	48338
48067	48112	48154	48195	48257	48296	48339

Above: Ex-Midland
Class 3F 0-6-0T No.
47250 [D. Smith

Right: Class 3F
0-6-0T No. 47667
[Alan Williams

Below: Class 8F
2-8-0 No. 48610
[A. W. Martin

48340	48389	48441	48504	48554	48644	48692
48342	48390	48442	48505	48555	48645	48693
48343	48391	48443	48506	48556	48646	48694
48344	48392	48444	48507	48557	48647	48695
48345	48393	48445	48509	48558	48648	48696
48346	48394	48446	48510	48559	48649	48697
48347	48395	48447	48511	48600	48650	48698
48348	48397	48448	48512	48601	48651	48699
48349	48398	48449	48513	48602	48652	48700
48350	48399	48450	48514	48603	48653	48701
48351	48400	48451	48515	48604	48654	48702
48352	48401	48452	48516	48605	48655	48703
48353	48402	48453	48517	48606	48656	48704
48354	48403	48454	48518	48607	48657	48705
48355	48404	48455	48519	48608	48658	48706
48356	48405	48456	48520	48609	48659	48707
48357	48406	48457	48521	48610	48660	48708
48358	48408	48458	48522	48611	48661	48709
48359	48409	48459	48523	48612	48662	48710
48360	48410	48460	48525	48613	48663	48711
48361	48411	48461	48526	48614	48664	48712
48362	48412	48462	48527	48615	48665	48713
48363	48413	48464	48528	48617	48666	48714
48364	48414	48465	48529	48618	48667	48715
48365	48415	48466	48530	48619	48668	48716
48366	48416	48467	48531	48620	48669	48717
48367	48417	48468	48532	48621	48670	48718
48368	48418	48469	48533	48622	48671	48719
48369	48419	48470	48534	48623	48672	48720
48370	48421	48471	48535	48624	48673	48721
48371	48422	48472	48536	48625	48674	48722
48372	48423	48473	48537	48626	48675	48723
48373	48424	48474	48538	48627	48676	48724
48374	48425	48475	48539	48628	48677	48725
48375	48426	48476	48540	48629	48678	48726
48376	48427	48477	48541	48630	48679	48727
48377	48428	48478	48542	48631	48680	48728
48378	48429	48479	48543	48632	48681	48729
48379	48430	48490	48544	48633	48682	48730
48380	48432	48491	48545	48634	48683	48731
48381	48433	48492	48546	48635	48684	48732
48382	48434	48493	48547	48636	48685	48733
48383	48435	48494	48548	48637	48686	48734
48384	48436	48495	48549	48638	48687	48735
48385	48437	48500	48550	48639	48688	48736
48386	48438	48501	48551	48640	48689	48737
48387	48439	48502	48552	48641	48690	48738
48388	48440	48503	48553	48643	48691	48739

48740	48745	48750	48755	48760	48765	48770
48741	48746	48751	48756	48761	48766	48771
48742	48747	48752	48757	48762	48767	48773
48743	48748	48753	48758	48763	48768	48774
48744	48749	48754	48759	48764	48769	48775

TOTAL: 644

7F   0-8-0

Introduced 1936. L.N.W. G2a class. Bowen-Cooke G1 superheated design of 1912, rebuilt with G2 boiler and Belpaire firebox.

Weight
Locomotive: 62 tons

Boiler pressure
175 lb sq in

Cylinders
20½″ × 24″

Driving wheel diameter
4′ 5½″

Tractive effort
28,045 lb

Valve gear
Joy (piston valves)

48895   49173   49361

TOTAL: 3

7F   0-8-0

Introduced 1921. Development of L.N.W. G2 class. Bowen-Cooke G1 superheated design of 1912 with higher pressure boiler. Many later rebuilt with Belpaire firebox.

Weight
Locomotive: 62 tons

Boiler pressure
175 lb sq in

Cylinders
20½″ × 24″

Driving wheel diameter
4′ 5½″

Tractive effort
28,045 lb

Valve gear
Joy (piston valves)

49407   49430

TOTAL: 2

0F   0-4-0ST

Introduced 1891. Aspinall L. & Y. Class 21.

Weight
21 tons 5 cwt

Boiler pressure
160 lb sq in NS

Cylinders
(O) 13″ × 18″

Driving wheel diameter
3′ 0⅝″

Tractive effort
11,335 lb

Valve gear
Stephenson

51218

TOTAL: 1

7F   2-8-0

Introduced 1914.   Fowler design for S. & D.J.   Taken into L.M.S.
   stock, 1930.

Weight
Locomotive: 64 tons 15 cwt

Boiler pressure
190 lb sq in

Cylinders
(O) 21″ × 28″

53807

Driving wheel diameter
4′ 8½″

Tractive effort
35,295 lb

Valve gear
Walschaerts (piston valves)

TOTAL: I

PRESERVED LOCOMOTIVES IN WORKING ORDER

4-2-2

Introduced 1886. Neilson & Co. design for the Caledonian Railway
incorporating Drummond details. Withdrawn as L.M.S. No. 14010
in 1935. Restored to Caledonian livery and returned to service for
special use 1958.

Weight
Locomotive and Tender: 75 tons

Boiler pressure
150 lb sq in NS

Cylinders
18″ × 26″

123

Driving wheel diameter
7′ 0″

Tractive effort
12,785 lb

Valve gear
Stephenson

4-6-0

Introduced 1894. Jones Highland Goods design. Withdrawn 1934 as
L.M.S. No. 17916 for preservation. Restored to original condition
and returned to service for special use 1959.

Weight
Locomotive: 56 tons

Boiler pressure
175 lb sq in NS

Cylinders
(O) 20″ × 26″

103

Driving wheel diameter
5′ 3″

Tractive effort
24,555 lb

Valve gear
Stephenson

Above: Ex-L.N.W. Class 7F 0-8-0 No. 49407 [*D. L. Percival*

Right: Ex-L. & Y. Class 0F 0-4-0ST No. 51218 [*G. T. Storer*

Below: Ex-S. & D. Class 7F 2-8-0 No. 53807 [*N. E. Preedy*

DEPARTMENTAL LOCOMOTIVE

2F   0-6-0ST

Introduced 1891. Aspinall rebuild of L. & Y. Barton Wright Class 23
0-6-0. Originally introduced 1877.

Weight
43 tons 17 cwt

Driving wheel diameter
4′ 6″

Boiler pressure
140 lb sq in NS

Tractive effort
17,545 lb

Cylinders
17½″ × 26″

Valve gear
Stephenson

11305

TOTAL: 1

LOCOMOTIVE SUPERINTENDENTS AND CHIEF MECHANICAL ENGINEERS
L.M.S.

George Hughes 1923–1925	Sir William Stanier ... 1932–1944
Sir Henry Fowler ... 1925–1931	Charles E. Fairburn ... 1944–1945
E. H. J. Lemon	H. G. Ivatt 1945–1951
(Sir Ernest Lemon) 1931–1932	

CALEDONIAN

Robert Sinclair
(First Loco. engineer)*   1847–1856
Benjamin Connor   ...   1856–1876
George Brittain   ...   1876–1882
Dugald Drummond   ...   1882–1890
Hugh Smellie   1890
J. Lambie   1890–1895
J. F. McIntosh   1895–1914
William Pickersgill   ...   1914–1923

GLASGOW & SOUTH WESTERN

Patrick Stirling   1853–1866
James Stirling   1866–1878
Hugh Smellie   1878–1890
James Manson   1890–1912
Peter Drummond   ...   1912–1918
R. H. Whitelegg   ...   1918–1923

*Exclusive of previous service with constituent company.

Above: Caledonian Railway No. 123 (restored to C.R. livery)
[*N. E. Preedy*

Right: Highland Railway No. 103 (restored to H.R. livery)
[*N. E. Preedy*

Below: Class 2F 0-6-0ST departmental locomotive No. 11305
[*I. G. Holt*

FURNESS

R. Mason	1890–1897
W. F. Pettigrew ...	1897–1918
D. J. Rutherford ...	1918–1923

LANCASHIRE & YORKSHIRE

Sir John Hawkshaw (Consultant),*
  Hurst and Jenkins successively
  to 1868

W. Hurst	1868–1876
W. Barton Wright ...	1876–1886
John A. F. Aspinall ...	1886–1899
H. A. Hoy	1899–1904
George Hughes	1904–1921

The L. & Y. amalgamated with
L.N.W.R. as from January 1st, 1922

LONDON & NORTH WESTERN

Francis Trevithick and
  J. E. McConnell, first
  loco. engineers, 1846,
  with Alexander Allan
  largely responsible for
  design at Crewe.*

John Ramsbottom ...	1857–1871
Francis William Webb	1871–1903
George Whale ...	1903–1909
Charles John Bowen-Cooke ...	1909–1920
Capt. Hewitt Pearson Montague Beames ...	1920–1921
George Hughes	1922

LONDON, TILBURY & SOUTHEND

Thomas Whitelegg ...	1880–1910
Robert Harben Whitelegg ...	1910–1912

(L.T. & S.R. absorbed by M.R.
and control of locos transferred
to Derby as from August, 1912.)

MARYPORT & CARLISLE

Hugh Smellie	1870–1878
J. Campbell	1878–
William Coulthard ...	* –1904
J. B. Adamson	1904–1923

HIGHLAND

William Stroudley (First loco engineer) ...	1866–1869
David Jones	1869–1896
Peter Drummond ...	1896–1911
F. G. Smith	1912–1915
C. Cumming	1915–1923

MIDLAND

Matthew Kirtley (First loco. engineer)	1844–1873
Samuel Waite Johnson	1873–1903
Richard Mountford Deeley	1903–1909
Henry Fowler	1909–1923

SOMERSET & DORSET JOINT

Until leased by Mid. and L. &
S. W. (as from 1st November 1875)
locomotives were bought from out-
side builders, principally George
England of Hatcham Iron Works, S.E.
After the above date, Derby and its
various Loco. Supts. and C.M.Es. have
acted for S. & D.J. aided by a resident
Loco. Supt. stationed at Highbridge
Works.

NORTH STAFFORDSHIRE

L. Clare	1876–1882
L. Longbottom	1882–1902
J. H. Adams	1902–1915
J. A. Hookham	1915–1923

W. Angus was Loco. Supt. at
Stoke prior to 1876. No earlier
records can be traced.

WIRRAL

Eric G. Barker	1892–1902
T. B. Hunter	1903–1923

Barker of the Wirral Railway is
noteworthy for originating the 4-4-4
tank type in this country (1896).

NORTH LONDON

(Worked by L. & N.W. by agreement
dated December, 1908.)

William Adams	1853–1873
J. C. Park	1873–1893
Henry J. Pryce ...	1893–1908

*Date of actual entry into office not known.

Ex-L.N.E.R. STEAM LOCOMOTIVES
Nos. 60001-69028

The numbers of locomotives in service have been checked in E.R. to July 25, 1964; N.E.R. to July 25, 1964; L.M.R. to July 11, 1964; and Sc.R. to July 25, 1964.

8P6F　　　　　　　**A4**　　　　　　　**4-6-2**

Introduced 1935. Gresley streamlined design with corridor tender (except those marked †). All fitted with double chimney.
*Inside cylinder reduced to 17″.

Weight
Locomotive: 102 tons 19 cwt
Tender: 64 tons 19 cwt
　　　　60 tons 7 cwt†

Boiler pressure
250 lb sq in

Cylinders
Three, 18½″ × 26″
Two, 18½″ × 26″ One, 17″ × 26″*

Driving wheel diameter
6′ 8″

Tractive effort
35,455 lb
33,616 lb*

Valve gear
Walschaerts (with derived motion and piston valves)

60001†	Sir Ronald Matthews	60016†	Silver King
60004	William Whitelaw	60019†	Bittern
60006†	Sir Ralph Wedgwood	60023†	Golden Eagle
60007	Sir Nigel Gresley	60024	Kingfisher
60009	Union of South Africa	60026†	Miles Beevor
60010	Dominion of Canada	60027	Merlin
60012*	Commonwealth of Australia	60031	Golden Plover
		60034†	Lord Faringdon

TOTAL: 15

7P6F　　　　　　　**A3**　　　　　　　**4-6-2**

Introduced 1927. Development of Gresley G.N. 180 lb. Pacific (introduced 1922. L.N.E.R. A1, later A10) with 220 lb pressure (60045–80, 60106/12 rebuilt from A10). Some have G.N.-type tender with coal rails, remainder L.N.E.R. pattern*. All fitted with double chimney.

Weight
Locomotive: 96 tons 5 cwt
Tender: 56 tons 6 cwt
　　　　57 tons 18 cwt*

Boiler pressure
220 lb sq in

Cylinders
Three, 19″ × 26″

Driving wheel diameter
6′ 8″

Tractive effort
32,910 lb

Valve gear
Walschaerts (with derived motion and piston valves)

Class A4 4-6-2 No. 60024 *Kingfisher*   [*D. J. Dippie*

Class A3 4-6-2 No. 60036 *Colombo*   [*G. H. Wheeler*

Class A1 4-6-2 No. 60154 *Bon Accord*   [*J. B. Bucknall*

60036	Colombo	60084*	Trigo
60041	Salmon Trout	60085	Manna
60045	Lemberg	60091*	Captain Cuttle
60051*	Blink Bonny	60092*	Fairway
60052	Prince Palatine	60100*	Spearmint
60062	Minoru	60106	Flying Fox
60071	Tranquil	60112	St. Simon
60080	Dick Turpin		

TOTAL: 15

8P6F   A1   4-6-2

Introduced 1948. Peppercorn development of Thompson Class A1/1 (Class A1/1 was rebuild of Gresley A10 No. 4470, B.R. No. 60113).

*Fitted with roller bearings.

All fitted with double chimney.

Weight
Locomotive: 104 tons 2 cwt
Tender: 60 tons 7 cwt

Boiler pressure
250 lb sq in

Cylinders
Three, 19″ × 26″

Driving wheel diameter
6′ 8″

Tractive effort
37,400 lb

Valve gear
Walschaerts (piston valves)

60114	W. P. Allen	60140	Balmoral
60116	Hal o' the Wynd	60141	Abbotsford
60117	Bois Roussel	60142	Edward Fletcher
60118	Archibald Sturrock	60145	Saint Mungo
60121	Silurian	60146	Peregrine
60124	Kenilworth	60147	North Eastern
60126	Sir Vincent Raven	60148	Aboyeur
60127	Wilson Worsdell	60150	Willbrook
60128	Bongrace	60151	Midlothian
60129	Guy Mannering	60152	Holyrood
60130	Kestrel	60154*	Bon Accord
60131	Osprey	60155*	Borderer
60132	Marmion	60156*	Great Central
60133	Pommern	60157*	Great Eastern
60134	Foxhunter	60158	Aberdonian
60138	Boswell		

TOTAL: 31

8P7F **A2** **4-6-2**

A2/3, introduced 1946. Development of Thompson Class A2/2 Fitted with double chimney.

*A2, introduced 1947. Peppercorn development of Class A2/2 with shorter wheelbase.

†A2, rebuilt with double chimney and multiple valve regulator.

Weight
Locomotive: 101 tons 10 cwt
          101 tons*†
Tender: 60 tons 7 cwt

Boiler pressure
250 lb sq in

Cylinders
Three, 19″ × 26″

Driving wheel diameter
6′ 2″

Tractive effort
40,430 lb

Valve gear
Walschaerts (piston valves)

60512 *Steady Aim*	60528* *Tudor Minstrel*
60522 *Straight Deal*	60530* *Sayajirao*
60524 *Herringbone*	60532† *Blue Peter*
60527* *Sun Chariot*	60535* *Hornet's Beauty*

TOTAL: 8

7P6F **V2** **2-6-2**

Introduced 1936. Gresley design.

*Fitted with double chimney

Weight
Locomotive: 93 tons 2 cwt
Tender: 52 tons

Boiler pressure
220 lb sq in

Cylinders
Three, 18½″ × 26″

Driving wheel diameter
6′ 2″

Tractive effort
33,730 lb

Valve gear
Walschaerts (with derived motion and piston valves)

60806	60813	60822	60828	60835	60837	60844
60808	60816	60824	60831	60836	60843	60846
60810	60818					

60847 *St. Peter's School York A.D. 627*

60859	60884	60901	60929	60944	60957	60970
60865	60885	60913	60931	60946	60961	60973
60868	60886	60919	60939	60952	60962	60976
60876	60891	60923	60940	60955	60963*	60982
60877	60895					

TOTAL: 47

Class A2/3 4-6-2 No. 60512 *Steady Aim*

[*P. J. Sharpe*

Class A2 4-6-2 No. 60535 *Hornets Beauty*

[*W. R. Devitt*

Class V2 2-6-2 No. 60847 *St. Peters School York A.D. 627* (with outside steam pipes)

[*G. H. Wheeler*

Introduced 1942. Thompson design.

Weight
Locomotive: 71 tons 3 cwt
Tender: 52 tons

Boiler pressure
225 lb sq in

Cylinders
(O) 20″ × 26″

Driving wheel diameter
6′ 2″

Tractive effort
26,880 lb

Valve gear
Walschaerts (piston valves)

61002	*Impala*	
61003	*Gazelle*	
61008	*Kudu*	
61010	*Wildebeeste*	
61012	*Puku*	
61013	*Topi*	
61014	*Oribi*	
61016	*Inyala*	
61017	*Bushbuck*	
61018	*Gnu*	
61019	*Nilghai*	
61021	*Reitbok*	

61022	*Sassaby*
61023	*Hirola*
61024	*Addax*
61026	*Ourebi*
61029	*Chamois*
61030	*Nyala*
61031	*Reedbuck*
61032	*Stembok*
61034	*Chiru*
61035	*Pronghorn*
61039	*Steinbok*
61040	*Roedeer*

61042	61070	61098	61115	61132	61148	61168
61049	61072	61099	61116	61133	61153	61172
61050	61076	61101	61120	61134	61157	61173
61051	61087	61102	61121	61138	61158	61176
61055	61089	61103	61123	61140	61161	61179
61058	61092	61105	61127	61141	61162	61180
61061	61093	61107	61129	61145	61165	61185
61062	61094	61110	61131	61147	61167	61188
61065	61097					

61189   *Sir William Gray*

61190	61194	61196	61199	61210	61214
61191	61195	61198	61208	61212	

61215   *William Henton Carver*

61216	61218	61220

61221   *Sir Alexander Erskine-Hill*

61223	61224	61225	61232

61237	*Geoffrey H. Kitson*	61245	*Murray of Elibank*
61238	*Leslie Runciman*	61248	*Geoffrey Gibbs*
61240	*Harry Hinchliffe*	61250	*A. Harold Bibby*
61244	*Strang Steel*		

Class V2 2-6-2 No. 60939

[*D. J. Dippie*

Class B1 4-6-0 No. 61308

[*D. C. Smith*

Class K1 2-6-0 No. 62064

[*J. B. Bucknall*

61255	61276	61304	61322	61344	61365	61390
61256	61278	61306	61324	61345	61367	61392
61257	61281	61307	61326	61347	61370	61394
61259	61285	61308	61327	61348	61372	61396
61261	61289	61309	61329	61349	61382	61397
61262	61291	61310	61330	61350	61384	61398
61263	61292	61313	61337	61353	61385	61400
61264	61293	61315	61338	61354	61386	61403
61268	61294	61319	61340	61357	61387	61404
61272	61299	61320	61342	61360	61388	61406
61274	61302	61321	61343	61361	61389	61407
61275	61303					

TOTAL: 189

5P6F   K1   2-6-0

Introduced 1949. Peppercorn development of Thompson K1/1 (rebuilt from Gresley K4) with increased length.

Weight
Locomotive: 66 tons 17 cwt
Tender: 44 tons 4 cwt

Boiler pressure
225 lb sq in

Cylinders
(O) 20″ × 26″

Driving wheel diameter
5′ 2″

Tractive effort
32,080 lb

Valve gear
Walschaerts (piston valves)

62001	62009	62021	62029	62043	62051	62061
62002	62010	62022	62030	62044	62054	62062
62003	62011	62023	62033	62045	62055	62063
62004	62012	62024	62035	62046	62056	62064
62005	62014	62025	62037	62047	62057	62065
62006	62015	62026	62040	62048	62058	62066
62007	62017	62027	62041	62049	62059	62067
62008	62020	62028	62042	62050	62060	62070

TOTAL: 56

6F   Q6   0-8-0

Introduced 1913. Raven N.E. design.

*Some locomotives are fitted with tender from withdrawn B15 locomotives.

Weight
Locomotive: 65 tons 18 cwt
Tender: 44 tons 2 cwt
      44 tons*

Boiler pressure
180 lb sq in

Cylinders
(O) 20″ × 26″

Driving wheel diameter
4′ 7½″

Tractive effort
28,800 lb

Valve gear
Stephenson (piston valves)

63341	63360	63379	63397	63411	63427	63444
63343	63361	63381	63398	63412	63429	63445
63344	63362	63382	63402	63413	63431	63446
63346	63363	63384	63403	63414	63432	63450
63347	63366	63386	63404	63417	63435	63453
63349	63367	63387	63405	63419	63436	63454
63351	63368	63389	63406	63420	63437	63455
63354	63371	63391	63407	63421	63438	63456
63357	63377	63394	63409	63423	63440	63458
63359	63378	63395	63410	63426	63443	63459

TOTAL: 70

8F (O1)
7F (O4)
O1 & O4
2-8-0

O4/1, introduced 1911. Robinson G.C. design with small boiler, Belpaire firebox, steam and vacuum brakes and water scoop.

*O4/3, introduced 1917. R.O.D. locomotives with steam brake only and no scoop.

†O4/6, introduced 1924. Rebuilt from O5 retaining higher cab.

‡O4/7, introduced 1939. Rebuilt with shortened O2-type boiler, retaining G.C. smokebox.

§O4/8, introduced 1944. Rebuilt with 100A (B1) boiler, retaining original cylinders.

(O4/4 were rebuilds with O2 boilers, since rebuilt again; O5 was a G.C. development of O4 with larger boiler and Belpaire firebox.)

Weight
Locomotive: 73 tons 4 cwt
         73 tons 4 cwt*†
         73 tons 17 cwt‡
         72 tons 10 cwt§
Tender: 48 tons 6 cwt (with scoop)
      47 tons 6 cwt (without
          scoop)

Boiler pressure
180 lb sq in

Cylinders
(O) 21″ × 26″

Driving wheel diameter
4′ 8″

Tractive effort
31,325 lb

Valve gear
Stephenson (piston valves)

Class Q6 0-8-0 No. 63423   *[T. C. Lawrence*

Class O4/1 2-8-0 No. 63586   *[P. J. Hughes*

Class O1 2-8-0 No. 63663   *[L. King*

¶O1, introduced 1944. Thompson rebuild with 100A boiler, Walschaerts valve gear and new cylinders.

Weight
Locomotive: 73 tons 6 cwt
Tender as O4

Boiler pressure
225 lb sq in

Cylinders
(O) 20″ × 26″

Driving wheel diameter
4′ 8″

Tractive effort
35,520 lb

Valve gear
Walschaerts (piston valves)

63571¶	63630¶	63674§	63706§	63764*	63807§	63863¶
63586	63636§	63675§	63707	63765§	63813*	63868¶
63589¶	63639§	63679§	63717§	63768¶	63816§	63873§
63590¶	63644§	63683§	63725¶	63770‡	63818§	63877§
63593	63646¶	63688§	63728§	63773¶	63819§	63878§
63606§	63650¶	63691§	63730§	63781§	63828§	63879¶
63607	63651§	63692	63732§	63785§	63842*	63882§
63612§	63653§	63697§	63734§	63786¶	63843‡	63893§
63613§	63661‡	63701*	63738§	63788§	63850§	63902†
63615‡	63663¶	63702*	63739§	63791§	63858§	63906†
63628§	63671	63703§	63741§	63793§	63861§	63913†

TOTAL: O1, 14; O4, 63

5F	**J37**	**0-6-0**

Introduced 1914. Reid N.B. design. Superheated development of J35.

Weight
Locomotive: 54 tons 14 cwt
Tender: 40 tons 19 cwt

Boiler pressure
180 lb sq in

Cylinders
19½″ × 26″

Driving wheel diameter
5′ 0″

Tractive effort
25,210 lb

Valve gear
Stephenson (piston valves)

64547	64569	64576	64591	64602	64614	64624
64552	64570	64577	64592	64606	64618	64625
64555	64571	64580	64595	64608	64620	64632
64558	64572	64585	64597	64610	64621	64636
64563	64573	64588	64599	64611	64623	

TOTAL: 34

Top: Class
O4/8 2-8-0
No. 63688
[P. J. Hughes

Centre: Class
J37 0-6-0 No.
64623
[R. B. Parr

Left: Class
J36 0-6-0 No.
65297
[I. G. Holt

2F   **J36**   **0-6-0**

Introduced 1888. Holmes N.B. design.

Weight   **Driving wheel diameter**
Locomotive: 41 tons 19 cwt   5′ 0″
Tender: 33 tons 9 cwt
                                    Tractive effort
Boiler pressure   19,690 lb
165 lb sq in NS
                                    Valve gear
Cylinders   Stephenson
18¼″ × 26″

65234   65243 *Maude*

65267   65282   65288   65297   65319   65327   65345

TOTAL: 9

5F   **J27**   **0-6-0**

Introduced 1906. W. Worsdell N.E. design developed from J26.
*Introduced 1921. Raven locomotive. Superheated, with piston
valves.
†Introduced 1943. Piston valves, but superheater removed.

Weight   **Driving wheel diameter**
Locomotive: 47 tons   4′ 7¼″
            49 tons 10 cwt*
Tender: 36 tons 19 cwt   **Tractive effort**
                                    24,640 lb
Boiler pressure
180 lb sq in SS   **Valve gear**
                                    Stephenson
Cylinders
18½″ × 26″

65788   65802   65815   65832   65845   65861†   65878†
65789   65804   65817   65833   65846   65862†   65879†
65790   65805   65819   65834   65851   65865†   65880*
65791   65808   65821   65835   65853   65869†   65882†
65792   65809   65822   65838   65855   65870†   65885†
65794   65811   65823   65841   65858   65872†   65892†
65795   65812   65825   65842   65859   65873†   65893†
65796   65813   65831   65844   65860†   65874†   65894†
65801   65814

TOTAL: 58

Top: Class J27 0-6-0
No. 65893
[R. B. Arthur

Centre: Class J38
0-6-0 No. 65929
[K. R. Pirt

Left: Class V3
2-6-2T No. 67628
[T. Booth

6F   J38   0-6-0

Introduced 1926. Gresley design. Predecessor of J39, with smaller wheels, boiler 6″ longer than J39 and smokebox 6″ shorter.
*Rebuilt with J39 boiler.

Weight
Locomotive: 58 tons 19 cwt
Tender: 44 tons 4 cwt

Boiler pressure
180 lb sq in

Cylinders
20″ × 26″

Driving wheel diameter
4′ 8″

Tractive effort
28,415 lb

Valve gear
Stephenson (piston valves)

65901	65908*	65912	65916	65920	65926*	65931
65903*	65909	65913	65917*	65921	65927*	65932
65905	65910	65914	65918*	65922	65929	65933
65906*	65911	65915	65919	65925	65930	65934
65907						

TOTAL: 29

4MT   V3   2-6-2T

Introduced 1939. Gresley design. Development of V1 introduced 1930, with higher pressure (locomotives numbered below 67682 rebuilt from V1).

Weight
86 tons 16 cwt

Boiler pressure
200 lb sq in

Cylinders
Three, 16″ × 26″

Driving wheel diameter
5′ 8″

Tractive effort
24,960 lb

Valve gear
Walschaerts (with derived motion and piston valves)

67620	67636	67640	67646	67684	67690	67691
67628	67638	67643	67678			

TOTAL: 11

4F   J94   0-6-0ST

Introduced 1943. Riddles Ministry of Supply design, purchased by L.N.E.R., 1946.

Weight
48 tons 5 cwt

Boiler pressure
170 lb sq in NS

Cylinders
18″ × 26″

Driving wheel diameter
4′ 3″

Tractive effort
23,870 lb

Valve gear
Stephenson

68006	68012	68019	68043	68050	68060	68068
68010	68013	68023	68047	68053	68062	68079
68011	68014	68037				

TOTAL: 17

| **2F** | **J72** | **0-6-0T** |

Introduced 1949. Development of W. Worsdell N. E. design of 1898.

Weight
38 tons 12 cwt

Boiler pressure
140 lb sq in NS

Cylinders
17″ × 24″

Driving wheel diameter
4′ 1¼″

Tractive effort
16,760 lb

Valve gear
Stephenson

| 69005 | 69016 | 69023 | 69028 |

TOTAL: 4

PRESERVED LOCOMOTIVES IN WORKING ORDER

| **IP** | **D40** | **4-4-0** |

Introduced 1920. Heywood G.N. of S. superheated development of Pickersgill 1899 design. Withdrawn 1958 as B.R. No. 62277 and restored to original condition, being returned to service for special use in 1959.

Weight
Locomotive: 48 tons 13 cwt
Tender: 37 tons 8 cwt

Boiler pressure
165 lb sq in

Cylinders
18″ × 26″

Driving wheel diameter
6′ 1″

Tractive effort
16,185 lb

Valve gear
Stephenson

49 *Gordon Highlander*

Right: Class J94
0-6-0ST No. 68043
[*M. York*

Centre: Class J72
0-6-0T No. 69008
(since withdrawn)
[*N. E. Preedy*

Bottom: Great
North of Scotland
Railway 4-4-0 No.
49 *Gordon High-
lander* (restored to
G.N.S.R. livery)
[*N. E. Preedy*

3P   **D34**   **4-4-0**

Introduced 1913. Reid N.B. "Glen" class. Withdrawn 1959 as B.R.
No. 62469 and restored to original livery. Returned to service for
special use in 1959.

Weight
Locomotive: 57 tons 4 cwt
Tender: 46 tons 13 cwt

Boiler pressure
165 lb sq in

Cylinders
20″ × 26″

Driving wheel diameter
6′ 0″

Tractive effort
20,260 lb

Valve gear
Stephenson (piston valves)

256   *Glen Douglas*

DEPARTMENTAL LOCOMOTIVES

Former running number in brackets

4F   **J50**   **0-6-0T**

*J50/2, introduced 1922. Gresley G.N. design (68911–17 rebuilt
from smaller J51, built 1915–22).
†J50/3, introduced 1926. Post-grouping development with detail
differences.

Weight
57 tons*
58 tons 3 cwt†

Boiler pressure
175 lb sq in NS

Cylinders
18½″ × 26″

Driving wheel diameter
4′ 8″

Tractive effort
23,635 lb

Valve gear
Stephenson

10*(68911)   12*(68917)   14†(68961)   15†(68971)   16†(68976)
11*(68914)   13*(68928)

TOTAL: 7

Class J50/2 0-6-0T No. 68917 (now departmental locomotive No. 12)   [R. K. Evans

CIVIL ENGINEER'S
DEPARTMENTAL
LOCOMOTIVE Nº 41

Class Y3 0-4-0T departmental locomotive No. 41   [H. N. James

Unclass.　　　　　Y3　　　　　0-4-0T

Introduced 1927.
Sentinel Wagon Works design. Two-speed Geared Sentinel locomotives.

Sprocket gear ratio
15:19

Weight
Locomotive: 20 tons 16 cwt

Boiler pressure
275 lb sq in

Cylinders
$6\frac{3}{4}'' \times 9''$

Driving wheel diameter
2' 6"

Tractive effort
Low gear: 15,960 lb
High gear: 5,960 lb

Valve gear
Poppet

40　(68173)　　41　(68177)

TOTAL: 2

ROUTE AVAILABILITY OF LOCOMOTIVES

R.A. No.	Ex-L.N.E.R.	Ex-L.M.S.	B.R.
1	Y3.	2MT (2-6-2T).	
2	J72.	2MT (2-6-0).	
3	J36.	1F (0-6-0T).	2MT (2-6-0), 2MT (2-6-2T).
4	D40.	4MT (2-6-0), 4MT (2-6-4T T.B.).	3MT (2-6-0), 4MT (2-6-0), 3MT (2-6-2T).
5	B1, J27, J94.	4F (0-6-0), 3F (0-6-0T), 4MT (2-6-4T P.B.).	4MT (2-6-4T).
6	D34, K1, O1, O4, WD, Q6, J50.	8F, 7F (0-8-0 L.N.W.).	
7	V3.	5MT (4-6-0), 5MT (2-6-0).	4MT (4-6-0), 5MT (4-6-0).
8	J37, J38.	6P (4-6-0 " Jubilee ").	6MT (4-6-2), 7MT (4-6-2).
9	A1, A2, A3, A4, V2.	7P (4-6-0 Rebuilt " Jubilee "), 7P (4-6-0 Rebuilt " Patriot "), 7P (4-6-0 " Royal Scot ").	9F (2-10-0).

LOCOMOTIVE SUPERINTENDENTS AND CHIEF MECHANICAL ENGINEERS

L.N.E.R.

| Sir Nigel Gresley | ... | 1923–1941 | E. Thompson | ... | ... | 1941–1946 |
| | A. H. Peppercorn | ... 1946–1949 | | | | |

GREAT NORTHERN

A. Sturrock	...	...	1850–1866
P. Stirling	...	...	1866–1895
H. A. Ivatt	...	...	1896–1911
H. N. Gresley	...	...	1911–1922

NORTH EASTERN

E. Fletcher	...	...	1854–1883
A. McDonnell*	...		1883–1884
T. W. Worsdell		...	1885–1890
W. Worsdell	...	...	1890–1910
Sir Vincent Raven		...	1910–1922

GREAT EASTERN

R. Sinclair	...	...	1862–1866
S. W. Johnson	...	...	1866–1873
W. Adams	...	...	1873–1878
M. Bromley	...	...	1878–1881
T. W. Worsdell	...		1881–1885
J. Holden	...	...	1885–1907
S. D. Holden	...	...	1908–1912
A. J. Hill	...	...	1912–1922

LANCASHIRE, DERBYSHIRE AND EAST COAST

| R. A. Thom | ... | ... | 1902–1907 |

MANCHESTER, SHEFFIELD AND LINCOLNSHIRE

| Richard Peacock | ... | | –1854 |
| W. G. Craig | ... | ... | 1854–1859 |

Charles Sacré	...	...	1859–1886
T. Parker	...	...	1886–1893
H. Pollitt	...	...	1893–1897

GREAT CENTRAL

| H. Pollitt | ... | ... | 1897–1900 |
| J. G. Robinson | ... | ... | 1900–1922 |

HULL AND BARNSLEY

| M. Stirling | ... | ... | 1885–1922 |

MIDLAND AND GREAT NORTHERN JOINT

| W. Marriott | ... | ... | 1884–1924 |

NORTH BRITISH

T. Wheatley†	...	...	1867–1874
D. Drummond	...	...	1875–1882
M. Holmes	...	...	1882–1903
W. P. Reid	...	...	1903–1919
W. Chalmers	...	...	1919–1922

GREAT NORTH OF SCOTLAND

D. K. Clark	...	...	1853–1855
J. F. Ruthven	...	...	1855–1857
W. Cowan	...	...	1857–1883
J. Manson	...	...	1883–1890
J. Johnson	...	...	1890–1894
W. Pickersgill	...	...	1894–1914
T. E. Heywood	...	...	1914–1922

---

* Between McDonnell and T. W. Worsdell there was an interval during which the office was covered by a Locomotive Committee.

† Previous to whom the records are indeterminate.

B.R. STEAM LOCOMOTIVES
Nos. 70000-92250

7P6F

4-6-2

Introduced 1951. Designed at Derby.

Weight
Locomotive: 94 tons 4 cwt

Boiler pressure
250 lb sq in

Cylinders
(O) 20″ × 28″

Driving wheel diameter
6′ 2″

Tractive effort
32,150 lb

Valve gear
Walschaerts (piston valves)

70000	Britannia	70028	Royal Star
70001	Lord Hurcomb	70029	Shooting Star
70002	Geoffrey Chaucer	70030	William Wordsworth
70003	John Bunyan	70031	Byron
70004	William Shakespeare	70032	Tennyson
70005	John Milton	70033	Charles Dickens
70006	Robert Burns	70034	Thomas Hardy
70007	Coeur-de-Lion	70035	Rudyard Kipling
70008	Black Prince	70036	Boadicea
70009	Alfred the Great	70037	Hereward the Wake
70010	Owen Glendower	70038	Robin Hood
70011	Hotspur	70039	Sir Christopher Wren
70012	John of Gaunt	70040	Clive of India
70013	Oliver Cromwell	70041	Sir John Moore
70014	Iron Duke	70042	Lord Roberts
70015	Apollo	70043	Lord Kitchener
70016	Ariel	70044	Earl Haig
70017	Arrow	70045	Lord Rowallan
70018	Flying Dutchman	70046	Anzac
70019	Lightning	70047	
70020	Mercury	70048	The Territorial Army 1908–1958
70021	Morning Star		
70022	Tornado	70049	Solway Firth
70023	Venus	70050	Firth of Clyde
70024	Vulcan	70051	Firth of Forth
70025	Western Star	70052	Firth of Tay
70026	Polar Star	70053	Moray Firth
70027	Rising Star	70054	Dornoch Firth

TOTAL: 55

Standard Class 7P6F 4-6-2 No. 70019 *Lightning*   [J. Hodge

Standard Class 6P5F 4-6-2 No. 72008 *Clan Macleod*   G. W. Morrison

Standard Class 5MT 4-6-0 No. 73014   [G. H. Wheeler

6P5F

4-6-2

Introduced 1952. Designed at Derby.

Weight
Locomotive: 86 tons 19 cwt

Driving wheel diameter
6′ 2″

Boiler pressure
225 lb sq in

Tractive effort
27,520 lb

Cylinders
(O) 19¼″ × 28″

Valve gear
Walschaerts (piston valves)

72005	*Clan Macgregor*	72008	*Clan Macleod*
72006	*Clan Mackenzie*	72009	*Clan Stewart*
72007	*Clan Mackintosh*		

TOTAL: 5

5MT

4-6-0

Introduced 1951. Designed at Doncaster.
*Introduced 1956. Fitted with Caprotti valve gear.

Weight
Locomotive: 76 tons 4 cwt

Driving wheel diameter
6′ 2″

Boiler pressure
225 lb sq in

Tractive effort
26,120 lb

Cylinders
(O) 19″ × 28″

Valve gear
Walschaerts (piston valves)

73000	73012	73023	73035	73046	73057	73068
73001	73013	73024	73036	73047	73058	73069
73002	73014	73025	73037	73048	73059	73070
73003	73015	73026	73038	73049	73060	73071
73004	73016	73028	73039	73050	73061	73072
73005	73017	73029	73040	73051	73062	73073
73006	73018	73030	73041	73052	73063	73074
73007	73019	73031	73042	73053	73064	73075
73008	73020	73032	73043	73054	73065	73077
73009	73021	73033	73044	73055	73066	73078
73010	73022	73034	73045	73056	73067	73079
73011						

73080	*Merlin*	73085	*Melisande*
73081	*Excalibur*	73086	*The Green Knight*
73082	*Camelot*	73087	*Linette*
73083	*Pendragon*	73088	*Joyous Gard*
73084	*Tintagel*	73089	*Maid of Astolat*

73090	73093	73096	73099	73102	73105	73108
73091	73094	73097	73100	73103	73106	73109
73092	73095	73098	73101	73104	73107	

73110	*The Red Knight*	73115	*King Pellinore*
73111	*King Uther*	73116	*Iseult*
73112	*Morgan le Fay*	73117	*Vivien*
73113	*Lyonnesse*	73118	*King Leodegrance*
73114	*Etarre*	73119	*Elaine*

73120	73128*	73136*	73144*	73151*	73158	73165
73121	73129*	73137*	73145*	73152*	73159	73166
73122	73130*	73138*	73146*	73153*	73160	73167
73123	73131*	73139*	73147*	73154*	73161	73168
73124	73132*	73140*	73148*	73155	73162	73169
73125*	73133*	73141*	73149*	73156	73163	73170
73126*	73134*	73142*	73150*	73157	73164	73171
73127*	73135*	73143*				

TOTAL: 170

4MT   4-6-0

Introduced 1951. Designed at Brighton.
*Introduced 1957. Fitted with double chimney.

Weight
Locomotive: 69 tons

Driving wheel diameter
5′ 8″

Boiler pressure
225 lb sq in

Tractive effort
25,100 lb

Cylinders
(O) 18″ × 28″

Valve gear
Walschaerts (piston valves)

75000	75012	75024	75036	75047	75058	75069*
75001	75013	75025	75037	75048	75059	75070*
75002	75014	75026*	75038	75049	75060	75071*
75003*	75015	75027	75039	75050	75061	75072*
75004	75016	75028	75040	75051	75062	75073*
75005*	75017	75029*	75041	75052	75063	75074*
75006*	75018	75030	75042	75053	75064	75075*
75007	75019	75031	75043	75054	75065*	75076*
75008*	75020*	75032	75044	75055	75066*	75077*
75009	75021	75033	75045	75056	75067*	75078*
75010	75022	75034	75046	75057	75068*	75079*
75011	75023	75035				

TOTAL: 80

4MT   2-6-0

Introduced 1953. Designed at Doncaster.

Weight
Locomotive: 59 tons 2 cwt

Driving wheel diameter
5′ 3″

Boiler pressure
225 lb sq in

Tractive effort
24,170 lb

Cylinders
(O) 17½″ × 26″

Valve gear
Walschaerts (piston valves)

76000	76005	76010	76015	76020	76025	76031
76001	76006	76011	76016	76021	76026	76032
76002	76007	76012	76017	76022	76027	76033
76003	76008	76013	76018	76023	76029	76034
76004	76009	76014	76019	76024	76030	76035

76036	76047	76058	76069	76080	76091	76105
76037	76048	76059	76070	76081	76092	76106
76038	76049	76060	76071	76082	76093	76107
76039	76050	76061	76072	76083	76094	76108
76040	76051	76062	76073	76084	76096	76109
76041	76052	76063	76074	76085	76098	76110
76042	76053	76064	76075	76086	76100	76111
76043	76054	76065	76076	76087	76101	76112
76044	76055	76066	76077	76088	76102	76113
76045	76056	76067	76078	76089	76103	76114
76046	76057	76068	76079	76090	76104	

TOTAL: 111

3MT   2-6-0

Introduced 1954. Designed at Swindon.

Weight
Locomotive: 57 tons 9 cwt

Driving wheel diameter
5′ 3″

Boiler pressure
200 lb sq in

Tractive effort
21,490 lb

Cylinders
(O) 17½″ × 26″

Valve gear
Walschaerts (piston valves)

77000	77003	77006	77009	77012	77015	77018
77001	77004	77007	77010	77013	77016	77019
77002	77005	77008	77011	77014	77017	

TOTAL: 20

2MT   2-6-0

Introduced 1953. Designed at Derby.

Weight
Locomotive: 49 tons 5 cwt

Driving wheel diameter
5′ 0″

Boiler pressure
200 lb sq in

Tractive effort
18,515 lb

Cylinders
(O) 16½″ × 24″

Valve gear
Walschaerts (piston valves)

78000	78010	78020	78029	78038	78047	78057
78001	78011	78021	78030	78039	78049	78058
78002	78012	78022	78031	78040	78050	78059
78003	78013	78023	78032	78041	78051	78060
78004	78014	78024	78033	78042	78052	78061
78005	78016	78025	78034	78043	78053	78062
78006	78017	78026	78035	78044	78054	78063
78007	78018	78027	78036	78045	78055	78064
78008	78019	78028	78037	78046	78056	

TOTAL: 62

Top: Standard Class 5MT 4-6-0 No. 73143 (with Caprotti valve gear) [*P. H. Wells*

Centre: Standard Class 4MT 4-6-0 No. 75029 (with double chimney)
[*G. W. Morrison*

Right: Standard Class 4MT 2-6-0 No. 76047
[*A. W. Martin*

Top: Standard
Class 3MT 2-6-0
No. 77009
[*R. A. Panting*

Centre: Standard
Class 2MT 2-6-0
No. 78047
[*D. Holmes*

Left: Standard
Class 4MT 2-6-4T
No. 80012
[*P. H. Wells*

4MT

2-6-4T

Introduced 1951. Designed at Brighton.

Weight
Locomotive: 88 tons 10 cwt

Boiler pressure
225 lb sq in

Cylinders
(O) 18" × 28"

Driving wheel diameter
5' 8"

Tractive effort
25,100 lb

Valve gear
Walschaerts (piston valves)

80000	80023	80046	80072	80093	80114	80135
80001	80024	80047	80073	80094	80115	80136
80002	80025	80051	80074	80095	80116	80137
80003	80026	80054	80075	80096	80117	80138
80004	80027	80055	80076	80097	80118	80139
80005	80028	80057	80077	80098	80119	80140
80006	80029	80058	80078	80099	80120	80141
80007	80031	80059	80079	80100	80121	80142
80009	80032	80060	80080	80101	80122	80143
80011	80033	80061	80081	80102	80123	80144
80012	80034	80062	80082	80104	80124	80145
80013	80035	80063	80083	80105	80126	80146
80014	80036	80064	80084	80106	80127	80147
80015	80037	80065	80085	80107	80128	80149
80016	80038	80066	80086	80108	80130	80150
80017	80039	80067	80088	80109	80131	80151
80018	80041	80068	80089	80110	80132	80152
80019	80042	80069	80090	80111	80133	80153
80020	80043	80070	80091	80112	80134	80154
80022	80045	80071	80092	80113		

TOTAL: 138

3MT

2-6-2T

Introduced 1952. Designed at Swindon.

Weight
Locomotive: 73 tons 10 cwt

Boiler pressure
200 lb sq in

Cylinders
(O) 17½" × 26"

Driving wheel diameter
5' 3"

Tractive effort
21,490 lb

Valve gear
Walschaerts (piston valves)

Left: Standard Class 3MT 2-6-2T No. 82016
[*G. W. Morrison*

Centre: Standard Class 2MT 2-6-2T No. 84004 [*I. G. Holt*

Bottom: Class WD 2-8-0 No. 90178
[*A. W. Martin*

82000	82009	82018	82024	82029	82034	82039
82001	82010	82019	82025	82030	82035	82040
82003	82011	82020	82026	82031	82036	82041
82004	82015	82021	82027	82032	82037	82042
82005	82016	82022	82028	82033	82038	82044
82006	82017	82023				

TOTAL: 38

2MT 2-6-2T

Introduced 1953. Designed at Derby.

Weight Locomotive: 63 tons 5 cwt	**Driving wheel diameter** 5' 0"
Boiler pressure 200 lb sq in	**Tractive effort** 18,515 lb
Cylinders (O) 16½" × 24"	**Valve gear** Walschaerts (piston valves)

84000	84004	84009	84014	84018	84022S	84025
84001	84005	84010	84015	84019	84023S	84026
84002	84006	84011	84016	84020	84024S	84028
84003	84008	84013	84017	84021S		

TOTAL: 26

8F WD 2-8-0

Introduced 1943. Riddles Ministry of Supply "Austerity" locomotives purchased by British Railways, 1948.

Weight Locomotive: 70 tons 5 cwt Tender: 55 tons 10 cwt	**Driving wheel diameter** 4' 8½"
Boiler pressure 225 lb sq in	**Tractive effort** 34,215 lb
Cylinders (O) 19" × 28"	**Valve gear** Walschaerts (piston valves)

90000	90008	90014	90025	90036	90041	90047
90001	90009	90016	90029	90037	90042	90051
90002	90010	90018	90030	90038	90043	90053
90005	90011	90020	90032	90039	90044	90054
90007	90013	90024	90035	90040	90045	90055

90056	90132	90220	90292	90361	90426	90496
90057	90133	90221	90293	90362	90427	90498
90059	90135	90222	90294	90363	90428	90501
90061	90136	90223	90295	90364	90429	90503
90063	90139	90225	90296	90365	90430	90506
90067	90140	90227	90297	90367	90432	90509
90068	90142	90229	90300	90368	90434	90510
90069	90146	90230	90301	90369	90437	90514
90070	90148	90232	90302	90370	90438	90515
90071	90149	90233	90304	90372	90439	90516
90072	90152	90235	90305	90373	90441	90517
90073	90153	90236	90306	90377	90442	90518
90074	90154	90240	90309	90378	90443	90519
90075	90155	90241	90310	90379	90444	90520
90076	90156	90242	90311	90380	90445	90521
90078	90158	90243	90314	90381	90448	90522
90080	90160	90246	90315	90382	90450	90528
90081	90164	90248	90316	90383	90451	90529
90082	90166	90252	90317	90384	90452	90533
90084	90168	90254	90318	90385	90454	90534
90085	90169	90255	90321	90386	90456	90535
90088	90171	90257	90322	90389	90457	90537
90089	90172	90258	90325	90390	90458	90538
90091	90175	90259	90327	90392	90459	90540
90092	90178	90261	90329	90393	90460	90541
90094	90180	90262	90330	90395	90462	90543
90096	90181	90264	90332	90396	90465	90545
90098	90183	90265	90333	90397	90466	90547
90099	90184	90266	90336	90398	90468	90551
90103	90185	90267	90337	90399	90469	90553
90104	90187	90268	90339	90401	90470	90556
90108	90188	90271	90340	90404	90471	90557
90112	90189	90272	90341	90405	90474	90558
90113	90190	90273	90342	90406	90476	90560
90115	90195	90274	90344	90407	90477	90561
90116	90199	90275	90345	90409	90478	90563
90117	90200	90276	90346	90410	90479	90567
90119	90202	90277	90347	90411	90480	90569
90120	90203	90279	90348	90412	90481	90572
90121	90204	90280	90349	90413	90482	90573
90122	90207	90281	90350	90415	90484	90577
90123	90210	90282	90351	90417	90485	90579
90124	90211	90283	90352	90418	90486	90580
90125	90212	90284	90353	90419	90488	90581
90126	90213	90285	90354	90420	90489	90584
90127	90215	90289	90357	90421	90491	90585
90130	90216	90290	90359	90422	90492	90586
90131	90217	90291	90360	90423	90493	90587

90588	90617	90636	90655	90678	90695	90714
90593	90619	90639	90656	90679	90697	90718
90596	90620	90640	90658	90680	90698	90719
90599	90621	90641	90660	90681	90699	90720
90600	90622	90642	90662	90682	90702	90721
90601	90625	90644	90664	90683	90703	90722
90602	90626	90645	90666	90684	90704	90723
90605	90627	90647	90668	90685	90706	90724
90606	90628	90649	90669	90686	90707	90725
90610	90629	90650	90670	90687	90709	90727
90611	90631	90651	90674	90688	90710	90730
90613	90632	90652	90675	90689	90711	90731
90615	90633	90654	90677	90694	90712	

TOTAL: 461

9F   2-10-0

Introduced 1954. Designed at Brighton.

*Introduced 1955. Fitted with Crosti boiler. Crosti pre-heater now sealed off for orthodox working.

†Introduced 1957. Fitted with double chimney.

‡Introduced 1958. Fitted with Mechanical Stoker and double chimney.

§Introduced 1960. Fitted with Giesl oblong ejector.

Weight
Locomotive: 86 tons 14 cwt
                90 tons 4 cwt*

Boiler pressure
250 lb sq in

Cylinders
(O) 20″ × 28″

Driving wheel diameter
5′ 0″

Tractive effort
39,670 lb

Valve gear
Walschaerts (piston valves)

92000†	92031	92063	92094	92124	92154	92190†
92001†	92032	92064	92095	92125	92155	92191†
92002	92033	92065	92096	92126	92156	92192†
92003	92035	92066	92097	92127	92157	92193†
92004	92036	92067	92098	92128	92158	92194†
92005	92037	92068	92099	92129	92159	92195†
92006†	92038	92069	92100	92130	92160	92196†
92007	92039	92070	92101	92131	92161	92197†
92008	92040	92071	92102	92132	92162	92198†
92009	92041	92072	92103	92133	92163	92199†
92010	92042	92073	92104	92134	92164	92200†
92011	92043	92074	92105	92135	92165‡	92201†
92012	92044	92075	92106	92136	92166‡	92202†
92013	92045	92076	92107	92137	92167‡	92203†
92014	92046	92077	92108	92138	92168	92204†
92015	92047	92078	92109	92139	92172	92205†
92016	92048	92079†	92110	92140	92173	92206†
92017	92049	92080	92111	92141	92174	92207†
92018	92050	92081	92112	92142	92178†	92208†
92019	92051	92082	92113	92143	92179	92209†
92020*	92052	92083	92114	92144	92180	92210†
92021*	92053	92084	92115	92145	92181	92211†
92022*	92054	92085	92116	92146	92182	92212†
92023*	92055	92086	92117	92147	92183†	92213†
92024*	92056	92087	92118	92148	92184†	92214†
92025*	92057	92088	92119	92149	92185†	92215†
92026*	92058	92089	92120	92150	92186†	92216†
92027*	92059	92090	92121	92151	92187†	92217†
92028*	92060	92091	92122	92152	92188†	92218†
92029*	92061	92092	92123	92153	92189†	92219†
92030	92062	92093				

92220† *Evening Star*   92221†   92222†

92223†	92227†	92231†	92235†	92239†	92243†	92247†
92224†	92228†	92232†	92236†	92240†	92244†	92248†
92225†	92229†	92233†	92237†	92241†	92245†	92249†
92226†	92230†	92234†	92238†	92242†	92246†	92250§

TOTAL: 244

Standard Class 9F 2-10-0 No. 92006

[*B. Stephenson*

Standard Class 9F 2-10-0 No. 92028 (with Crosti boiler)

[*J. K. Morton*

Standard Class 9F 2-10-0 No. 92097 (fitted with air-pumps for working Tyne Dock-Consett iron ore trains)

[*V. C. Allen*

BRITISH RAILWAYS STANDARD TENDERS

N.B.—*These pairings are not permanent and are liable to alteration with changed operating conditions.*

Type	Capacity Water galls	Coal tons	Weight in full W.O. tons	cwt	Locomotives to which originally allocated
BRI ...	4,250	7	49	3	70000–24/30–44 72000–9 73000–49
BRIA ...	5,000	7	52	10	70025–9
BRIB ...	4,725	7	50	5	92020–9/60–6/97–99 73080–9 73100–9/20–34/45–71 75065–79 76053–69
BRIC ...	4,725	9	53	5	92015–9/45–59/77–86 92100–39/50–64 73065–79/90–9 73135–44
BRID ...	4,725	9	54	10	70045–54
BRIF ...	5,625	7	55	5	92010–4/30–44/67–76 92087–96 92140–9/68–92202 73110–9
BRIG ...	5,000	7	52	10	92000–9 73050–2 92203–50
BRIH ...	4,250	7	49	3	73053–64
BRIK ...	4,325	9	52	7	92165–7
BR2 ...	3,500	6	42	3	75000–49 76000–44
BR2A ...	3,500	6	42	3	75050–64 76045–52/70–76114 77000–19
BR3 ...	3,000	4	36	17	78000–64

B.R. DIESEL LOCOMOTIVES

BRITISH RAILWAYS diesel locomotives are listed in this publication in numerical order and classified by make. In 1957 the then British Transport Commission announced a new numbering system for all diesel locomotives, involving the use of the prefix "D" for all such locomotives, followed by a number which would not only identify the locomotive, but would also indicate its power range; at the same time, the power of main-line locomotives was to be indicated by Type numbers in the following ranges:—

Type of Locomotive	Horsepower
1	800–1,000
2	1,000–1,365
3	1,500–1,750
4	2,000–2,750
5	3,000+

Subsequently new batches of locomotives have been delivered and numbered outside the original groups for the type so that it is not always possible to ascertain the power of a locomotive solely by its number. Locomotives built before nationalisation, or after nationalisation to company designs, are numbered in a separate series commencing at 10000 without a prefix "D". Early British Railways diesel shunters were numbered in this series but have since been renumbered into the "D" series.

The heading to each class shows the type designation, the principal manufacturer and the wheel arrangement.

Diesel (and electric) locomotive wheel arrangements are described by a development of the Continental notation. This calculates by axles and not by wheels, and uses letters instead of numerals to denote driving axles ("A" = 1, "B" = 2, "C" = 3, etc.) and numerals only for non-powered axles. An indication of the grouping of axles is given, but powered and non-powered axles may be found in the same group. Thus, diesel-electric locomotive No. D5500 is described as an A1A-A1A, indicating that it is mounted on two six-wheel bogies, each of which has a non-powered axle in the centre and a motored axle at either end. Groups of axles are separated by a hyphen if they are quite independent of each other, but by a "plus" sign in cases where powered bogies are linked by an articulated joint to take certain stresses. If all axles on a bogie or frame unit are individually powered, a suffix letter "o" is added to the descriptive letter.

The sub-headings give brief technical details of each type. Reference marks are shown in the details and against the locomotives concerned (if known) where equipment varies from the main batch.

Birmingham R.C. & W. Co. Type 2s Nos. D5381 and D5383

[A. Swain

COUPLING OF DIESEL LOCOMOTIVES

Although several diesel locomotives may be coupled together and driven by one man in the leading cab, for various reasons it is not possible for all types of diesel units to work together. In order to distinguish locomotives that can run together, all have painted above each buffer a colour code symbol. This is repeated as a miniature symbol on the plug socket covers. Only units bearing the same symbol may run in multiple and be controlled from the leading cab.

Type of Locomotive	*Coupling symbol*
All diesel-electric locomotives with electro-pneumatic control	Blue star ✱
All diesel-electric locomotives with electro-magnetic control.	Red circle ●
Diesel-hydraulic locomotives Nos. D600-4, D6300-5.	Orange square □
Diesel-hydraulic locomotives Nos. D803-70, D6306-57 (Nos. D800-2 cannot work in multiple).	White diamond ◇
Diesel-hydraulic locomotives Nos. D7000-7100.	Yellow triangle △
Ex-L.M.S. diesel-electric locomotive No. 10001 and diesel-electric locomotives Nos. D8500-8615.	Red diamond ◆

DIESEL LOCOMOTIVES

The lists of numbers include all locomotives on order at the time of going to press. For details of delivery, see the Motive Power Change list each month in Modern Railways.

Type 4   British Railways   ICo-Col

"Peak"   *

Introduced
1959

Engine
*Sulzer 12-cyl 12LDA28-A twin-bank pressure charged of 2,300 b.h.p. at 750 r.p.m.
Sulzer 12LDA28-B, with inter-cooling of 2,500 b.h.p. at 750 r.p.m.

Weight
138 tons 2 cwt

Maximum tractive effort
70,000 lb

Total b.h.p.
2,300*
2,500

Transmission
Electric. Six Crompton Parkinson 305 h.p. axle-hung nose-suspended traction motors
†Six Brush traction motors

Driving wheel diameter
3' 9"

D1* *Scafell Pike*	D6* *Whernside*
D2* *Helvellyn*	D7* *Ingleborough*
D3* *Skiddaw*	D8* *Penyghent*
D4* *Great Gable*	D9* *Snowdon*
D5* *Cross Fell*	D10* *Tryfan*

D11	D17	D23	D29	D35	D41	D47
D12	D18	D24	D30	D36	D42	D48
D13	D19	D25	D31	D37	D43	D49
D14	D20	D26	D32	D38	D44	D50
D15	D21	D27	D33	D39	D45	D51
D16	D22	D28	D34	D40	D46	

D52   *The Lancashire Fusilier*
D53
D54   *The Royal Pioneer Corps*
D55
D56   *The Bedfordshire and Hertfordshire Regiment (T.A.)*
D57
D58   *The King's Own Royal Border Regiment*
D59   *The Royal Warwickshire Fusilier*
D60   *Lytham St. Annes*
D61   D62   D63   D64
D65   *Grenadier Guardsman*

D66	D71	D76	D81	D86	D91	D96
D67	D72	D77	D82	D87	D92	D97
D68	D73	D78	D83	D88	D93	D98
D69	D74	D79	D84	D89	D94	D99
D70	D75	D80	D85	D90	D95	

D100   *Sherwood Forester*

British Railways Type 4 2,500 b.h.p. diesel-electric 1Co-Col No. D193 *[P J. Sharpe*

English Electric Type 4 2,000 b.h.p. diesel-electric 1Co-Col No. D230 *Scythia*
[B. Stephenson

English Electric Type 4 2,000 b h.p. diesel-electric 1Co-Col No. D325 *[N. E. Preedy*

D101	D110	D119	D128	D137	D146†	D155†
D102	D111	D120	D129	D138†	D147†	D156†
D103	D112	D121	D130	D139†	D148†	D157†
D104	D113	D122	D131	D140†	D149†	D158†
D105	D114	D123	D132	D141†	D150†	D159†
D106	D115	D124	D133	D142†	D151†	D160†
D107	D116	D125	D134	D143†	D152†	D161†
D108	D117	D126	D135	D144†	D153†	D162†
D109	D118	D127	D136	D145†	D154†	

D163† *Leicestershire and Derbyshire Yeomanry*

D164†	D169†	D174†	D178†	D182†	D186†	D190†
D165†	D170†	D175†	D179†	D183†	D187†	D191†
D166†	D171†	D176†	D180†	D184†	D188†	D192†
D167†	D172†	D177†	D181†	D185†	D189†	D193†
D168†	D173†					

Type 4   English Electric   ICo-CoI

Introduced
1958

Total b.h.p.
2,000

Engine
English Electric 16-cyl 16SVT Mk. II
of 2,000 b.h.p. at 850 r.p.m.

Transmission
Electric. Six English Electric nose
suspended traction motors

Weight
133 tons

Driving wheel diameter
3′ 9″

Maximum tractive effort
52,000 lb

| D200 | D202 | D204 | D206 | D207 | D208 | D209 |
| D201 | D203 | D205 | | | | |

D210	*Empress of Britain*		D224	*Lucania*
D211	*Mauretania*		D225	*Lusitania*
D212	*Aureol*		D226	
D213	*Andania*		D227	*Parthia*
D214	*Antonia*		D228	*Samaria*
D215	*Aquitania*		D229	*Saxonia*
D216	*Campania*		D230	*Scythia*
D217	*Carinthia*		D231	*Sylvania*
D218	*Carmania*		D232	*Empress of Canada*
D219	*Caronia*		D233	*Empress of England*
D220	*Franconia*		D234	*Accra*
D221	*Ivernia*		D235	*Apapa*
D222	*Laconia*		D236	
D223	*Lancastria*			

D237	D261	D285	D308	D331	D354	D377
D238	D262	D286	D309	D332	D355	D378
D239	D263	D287	D310	D333	D356	D379
D240	D264	D288	D311	D334	D357	D380
D241	D265	D289	D312	D335	D358	D381
D242	D266	D290	D313	D336	D359	D382
D243	D267	D291	D314	D337	D360	D383
D244	D268	D292	D315	D338	D361	D384
D245	D269	D293	D316	D339	D362	D385
D246	D270	D294	D317	D340	D363	D386
D247	D271	D295	D318	D341	D364	D387
D248	D272	D296	D319	D342	D365	D388
D249	D273	D297	D320	D343	D366	D389
D250	D274	D298	D321	D344	D367	D390
D251	D275	D299	D322	D345	D368	D391
D252	D276	D300	D323	D346	D369	D392
D253	D277	D301	D324	D347	D370	D393
D254	D278	D302	D325	D348	D371	D394
D255	D279	D303	D326	D349	D372	D395
D256	D280	D304	D327	D350	D373	D396
D257	D281	D305	D328	D351	D374	D397
D258	D282	D306	D329	D352	D375	D398
D259	D283	D307	D330	D353	D376	D399
D260	D284					

Type 4   North British   A1A-A1A

"Warship"

Introduced
1958

Engines
Two N.B.L./M.A.N. 12-cyl L12V 18/21S of 1,000 b.h.p.

Weight
117 tons 8 cwt

Maximum tractive effort
50,000 lb

Total b.h.p.
2,000

Transmission
Hydraulic. Two Hardy Spicer cardan shafts to Voith-North British type L306r hydraulic transmissions, each containing three torque converters

Driving wheel diameter
3' 7"

D600 *Active*
D601 *Ark Royal*
D602 *Bulldog*

D603 *Conquest*
D604 *Cossack*

North British Type 4 2,000 b.h.p. diesel-hydraulic A1A-A1A No. D601 *Ark Royal*
[*B. Roberts*

North British Type 4 2,200 b.h.p. diesel-hydraulic B-B No. D862 *Viking* [*C. T. Verrall*

Nameplate of British Railways Type 4 2,200 b.h.p. diesel-hydraulic B-B No. D868
Zephyr
[*A. Swain*

Type 4   British Railways   B-B

"Warship" ◇

Introduced
1958

Engines
Two Bristol Siddeley-Maybach MD 650 V-type of 1,152 b.h.p. at 1,530 r.p.m. (*1,056 b.h.p. at 1,400 r.p.m.) † Two Paxman 12-cyl high-speed 12 YJXL of 1,200 b.h.p. at 1,500 r.p.m.

Weight
78 tons

Maximum tractive effort
52,400 lb

Total b.h.p.
2,000*
2,200
2,400†

Transmission
Hydraulic. Two Mekydro type K104 hydraulic transmissions containing permanently filled single torque converter and four-speed automatic gearbox

Driving wheel diameter
3' 3¼"

* These locomotives may not be coupled in multiple.

D800*	Sir Brian Robertson	D816	Eclipse
D801*	Vanguard	D817	Foxhound
D802*	Formidable	D818	Glory
D803	Albion	D819	Goliath
D804	Avenger	D820	Grenville
D805	Benbow	D821	Greyhound
D806	Cambrian	D822	Hercules
D807	Caradoc	D823	Hermes
D808	Contaur	D824	Highflyer
D809	Champion	D825	Intrepid
D810	Cockade	D826	Jupiter
D811	Daring	D827	Kelly
D812	Royal Naval Reserve 1859-1959	D828	Magnificent
		D829	Magpie
D813	Diadem	D830†	Majestic
D814	Dragon	D831	Monarch
D815	Druid	D832	Onslaught

Class continued with D866

Type 4   North British   B-B

"Warship" ◇

Introduced
1960

Engines
Two N.B.L./M.A.N. 12-cyl L12V18/21BS of 1,100 b.h.p.

Weight
79 tons 10 cwt

Maximum tractive effort
53,400 lb

Total b.h.p.
2,200

Transmission
Hydraulic. Voith

Driving wheel diameter
3' 3¼"

D833	*Panther*	D850	*Swift*
D834	*Pathfinder*	D851	*Temeraire*
D835	*Pegasus*	D852	*Tenacious*
D836	*Powerful*	D853	*Thruster*
D837	*Ramillies*	D854	*Tiger*
D838	*Rapid*	D855	*Triumph*
D839	*Relentless*	D856	*Trojan*
D840	*Resistance*	D857	*Undaunted*
D841	*Roebuck*	D858	*Valorous*
D842	*Royal Oak*	D859	*Vanquisher*
D843	*Sharpshooter*	D860	*Victorious*
D844	*Spartan*	D861	*Vigilant*
D845	*Sprightly*	D862	*Viking*
D846	*Steadfast*	D863	*Warrior*
D847	*Strongbow*	D864	*Zambesi*
D848	*Sultan*	D865	*Zealous*
D849	*Superb*		

Type 4   British Railways   B-B

❖

Class continued from D832

D866	*Zebra*	D869	*Zest*
D867	*Zenith*	D870	*Zulu*
D868	*Zephyr*		

Type 4   British Railways   C-C

"Western"

Introduced
1961

Engines
Two Maybach MD655 V-type of
1,350 h.p. at 1,500 r.p.m.

Weight
108 tons

Maximum tractive effort
72,600 lb

Total b.h.p.
2,700

Transmission
Hydraulic. Two Voith-North British
L630rV hydraulic transmissions, each
containing three torque coverters

Driving wheel diameter
3′ 7″

D1000	*Western Enterprise*	D1007	*Western Talisman*
D1001	*Western Pathfinder*	D1008	*Western Harrier*
D1002	*Western Explorer*	D1009	*Western Invader*
D1003	*Western Pioneer*	D1010	*Western Campaigner*
D1004	*Western Crusader*	D1011	*Western Thunderer*
D1005	*Western Venturer*	D1012	*Western Firebrand*
D1006	*Western Stalwart*	D1013	*Western Ranger*

D1014	*Western Leviathan*			D1044	*Western Duchess*	
D1015	*Western Champion*			D1045	*Western Viscount*	
D1016	*Western Gladiator*			D1046	*Western Marquis*	
D1017	*Western Warrior*			D1047	*Western Lord*	
D1018	*Western Buccaneer*			D1048	*Western Lady*	
D1019	*Western Challenger*			D1049	*Western Monarch*	
D1020	*Western Hero*			D1050	*Western Ruler*	
D1021	*Western Cavalier*			D1051	*Western Ambassador*	
D1022	*Western Sentinel*			D1052	*Western Viceroy*	
D1023	*Western Fusilier*			D1053	*Western Patriarch*	
D1024	*Western Huntsman*			D1054	*Western Governor*	
D1025	*Western Guardsman*			D1055	*Western Advocate*	
D1026	*Western Centurion*			D1056	*Western Sultan*	
D1027	*Western Lancer*			D1057	*Western Chieftain*	
D1028	*Western Hussar*			D1058	*Western Nobleman*	
D1029	*Western Legionnaire*			D1059	*Western Empire*	
D1030	*Western Musketeer*			D1060	*Western Dominion*	
D1031	*Western Rifleman*			D1061	*Western Envoy*	
D1032	*Western Marksman*			D1062	*Western Courier*	
D1033	*Western Trooper*			D1063	*Western Monitor*	
D1034	*Western Dragoon*			D1064	*Western Regent*	
D1035	*Western Yeoman*			D1065	*Western Consort*	
D1036	*Western Emperor*			D1066	*Western Prefect*	
D1037	*Western Empress*			D1067	*Western Druid*	
D1038	*Western Sovereign*			D1068	*Western Reliance*	
D1039	*Western King*			D1069	*Western Vanguard*	
D1040	*Western Queen*			D1070	*Western Gauntlet*	
D1041	*Western Prince*			D1071	*Western Renown*	
D1042	*Western Princess*			D1072	*Western Glory*	
D1043	*Western Duke*			D1073	*Western Bulwark*	

Type 4   Brush   Co-Co

Introduced
1962

Total b.h.p.
2,750
*2,650

Engine
Sulzer 12-cyl 12LDA28-C twin-bank, pressure-charged, of 2,750 b.h.p. at 800 r.p.m.
*Sulzer 12-cyl 12LVA24 of 2,650 b.h.p. at 1,050 r.p.m.

Transmission
Electric. Six axle-hung, nose-suspended Brush traction motors

Weight
114 tons

Driving wheel diameter
3′ 9″

Maximum tractive effort
55,000 lb

D1500	D1504	D1508	D1512	D1516	D1520	D1524
D1501	D1505	D1509	D1513	D1517	D1521	D1525
D1502	D1506	D1510	D1514	D1518	D1522	D1526
D1503	D1507	D1511	D1515	D1519	D1523	D1527

British Railways Type 4 2,700 b.h.p. diesel-hydraulic C-C No. D1054 *Western Governor*
[*A. Swain*

Brush Type 4 2,750 b.h.p. diesel-electric Co-Co No. D1579 [*P. H. Wells*

Brush Type 4 2,750 b.h.p. diesel-electric Co-Co No. D1733 (in experimental blue livery)
[*J. W. Ellson*

D1528	D1576	D1624	D1672	D1720	D1768	D1816
D1529	D1577	D1625	D1673	D1721	D1769	D1817
D1530	D1578	D1626	D1674	D1722	D1770	D1818
D1531	D1579	D1627	D1675	D1723	D1771	D1819
D1532	D1580	D1628	D1676	D1724	D1772	D1820
D1533	D1581	D1629	D1677	D1725	D1773	D1821
D1534	D1582	D1630	D1678	D1726	D1774	D1822
D1535	D1583	D1631	D1679	D1727	D1775	D1823
D1536	D1584	D1632	D1680	D1728	D1776	D1824
D1537	D1585	D1633	D1681	D1729	D1777	D1825
D1538	D1586	D1634	D1682	D1730	D1778	D1826
D1539	D1587	D1635	D1683	D1731	D1779	D1827
D1540	D1588	D1636	D1684	D1732	D1780	D1828
D1541	D1589	D1637	D1685	D1733	D1781	D1829
D1542	D1590	D1638	D1686	D1734	D1782	D1830
D1543	D1591	D1639	D1687	D1735	D1783	D1831
D1544	D1592	D1640	D1688	D1736	D1784	D1832
D1545	D1593	D1641	D1689	D1737	D1785	D1833
D1546	D1594	D1642	D1690	D1738	D1786	D1834
D1547	D1595	D1643	D1691	D1739	D1787	D1835
D1548	D1596	D1644	D1692	D1740	D1788	D1836
D1549	D1597	D1645	D1693	D1741	D1789	D1837
D1550	D1598	D1646	D1694	D1742	D1790	D1838
D1551	D1599	D1647	D1695	D1743	D1791	D1839
D1552	D1600	D1648	D1696	D1744	D1792	D1840
D1553	D1601	D1649	D1697	D1745	D1793	D1841
D1554	D1602	D1650	D1698	D1746	D1794	D1842
D1555	D1603	D1651	D1699	D1747	D1795	D1843
D1556	D1604	D1652	D1700	D1748	D1796	D1844
D1557	D1605	D1653	D1701	D1749	D1797	D1845
D1558	D1606	D1654	D1702*	D1750	D1798	D1846
D1559	D1607	D1655	D1703*	D1751	D1799	D1847
D1560	D1608	D1656	D1704*	D1752	D1800	D1848
D1561	D1609	D1657	D1705*	D1753	D1801	D1849
D1562	D1610	D1658	D1706*	D1754	D1802	D1850
D1563	D1611	D1659	D1707	D1755	D1803	D1851
D1564	D1612	D1660	D1708	D1756	D1804	D1852
D1565	D1613	D1661	D1709	D1757	D1805	D1853
D1566	D1614	D1662	D1710	D1758	D1806	D1854
D1567	D1615	D1663	D1711	D1759	D1807	D1855
D1568	D1616	D1664	D1712	D1760	D1808	D1856
D1569	D1617	D1665	D1713	D1761	D1809	D1857
D1570	D1618	D1666	D1714	D1762	D1810	D1858
D1571	D1619	D1667	D1715	D1763	D1811	D1859
D1572	D1620	D1668	D1716	D1764	D1812	D1860
D1573	D1621	D1669	D1717	D1765	D1813	D1861
D1574	D1622	D1670	D1718	D1766	D1814	D1862
D1575	D1623	D1671	D1719	D1767	D1815	D1863

D1864	D1883	D1902	D1920	D1938	D1956	D1974
D1865	D1884	D1903	D1921	D1939	D1957	D1975
D1866	D1885	D1904	D1922	D1940	D1958	D1976
D1867	D1886	D1905	D1923	D1941	D1959	D1977
D1868	D1887	D1906	D1924	D1942	D1960	D1978
D1869	D1888	D1907	D1925	D1943	D1961	D1979
D1870	D1889	D1908	D1926	D1944	D1962	D1980
D1871	D1890	D1902	D1927	D1945	D1963	D1981
D1872	D1891	D1910	D1928	D1946	D1964	D1982
D1873	D1892	D1911	D1929	D1947	D1965	D1983
D1874	D1893	D1912	D1930	D1948	D1966	D1984
D1875	D1894	D1913	D1931	D1949	D1967	D1985
D1876	D1895	D1914	D1932	D1950	D1968	D1986
D1877	D1896	D1915	D1933	D1951	D1969	D1987
D1878	D1897	D1916	D1934	D1952	D1970	D1988
D1879	D1898	D1917	D1935	D1953	D1971	D1989
D1880	D1899	D1918	D1936	D1954	D1972	D1990
D1881	D1900	D1919	D1937	D1955	D1973	D1991
D1882	D1901					

Shunter   British Railways   0-6-0

Introduced
1957

Engine
Gardner 8L3 of 204 b.h.p. at 1,200 r.p.m.

Weight
30 tons 16 cwt

Maximum tractive effort
15,650 lb

Total b.h.p.
204

Transmission
Mechanical. Vulcan-Sinclair type 23 fluid coupling. Wilson-Drewry C.A.5 type five-speed epicyclic gearbox. Type RF II spiral bevel reverse and final drive unit.

Driving wheel diameter
3' 7"

D2000	D2012	D2024	D2036	D2048	D2060	D2072
D2001	D2013	D2025	D2037	D2049	D2061	D2073
D2002	D2014	D2026	D2038	D2050	D2062	D2074
D2003	D2015	D2027	D2039	D2051	D2063	D2075
D2004	D2016	D2028	D2040	D2052	D2064	D2076
D2005	D2017	D2029	D2041	D2053	D2065	D2077
D2006	D2018	D2030	D2042	D2054	D2066	D2078
D2007	D2019	D2031	D2043	D2055	D2067	D2079
D2008	D2020	D2032	D2044	D2056	D2068	D2080
D2009	D2021	D2033	D2045	D2057	D2069	D2081
D2010	D2022	D2034	D2046	D2058	D2070	D2082
D2011	D2023	D2035	D2047	D2059	D2071	D2083

D2084	D2101	D2118	D2135	D2152	D2169	D2186
D2085	D2102	D2119	D2136	D2153	D2170	D2187
D2086	D2103	D2120	D2137	D2154	D2171	D2188
D2087	D2104	D2121	D2138	D2155	D2172	D2189
D2088	D2105	D2122	D2139	D2156	D2173	D2190
D2089	D2106	D2123	D2140	D2157	D2174	D2191
D2090	D2107	D2124	D2141	D2158	D2175	D2192
D2091	D2108	D2125	D2142	D2159	D2176	D2193
D2092	D2109	D2126	D2143	D2160	D2177	D2194
D2093	D2110	D2127	D2144	D2161	D2178	D2195
D2094	D2111	D2128	D2145	D2162	D2179	D2196
D2095	D2112	D2129	D2146	D2163	D2180	D2197
D2096	D2113	D2130	D2147	D2164	D2181	D2198
D2097	D2114	D2131	D2148	D2165	D2182	D2199
D2098	D2115	D2132	D2149	D2166	D2183	
D2099	D2116	D2133	D2150	D2167	D2184	
D2100	D2117	D2134	D2151	D2168	D2185	

Class continued with D2372

Shunter   Drewry   0-6-0

Introduced
1952

Total b.h.p.
204

Engine
Gardner 8L3 of 204 b.h.p. at 1,200 r.p.m.

Transmission
Mechanical, Vulcan-Sinclair type 23 fluid coupling. Wilson-Drewry C.A.5 type five-speed epicyclic gearbox. Type RF 11 spiral bevel reverse and final drive unit

Weight
29 tons 15 cwt

Maximum tractive effort
16,850 lb

Driving wheel diameter
3′ 3″

D2200	D2203	D2205	D2207	D2209	D2211	D2213
D2201	D2204	D2206	D2208	D2210	D2212	D2214
D2202						

Shunter   Drewry   0-6-0

Introduced
1955

Total b.h.p.
204

Engine
Gardner 8L3 of 204 b.h.p. at 1,200 r.p.m.

Transmission
Mechanical. Vulcan-Sinclair type 23 fluid coupling. Wilson-Drewry C.A.5 type five-speed epicyclic gearbox. Type RF 11 spiral bevel reverse and final drive unit

Weight
29 tons 15 cwt

Maximum tractive effort
15,650 lb

Driving wheel diameter
3′ 6″

D2215	D2224	D2233	D2242	D2250	D2258	D2266
D2216	D2225	D2234*	D2243	D2251	D2259	D2267
D2217	D2226	D2235	D2244	D2252	D2260	D2268
D2218	D2227	D2236	D2245	D2253	D2261	D2269
D2219	D2228	D2237	D2246	D2254	D2262	D2270
D2220	D2229	D2238	D2247	D2255	D2263	D2271
D2221	D2230	D2239	D2248	D2256	D2264	D2272
D2222	D2231	D2240	D2249	D2257	D2265	D2273
D2223	D2232	D2241				

* D2234 *still carries its original number,* 11153.

Shunter   Drewry   0-6-0

Introduced
1959

Engine
Gardner 8L3 of 204 b.h.p. at 1,200
r.p.m.

Weight
29 tons 15 cwt

Maximum tractive effort
16,850 lb

Total b.h.p.
204

Transmission
Mechanical. Vulcan-Sinclair type 23
fluid coupling. Wilson-Drewry C.A.5
type five-speed epicyclic gearbox.
Type RF II spiral bevel reverse and
final drive unit

Driving wheel diameter
3' 7"

D2274	D2284	D2294	D2304	D2314	D2323	D2332
D2275	D2285	D2295	D2305	D2315	D2324	D2333
D2276	D2286	D2296	D2306	D2316	D2325	D2334
D2277	D2287	D2297	D2307	D2317	D2326	D2335
D2278	D2288	D2298	D2308	D2318	D2327	D2336
D2279	D2289	D2299	D2309	D2319	D2328	D2337
D2280	D2290	D2300	D2310	D2320	D2329	D2338
D2281	D2291	D2301	D2311	D2321	D2330	D2339
D2282	D2292	D2302	D2312	D2322	D2331	D2340
D2283	D2293	D2303	D2313			

Shunter   British Railways   0-6-0

Class continued from D2199

D2372	D2376	D2380	D2384	D2388	D2392	D2396
D2373	D2377	D2381	D2385	D2389	D2393	D2397
D2374	D2378	D2382	D2386	D2390	D2394	D2398
D2375	D2379	D2383	D2387	D2391	D2395	D2399

British Railways 204 b.h.p. diesel-mechanical 0-6-0 No. D2029   [*B. Roberts*

Drewry 204 b.h.p. diesel-mechanical 0-6-0 No. D2334   [*M. York*

Barclay 204 b.h.p. diesel-mechanical 0-6-0 No. D2409 [P. Burhouse

Barclay 204 b.h.p. diesel-mechanical 0-6-0 No. D2429 [B. Alderwick

Shunter   Barclay   0-6-0

Introduced
1956

Engine
Gardner 8L3 of 204 b.h.p. at 1,200 r.p.m.

Weight
32 tons

Maximum tractive effort
15,340 lb.

Total b.h.p.
204

Transmission
Mechanical. Vulcan-Sinclair type 23 fluid coupling. Wilson C.A.4 type four-speed epicyclic gearbox. Wiseman type 15 RLGB reverse and final drive unit

Driving wheel diameter
3' 6"

D2400	D2402	D2404	D2406	D2407	D2408	D2409
D2401	D2403	D2405				

Shunter   Barclay   0-4-0

Introduced
1958

Engine
Gardner 8L3 of 204 b.h.p. at 1,200 r.p.m.

Weight
35 tons

Maximum tractive effort
20,000 lb

Total b.h.p.
204

Transmission
Mechanical. Vulcan-Sinclair type 23 fluid coupling. Wilson-Drewry C.A.5 type five-speed epicyclic gearbox. Wiseman type 15 R.L.G.B. reverse and final drive unit

Driving wheel diameter
3' 7"

D2410	D2415	D2420	D2425	D2430	D2435	D2440
D2411	D2416	D2421	D2426	D2431	D2436	D2441
D2412	D2417	D2422	D2427	D2432	D2437	D2442
D2413	D2418	D2423	D2428	D2433	D2438	D2443
D2414	D2419	D2424	D2429	D2434	D2439	D2444

Shunter   Hudswell-Clarke   0-6-0

Introduced
1956

Engine
Gardner 8L3 of 204 b.h.p. at 1,200 r.p.m.

Weight
36 tons 7 cwt
*34 tons 4 cwt

Maximum tractive effort
16,100 lb

Total b.h.p.
204

Transmission
Mechanical. S.C.R.5 type 23 scoop control fluid coupling. Three-speed (*four-speed) "SSS Power-flow" double synchro-type gearbox and final drive

Driving wheel diameter
3' 6"

D2500	D2503	D2506	D2509	D2512*	D2515*	D2518*
D2501	D2504†	D2507	D2510*	D2513*	D2516*	D2519*
D2502	D2505	D2508	D2511*	D2514*	D2517*	

† D2504 *still carries its original number,* 11120

Shunter   Hunslet   0-6-0

Introduced
1955

Engine
Gardner 8L3 of 204 b.h.p. at 1,200 r.p.m.

Weight
30 tons

Maximum tractive effort
14,500 lb

Total b.h.p.
204

Transmission
Mechanical. Hunslet patent friction clutch. Hunslet four-speed gearbox incorporating reverse and final drive gears

Driving wheel diameter
3′ 4″*
3′ 9″*

D2550	D2560†	D2570	D2580*	D2590*	D2599*	D2608*
D2551	D2561	D2571	D2581*	D2591*	D2600*	D2609*
D2552	D2562	D2572	D2582*	D2592*	D2601*	D2610*
D2553	D2563†	D2573	D2583*	D2593*	D2602*	D2611*
D2554	D2564	D2574*	D2584*	D2594*	D2603*	D2613*
D2555	D2565	D2575*	D2585*	D2595*	D2604*	D2614*
D2556	D2566	D2576*	D2586*	D2596*	D2605*	D2616*
D2557	D2567	D2577*	D2587*	D2597*	D2606*	D2617*
D2558	D2568	D2578*	D2588*	D2598*	D2607*	D2618*
D2559	D2569†	D2579*	D2589*			

† *These locomotives still carry their original numbers:* D2560 (11163), D2563 (11166), D2569 (11172)

Shunter   North British   0-4-0

Introduced
1953

Engine
Paxman 6RPH of 200 b.h.p. at 1,000 r.p.m.

Weight
32 tons

Maximum tractive effort
21,500 lb

Total b.h.p.
200

Transmission
Hydraulic. Voith-North British hydraulic torque converter type L33YU. North British bevel gears and reversing dog clutch coupled through reduction gearing to jackshaft

Driving wheel diameter
3′ 6″

D2701	D2702	D2703	D2704	D2705	D2706	D2707

udswell-Clarke 204 b.h.p. diesel-mechanical 0-6-0 No. D2503 [*P. H. Wells*

Hunslet 204 b.h.p. diesel-mechanical 0-6-0 No. D2573 [*M. P. Jacobs*

North British 200 b.h.p. diesel-hydraulic 0-4-0 No. 11706 (since renumbered D2706)
[F. W. Day

North British 225 b.h.p. diesel-hydraulic 0-4-0 No. D2763   [P. Ransome-Wallis

Shunter   North British   0-4-0

Introduced
1957

Engine
N.B.L./M.A.N. W6V 17.5/22A of 225 b.h.p. at 1,100 r.p.m. (12 hr rating)

Weight
30 tons

Maximum tractive effort
20,080 lb

Total b.h.p.
225

Transmission
Hydraulic. Voith-North British hydraulic torque converter type LCCYU. North British bevel gears and reversing dog clutch coupled through reduction gearing to jackshaft

Driving wheel diameter
3′ 6″

D2708	D2719	D2730	D2741	D2751	D2761	D2771
D2709	D2720	D2731	D2742	D2752	D2762	D2772
D2710	D2721	D2732	D2743	D2753	D2763	D2773
D2711	D2722	D2733	D2744	D2754	D2764	D2774
D2712	D2723	D2734	D2745	D2755	D2765	D2775
D2713	D2724	D2735	D2746	D2756	D2766	D2776
D2714	D2725	D2736	D2747	D2757	D2767	D2777
D2715	D2726	D2737	D2748	D2758	D2768	D2778
D2716	D2727	D2738	D2749	D2759	D2769	D2779
D2717	D2728	D2739	D2750	D2760	D2770	D2780
D2718	D2729	D2740				

Shunter   Yorkshire Engine Co.   0-4-0

Introduced
1960

Engine
Rolls-Royce C6NFL of 179 h.p. at 1,800 r.p.m.

Weight
28 tons

Maximum tractive effort
15,000 lb

Total b.h.p.
170

Transmission
Hydraulic. Rolls-Royce 3-stage torque converter, Series 10,000. Yorkshire Engine Co. axle-hung double-reduction final drive with reversing mechanism

Driving wheel diameter
3′ 6″

D2850	D2853	D2856	D2859	D2862	D2865	D2868
D2851	D2854	D2857	D2860	D2863	D2866	D2869
D2852	D2855	D2858	D2861	D2864	D2867	

Yorkshire Engine Co. 170 b.h.p. diesel-hydraulic 0-4-0 No. D2868   [B. Roberts

North British 330 b.h.p. diesel-hydraulic 0-4-0 No. D2910   [R. J. Buckley

Shunter   North British   0-4-0

Introduced
1958

Engine
N.B.L./M.A.N. W6V 17.5/22 AS,
super-charged

Weight
36 tons

Maximum tractive effort
24,100 lb

Total b.h.p.
330

Transmission
Hydraulic. Voith-North British hydraulic torque converter type L24V. North British spiral bevel gears, reversing and reduction gears to jackshaft

Driving wheel diameter
3′ 9″

D2900	D2902	D2904	D2906	D2908	D2910	D2912
D2901	D2903	D2905	D2907	D2909	D2911	D2913

Shunter   Hunslet   0-4-0

Introduced
1955

Engine
Gardner 6L3 of 153 b.h.p. at 1,200 r.p.m.

Weight
22 tons 9 cwt

Maximum tractive effort
10,800 lb

Total b.h.p.
153

Transmission
Mechanical. Hunslet patent friction clutch and four-speed gearbox incorporating reverse and final drive gears

Driving wheel diameter
3′ 4″

D2950	D2951	D2952

Shunter   Barclay   0-4-0

Introduced
1956

Engine
Gardner 6L3 of 153 b.h.p. at 1,200 r.p.m.

Weight
25 tons

Maximum tractive effort
12,750 lb

Total b.h.p.
153

Transmission
Mechanical. Vulcan-Sinclair rigid type hydraulic coupling. Wilson S.E. 4 type four-speed epicyclic gearbox. Wiseman type 15 RLGB reverse and final drive unit

Driving wheel diameter
3′ 2″

D2953	D2954	D2955	D2956

Shunter Ruston & Hornsby 0-4-0

Introduced
1956

Engine
Ruston 6VPHL of 165 b.h.p. at 1,250 r.p.m. (1 hr rating)

Weight
28 tons

Maximum tractive effort
14,350 lb

Total b.h.p.
165

Transmission
Mechanical. Oil pressure-operated S.L.M. type friction clutches incorporated in Ruston constant mesh type gearbox. Reverse gear and final drive unit incorporating bevel gears and dog clutches and reduction gear to final drive

Driving wheel diameter
3' 4"

D2957   D2958

Shunter Ruston & Hornsby 0-6-0

Introduced
1962

Engine
Paxman 6-cyl RPHL

Weight
42 tons 5 cwt

Maximum tractive effort
28,240 lb

Total b.h.p.
275

Transmission
Electric. A.E.I. type RTA 6652 traction motor, spigot-mounted on a double-reduction axle-hung final drive gearbox

Driving wheel diameter
3' 6"

| D2985 | D2987 | D2989 | D2991 | D2993 | D2995 | D2997 |
| D2986 | D2988 | D2990 | D2992 | D2994 | D2996 | D2998 |

Shunter Brush 0-4-0

Introduced
1960

Engine
Petter-McLaren 6-cyl LE6 of 180 b.h.p. at 1,800 r.p.m.

Weight
30 tons

Maximum tractive effort
19,200 lb

Total b.h.p.
180

Transmission
Electric. One axle-hung nose-suspended traction motor

Driving wheel diameter
3' 6"

D2999

Ruston & Hornsby 165 b.h.p. diesel-mechanical 0-4-0 No. 11508 (since renumbered D2958)
[A. W. *Martin*

Ruston & Hornsby 275 b.h.p. diesel-electric 0-6-0 No. D2986 [*British Railways*

Locomotives D3000-D3336 were originally numbered 13000-13336 and are being renumbered as they are overhauled.

Introduced
1953

Total b.h.p.
350

Engine
English Electric 6-cyl 6KT of 350 b.h.p. at 630 r.p.m.

Transmission
Electric. Two English Electric nose-suspended traction motors. Double reduction gear drive

Weight
49 tons

Driving wheel diameter
4′ 6″

Maximum tractive effort
35,000 lb

Note: Nos. D3000-91 and D3102-3116 fitted for vacuum brake operation.

D3000	D3017	D3034	D3051	D3068	D3085	D3101
D3001	D3018	D3035	D3052	D3069	D3086	D3102
D3002	D3019	D3036	D3053	D3070	D3087	D3103
D3003	D3020	D3037	D3054	D3071	D3088	D3104
D3004	D3021	D3038	D3055	D3072	D3089	D3105
D3005	D3022	D3039	D3056	D3073	D3090	D3106
D3006	D3023	D3040	D3057	D3074	D3091	D3107
D3007	D3024	D3041	D3058	D3075	D3092	D3108
D3008	D3025	D3042	D3059	D3076	D3093	D3109
D3009	D3026	D3043	D3060	D3077	D3094	D3110
D3010	D3027	D3044	D3061	D3078	D3095	D3111
D3011	D3028	D3045	D3062	D3079	D3096	D3112
D3012	D3029	D3046	D3063	D3080	D3097	D3113
D3013	D3030	D3047	D3064	D3081	D3098	D3114
D3014	D3031	D3048	D3065	D3082	D3099	D3115
D3015	D3032	D3049	D3066	D3083	D3100	D3116
D3016	D3033	D3050	D3067	D3084		

Shunter   British Railways   0-6-0

Introduced
1955

Total b.h.p.
350

Engine
Crossley 6-cyl ESNT 6 of 350 b.h.p. at 825 r.p.m. (continuous rating)

Transmission
Electric. Two Crompton Parkinson nose-suspended traction motors. Double reduction gear drive

Weight
47 tons 10 cwt

Driving wheel diameter
4′ 6″

Maximum tractive effort
35,000 lb

D3117	D3119	D3121	D3123	D3124	D3125	D3126
D3118	D3120	D3122				

Shunter　　British Railways　　0-6-0

Introduced
1953

Engine
English Electric 6-cyl 6KT of 350 b.h.p. at 680 r.p.m.

Weight
48 tons

Maximum tractive effort
35,000 lb

Total b.h.p.
350

Transmission
Electric. Two English Electric nose-suspended traction motors. Double reduction gear drive

Driving wheel diameter
4′ 6″

Fitted for vacuum brake operation

| D3127 | D3129 | D3131 | D3133 | D3134 | D3135 | D3136 |
| D3128 | D3130 | D3132 | | | | |

Shunter　　British Railways　　0-6-0

Introduced
1955

Engine
Blackstone 6-cyl ER6T of 350 b.h.p. at 750 r.p.m.

Weight
47 tons 10 cwt

Maximum tractive effort
35,000 lb

Total b.h.p.
350

Transmission
Electric. Two G.E.C. nose-suspended traction motors. Double reduction gear drive

Driving wheel diameter
4′ 6″

Fitted for vacuum brake operation

D3137	D3140	D3142	D3144	D3146	D3148	D3150
D3138	D3141	D3143	D3145	D3147	D3149	D3151
D3139						

Shunter　　British Railways　　0-6-0

Introduced
1955

Engine
Blackstone 6-cyl ER6T of 350 b.h.p. at 750 r.p.m.

Weight
47 tons

Maximum tractive effort
35,000 lb

Total b.h.p.
350

Transmission
Electric. Two B.T.H. nose-suspended traction motors. Double reduction gear drive

Driving wheel diameter
4′ 6″

D3152	D3155	D3157	D3159	D3161	D3163	D3165
D3153	D3156	D3158	D3160	D3162	D3164	D3166
D3154						

D3167	D3206	D3245	D3284	D3323	D3362	D3401
D3168	D3207	D3246	D3285	D3324	D3363	D3402
D3169	D3208	D3247	D3286	D3325	D3364	D3403
D3170	D3209	D3248	D3287	D3326	D3365	D3404
D3171	D3210	D3249	D3288	D3327	D3366	D3405
D3172	D3211	D3250	D3289	D3328	D3367	D3406
D3173	D3212	D3251	D3290	D3329	D3368	D3407
D3174	D3213	D3252	D3291	D3330	D3369	D3408
D3175	D3214	D3253	D3292	D3331	D3370	D3409
D3176	D3215	D3254	D3293	D3332	D3371	D3410
D3177	D3216	D3255	D3294	D3333	D3372	D3411
D3178	D3217	D3256	D3295	D3334	D3373	D3412
D3179	D3218	D3257	D3296	D3335	D3374	D3413
D3180	D3219	D3258	D3297	D3336	D3375	D3414
D3181	D3220	D3259	D3298	D3337	D3376	D3415
D3182	D3221	D3260	D3299	D3338	D3377	D3416
D3183	D3222	D3261	D3300	D3339	D3378	D3417
D3184	D3223	D3262	D3301	D3340	D3379	D3418
D3185	D3224	D3263	D3302	D3341	D3380	D3419
D3186	D3225	D3264	D3303	D3342	D3381	D3420
D3187	D3226	D3265	D3304	D3343	D3382	D3421
D3188	D3227	D3266	D3305	D3344	D3383	D3422
D3189	D3228	D3267	D3306	D3345	D3384	D3423
D3190	D3229	D3268	D3307	D3346	D3385	D3424
D3191	D3230	D3269	D3308	D3347	D3386	D3425
D3192	D3231	D3270	D3309	D3348	D3387	D3426
D3193	D3232	D3271	D3310	D3349	D3388	D3427
D3194	D3233	D3272	D3311	D3350	D3389	D3428
D3195	D3234	D3273	D3312	D3351	D3390	D3429
D3196	D3235	D3274	D3313	D3352	D3391	D3430
D3197	D3236	D3275	D3314	D3353	D3392	D3431
D3198	D3237	D3276	D3315	D3354	D3393	D3432
D3199	D3238	D3277	D3316	D3355	D3394	D3433
D3200	D3239	D3278	D3317	D3356	D3395	D3434
D3201	D3240	D3279	D3318	D3357	D3396	D3435
D3202	D3241	D3280	D3319	D3358	D3397	D3436
D3203	D3242	D3281	D3320	D3359	D3398	D3437
D3204	D3243	D3282	D3321	D3360	D3399	D3438
D3205	D3244	D3283	D3322	D3361	D3400	

D3439	D3442	D3444	D3446	D3448	D3450	D3452
D3440	D3443	D3445	D3447	D3449	D3451	D3453
D3441						

British Railways 350 b.h.p. diesel-electric 0-6-0 No. D3379 [R. J. Buckley

British Railways Type 2 1,160 b.h.p. diesel-electric Bo-Bo No. D5056 [B. Roberts

British Railways Type 2 1,250 b.h.p. diesel-electric Bo-Bo No. D5188 [F. W. Day

D3454-D3472: for particulars see D3127-D3136

D3454	D3457	D3460	D3463	D3466	D3469	D3471
D3455	D3458	D3461	D3464	D3467	D3470	D3472
D3456	D3459	D3462	D3465	D3468		

D3473-D3502: for particulars see D3137-D3151

D3473	D3478	D3483	D3487	D3491	D3495	D3499
D3474	D3479	D3484	D3488	D3492	D3496	D3500
D3475	D3480	D3485	D3489	D3493	D3497	D3501
D3476	D3481	D3486	D3490	D3494	D3498	D3502
D3477	D3482					

D3503-D3611: for particulars see D3127-D3136

D3503	D3519	D3535	D3551	D3567	D3582	D3597
D3504	D3520	D3536	D3552	D3568	D3583	D3598
D3505	D3521	D3537	D3553	D3569	D3584	D3599
D3506	D3522	D3538	D3554	D3570	D3585	D3600
D3507	D3523	D3539	D3555	D3571	D3586	D3601
D3508	D3524	D3540	D3556	D3572	D3587	D3602
D3509	D3525	D3541	D3557	D3573	D3588	D3603
D3510	D3526	D3542	D3558	D3574	D3589	D3604
D3511	D3527	D3543	D3559	D3575	D3590	D3605
D3512	D3528	D3544	D3560	D3576	D3591	D3606
D3513	D3529	D3545	D3561	D3577	D3592	D3607
D3514	D3530	D3546	D3562	D3578	D3593	D3608
D3515	D3531	D3547	D3563	D3579	D3594	D3609
D3516	D3532	D3548	D3564	D3580	D3595	D3610
D3517	D3533	D3549	D3565	D3581	D3596	D3611
D3518	D3534	D3550	D3566			

D3612-D3651: for particulars see D3137-D3151

D3612	D3618	D3624	D3630	D3636	D3642	D3647
D3613	D3619	D3625	D3631	D3637	D3643	D3648
D3614	D3620	D3626	D3632	D3638	D3644	D3649
D3615	D3621	D3627	D3633	D3639	D3645	D3650
D3616	D3622	D3628	D3634	D3640	D3646	D3651
D3617	D3623	D3629	D3635	D3641		

D3652-D4048: for particulars see D3127-D3136

D3652	D3658	D3664	D3670	D3676	D3682	D3688
D3653	D3659	D3665	D3671	D3677	D3683	D3689
D3654	D3660	D3666	D3672	D3678	D3684	D3690
D3655	D3661	D3667	D3673	D3679	D3685	D3691
D3656	D3662	D3668	D3674	D3680	D3686	D3692
D3657	D3663	D3669	D3675	D3681	D3687	D3693

D3694	D3742	D3790	D3838	D3886	D3934	D3982
D3695	D3743	D3791	D3839	D3887	D3935	D3983
D3696	D3744	D3792	D3840	D3888	D3936	D3984
D3697	D3745	D3793	D3841	D3889	D3937	D3985
D3698	D3746	D3794	D3842	D3890	D3938	D3986
D3699	D3747	D3795	D3843	D3891	D3939	D3987
D3700	D3748	D3796	D3844	D3892	D3940	D3988
D3701	D3749	D3797	D3845	D3893	D3941	D3989
D3702	D3750	D3798	D3846	D3894	D3942	D3990
D3703	D3751	D3799	D3847	D3895	D3943	D3991
D3704	D3752	D3800	D3848	D3896	D3944	D3992
D3705	D3753	D3801	D3849	D3897	D3945	D3993
D3706	D3754	D3802	D3850	D3898	D3946	D3994
D3707	D3755	D3803	D3851	D3899	D3947	D3995
D3708	D3756	D3804	D3852	D3900	D3948	D3996
D3709	D3757	D3805	D3853	D3901	D3949	D3997
D3710	D3758	D3806	D3854	D3902	D3950	D3998
D3711	D3759	D3807	D3855	D3903	D3951	D3999
D3712	D3760	D3808	D3856	D3904	D3952	D4000
D3713	D3761	D3809	D3857	D3905	D3953	D4001
D3714	D3762	D3810	D3858	D3906	D3954	D4002
D3715	D3763	D3811	D3859	D3907	D3955	D4003
D3716	D3764	D3812	D3860	D3908	D3956	D4004
D3717	D3765	D3813	D3861	D3909	D3957	D4005
D3718	D3766	D3814	D3862	D3910	D3958	D4006
D3719	D3767	D3815	D3863	D3911	D3959	D4007
D3720	D3768	D3816	D3864	D3912	D3960	D4008
D3721	D3769	D3817	D3865	D3913	D3961	D4009
D3722	D3770	D3818	D3866	D3914	D3962	D4010
D3723	D3771	D3819	D3867	D3915	D3963	D4011
D3724	D3772	D3820	D3868	D3916	D3964	D4012
D3725	D3773	D3821	D3869	D3917	D3965	D4013
D3726	D3774	D3822	D3870	D3918	D3966	D4014
D3727	D3775	D3823	D3871	D3919	D3967	D4015
D3728	D3776	D3824	D3872	D3920	D3968	D4016
D3729	D3777	D3825	D3873	D3921	D3969	D4017
D3730	D3778	D3826	D3874	D3922	D3970	D4018
D3731	D3779	D3827	D3875	D3923	D3971	D4019
D3732	D3780	D3828	D3876	D3924	D3972	D4020
D3733	D3781	D3829	D3877	D3925	D3973	D4021
D3734	D3782	D3830	D3878	D3926	D3974	D4022
D3735	D3783	D3831	D3879	D3927	D3975	D4023
D3736	D3784	D3832	D3880	D3928	D3976	D4024
D3737	D3785	D3833	D3881	D3929	D3977	D4025
D3738	D3786	D3834	D3882	D3930	D3978	D4026
D3739	D3787	D3835	D3883	D3931	D3979	D4027
D3740	D3788	D3836	D3884	D3932	D3980	D4028
D3741	D3789	D3837	D3885	D3933	D3981	D4029

D4030	D4033	D4036	D4039	D4042	D4045	D4047
D4031	D4034	D4037	D4040	D4043	D4046	D4048
D4032	D4035	D4038	D4041	D4044		

D4049–D4094: for particulars see D3137–D3151

D4049	D4056	D4063	D4070	D4077	D4083	D4089
D4050	D4057	D4064	D4071	D4078	D4084	D4090
D4051	D4058	D4065	D4072	D4079	D4085	D4091
D4052	D4059	D4066	D4073	D4080	D4086	D4092
D4053	D4060	D4067	D4074	D4081	D4087	D4093
D4054	D4061	D4068	D4075	D4082	D4088	D4094
D4055	D4062	D4069	D4076			

D4095–D4192

D4095	D4109	D4123	D4137	D4151	D4165	D4179
D4096	D4110	D4124	D4138	D4152	D4166	D4180
D4097	D4111	D4125	D4139	D4153	D4167	D4181
D4098	D4112	D4126	D4140	D4154	D4168	D4182
D4099	D4113	D4127	D4141	D4155	D4169	D4183
D4100	D4114	D4128	D4142	D4156	D4170	D4184
D4101	D4115	D4129	D4143	D4157	D4171	D4185
D4102	D4116	D4130	D4144	D4158	D4172	D4186
D4103	D4117	D4131	D4145	D4159	D4173	D4187
D4104	D4118	D4132	D4146	D4160	D4174	D4188
D4105	D4119	D4133	D4147	D4161	D4175	D4189
D4106	D4120	D4134	D4148	D4162	D4176	D4190
D4107	D4121	D4135	D4149	D4163	D4177	D4191
D4108	D4122	D4136	D4150	D4164	D4178	D4192

Type 2　　　British Railways　　　Bo-Bo ✷

Introduced
1958

Engine
Sulzer 6-cyl 6LDA28 of 1,160 b.h.p. at 750 r.p.m.
††Sulzer 6-cyl 6LDA28-B of 1,250 b.h.p. at 750 r.p.m.

Weight
75 tons
72 tons 17 cwt*†

Maximum tractive effort
40,000 lb
‡45,000 lb

Total b.h.p.
1,160
1,160*
1,250††‡§

Transmission
Electric. Four B.T.H. axle-hung, nose-suspended traction motors of 213 h.p. (continuous rating)
‡§Four A.E.I. 253 AY nose-suspended traction motors

Driving wheel diameter
3′ 9″

152

D5000	D5043	D5086	D5129*	D5172†	D5215‡	D5258§
D5001	D5044	D5087	D5130*	D5173†	D5216‡	D5259§
D5002	D5045	D5088	D5131*	D5174†	D5217‡	D5260§
D5003	D5046	D5089	D5132*	D5175†	D5218‡	D5261§
D5004	D5047	D5090	D5133*	D5176†	D5219‡	D5262§
D5005	D5048	D5091	D5134*	D5177‡	D5220‡	D5263§
D5006	D5049	D5092	D5135*	D5178‡	D5221‡	D5264§
D5007	D5050	D5093	D5136*	D5179‡	D5222‡	D5265§
D5008	D5051	D5094*	D5137*	D5180‡	D5223‡	D5266§
D5009	D5052	D5095*	D5138*	D5181‡	D5224‡	D5267§
D5010	D5053	D5096*	D5139*	D5182‡	D5225‡	D5268§
D5011	D5054	D5097*	D5140*	D5183‡	D5226‡	D5269§
D5012	D5055	D5098*	D5141*	D5184‡	D5227‡	D5270§
D5013	D5056	D5099*	D5142*	D5185‡	D5228‡	D5271§
D5014	D5057	D5100*	D5143*	D5186‡	D5229‡	D5272§
D5015	D5058	D5101*	D5144*	D5187‡	D5230‡	D5273§
D5016	D5059	D5102*	D5145*	D5188‡	D5231‡	D5274§
D5017	D5060	D5103*	D5146*	D5189‡	D5232‡	D5275§
D5018	D5061	D5104*	D5147*	D5190‡	D5233§	D5276§
D5019	D5062	D5105*	D5148*	D5191‡	D5234§	D5277§
D5020	D5063	D5106*	D5149*	D5192‡	D5235§	D5278§
D5021	D5064	D5107*	D5150*	D5193‡	D5236§	D5279§
D5022	D5065	D5108*	D5151†	D5194‡	D5237§	D5280§
D5023	D5066	D5109*	D5152†	D5195‡	D5238§	D5281§
D5024	D5067	D5110*	D5153†	D5196‡	D5239§	D5282§
D5025	D5068	D5111*	D5154†	D5197‡	D5240§	D5283§
D5026	D5069	D5112*	D5155†	D5198‡	D5241§	D5284§
D5027	D5070	D5113*	D5156†	D5199‡	D5242§	D5285§
D5028	D5071	D5114*	D5157†	D5200‡	D5243§	D5286§
D5029	D5072	D5115*	D5158†	D5201‡	D5244§	D5287§
D5030	D5073	D5116*	D5159†	D5202‡	D5245§	D5288§
D5031	D5074	D5117*	D5160†	D5203‡	D5246§	D5289§
D5032	D5075	D5118*	D5161†	D5204‡	D5247§	D5290§
D5033	D5076	D5119*	D5162†	D5205‡	D5248§	D5291§
D5034	D5077	D5120*	D5163†	D5206‡	D5249§	D5292§
D5035	D5078	D5121*	D5164†	D5207‡	D5250§	D5293§
D5036	D5079	D5122*	D5165†	D5208‡	D5251§	D5294§
D5037	D5080	D5123*	D5166†	D5209‡	D5252§	D5295§
D5038	D5081	D5124*	D5167†	D5210‡	D5253§	D5296§
D5039	D5082	D5125*	D5168†	D5211‡	D5254§	D5297§
D5040	D5083	D5126*	D5169†	D5212‡	D5255§	D5298§
D5041	D5084	D5127*	D5170†	D5213‡	D5256§	D5299§
D5042	D5085	D5128*	D5171†	D5214‡	D5257§	

Class continued with D7500

Type 2   Birmingham   Bo-Bo
R.C. & W. Co.

Introduced
1958

Engine
Sulzer 6-cyl 6LDA28 of 1,160 b.h.p.
at 750 r.p.m.
† Sulzer 6-cyl 6LDA28-B of 1,250
b.h.p. at 750 r.p.m.

Weight
74 tons
77 tons 10 cwt*
72 tons 10 cwt†

Maximum tractive effort
42,000 lb

Total b.h.p.   *
1,160
1,250†

Transmission
Electric. Four Crompton Parkinson
axle-hung, nose-suspended traction
motors
†Four G.E.C. axle-hung, nose-
suspended traction motors

Driving wheel diameter
3′ 7″

D5300*	D5317*	D5334	D5351†	D5368†	D5384†	D5400†
D5301*	D5318*	D5335	D5352†	D5369†	D5385†	D5401†
D5302*	D5319*	D5336	D5353†	D5370†	D5386†	D5402†
D5303*	D5320	D5337	D5354†	D5371†	D5387†	D5403†
D5304*	D5321	D5338	D5355†	D5372†	D5388†	D5404†
D5305*	D5322	D5339	D5356†	D5373†	D5389†	D5405†
D5306*	D5323	D5340	D5357†	D5374†	D5390†	D5406†
D5307*	D5324	D5341	D5358†	D5375†	D5391†	D5407†
D5308*	D5325	D5342	D5359†	D5376†	D5392†	D5408†
D5309*	D5326	D5343	D5360†	D5377†	D5393†	D5409†
D5310*	D5327	D5344	D5361†	D5378†	D5394†	D5410†
D5311*	D5328	D5345	D5362†	D5379†	D5395†	D5411†
D5312*	D5329	D5346	D5363†	D5380†	D5396†	D5412†
D5313*	D5330	D5347†	D5364†	D5381†	D5397†	D5413†
D5314*	D5331	D5348†	D5365†	D5382†	D5398†	D5414†
D5315*	D5332	D5349†	D5366†	D5383†	D5399†	D5415†
D5316*	D5333	D5350†	D5367†			

Type 2 or 3†   Brush   A1A-A1A

Introduced
1957

Engine
Mirrlees, Bickerton & Day 12-cyl
JVS12T of 1,250*, 1,365 or 1,600†
b.h.p. at 850*, 900 or 950† r.p.m.
‡Temporarily uprated to 2,000 b.h.p.
§ English Electric 12-cyl 12SV of
1,470 b.h.p.

Weight
104 tons

Maximum tractive effort
42,000 lb

Total b.h.p.   ●* *
1,250*
1,365
1,600†
2,000‡
1,470§

Transmission
Electric. Four Brush traction motors.
single reduction gear drive

Driving wheel diameter
3′ 7″

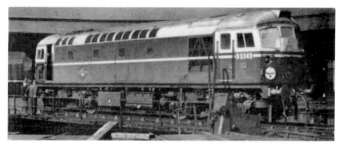

Birmingham R.C. & W. Co. Type 2 1,160 b.h.p. diesel-electric Bo-Bo No. D5345
[*P. H. Groom*

Brush Type 2 1,365 b.h.p. diesel-electric AIA-AIA No. D5522   [*J. C. Beckett*

Brush Type 2 1,365 b.h.p. diesel-electric AIA-AIA No. D5533   [*P. J. Sharpe*

D5500*	D5529	D5558	D5587	D5616	D5644	D5672
D5501*	D5530	D5559	D5588	D5617	D5645	D5673
D5502*	D5531	D5560	D5589	D5618	D5646	D5674
D5503*	D5532	D5561	D5590	D5619	D5647	D5675
D5504*	D5533	D5562	D5591	D5620	D5648	D5676
D5505*	D5534	D5563	D5592	D5621	D5649	D5677§
D5506*	D5535	D5564	D5593	D5622	D5650	D5678
D5507*	D5536	D5565	D5594	D5623	D5651	D5679
D5508*	D5537	D5566	D5595	D5624	D5652	D5680
D5509*	D5538	D5567	D5596	D5625	D5653	D5681
D5510*	D5539	D5568	D5597	D5626	D5654	D5682
D5511*	D5540	D5569	D5598	D5627	D5655†	D5683
D5512*	D5541	D5570	D5599	D5628	D5656†	D5684
D5513*	D5542	D5571	D5600	D5629	D5657†	D5685
D5514*	D5543	D5572	D5601	D5630	D5658†	D5686
D5515*	D5544	D5573	D5602	D5631	D5659†	D5687
D5516*	D5545†	D5574	D5603	D5632	D5660†	D5688
D5517*	D5546	D5575	D5604	D5633	D5661†	D5689
D5518*	D5547	D5576	D5605	D5634	D5662†	D5690
D5519*	D5548	D5577	D5606	D5635	D5663†	D5691
D5520	D5549	D5578	D5607	D5636	D5664†	D5692
D5521	D5550	D5579	D5608	D5637	D5665†	D5693
D5522	D5551	D5580	D5609	D5638	D5666†	D5694
D5523	D5552	D5581	D5610	D5639	D5667†	D5695
D5524	D5553	D5582	D5611	D5640	D5668†	D5696
D5525	D5554	D5583	D5612	D5641	D5669†	D5697
D5526	D5555	D5584	D5613	D5642	D5670†	D5698
D5527	D5556	D5585	D5614	D5643	D5671	D5699
D5528	D5557	D5586	D5615			

Class continued with D5800

Type 2 — Metropolitan Vickers — Co-Bo ●

Introduced
1958

Total b.h.p.
1,200

Engine
Crossley 8-cyl HST V8 of 1,200 b.h.p. at 625 r.p.m. (continuous)

Transmission
Electric. Five Metropolitan-Vickers axle-hung nose-suspended traction motors

Weight
97 tons

Driving wheel diameter
3' 3½"

Maximum tractive effort
50,000 lb

D5700	D5703	D5706	D5709	D5712	D5715	D5718
D5701	D5704	D5707	D5710	D5713	D5716	D5719
D5702	D5705	D5708	D5711	D5714	D5717	

Above: Metropolitan-Vickers Type 2 1,200 b.h.p. diesel-electric Co-Bo No. D5710
[*P. J. Sharpe*

Right: English Electric Type 2 1,100 b.h.p. diesel-electric Bo-Bo No. D5904
[*D. L. Percival*

Below: North British Type 2 1,350 b.h.p. diesel-electric Bo-Bo No. D6123
[*R. A. Panting*

Type 2   Brush   A1A-A1A

Class continued from D5699   ✱

D5800	D5809	D5818	D5827	D5836	D5845	D5854
D5801	D5810	D5819	D5828	D5837	D5846	D5855
D5802	D5811	D5820	D5829	D5838	D5847	D5856
D5803	D5812	D5821	D5830	D5839	D5848	D5857
D5804	D5813	D5822	D5831	D5840	D5849	D5858
D5805	D5814	D5823	D5832	D5841	D5850	D5859
D5806	D5815	D5824	D5833	D5842	D5851	D5860
D5807	D5816	D5825	D5834	D5843	D5852	D5861
D5808	D5817	D5826	D5835‡	D5844	D5853	D5862

Type 2   English Electric   Bo-Bo

Introduced
1959   ✱

Engine
Napier 9-cyl "Deltic" T9-29 two-stroke, pressure-charged, of 1,100 b.h.p. at 1,600 r.p.m.

Weight
73 tons 17 cwt

Maximum tractive effort
47,000 lb

Total b.h.p.
1,100

Transmission
Electric. Four English Electric axle-hung nose-suspended traction motors

Driving wheel diameter
3' 7"

D5900	D5902	D5904	D5906	D5907	D5908	D5909
D5901	D5903	D5905				

Type 2   North British   Bo-Bo

Introduced
1959   ● ✱*

Engine
N.B.L./M.A.N. 12-cyl L12V18/21S, pressure-charged, of 1,000 or 1,100* b.h.p.
†Paxman

Weight
72 tons 10 cwt

Maximum tractive effort
45,000 lb

Total b.h.p.
1,000
1,100*
1,350†

Transmission
Electric. Four G.E.C. nose-suspended traction motors

Driving wheel diameter
3' 7"

D6100	D6103	D6106	D6109	D6112	D6115	D6118
D6101	D6104*	D6107	D6110	D6113	D6116	D6119
D6102	D6105	D6108	D6111	D6114	D6117	D6120

D6121	D6127	D6133*	D6138*	D6143*	D6148*	D6153*
D6122*	D6128	D6134	D6139*	D6144*	D6149*	D6154*
D6123†	D6129	D6135*	D6140*	D6145*	D6150*	D6155*
D6124	D6130	D6136	D6141*	D6146*	D6151*	D6156*
D6125	D6131	D6137	D6142*	D6147*	D6152*	D6157*
D6126	D6132					

Type 2 — North British — B-B

Introduced
1959

Engine
N.B.L./M.A.N. 12-cyl L12VI8/21M of 1,000* or 1,100 b.h.p.

Weight
68 tons*
65 tons

Maximum tractive effort
40,000 lb

Total b.h.p.   □* ◇
1,000*
1,100

Transmission
Hydraulic. Voith-N.B.L. L.T.306r hydraulic transmission and cardan shafts to primary gear-boxes on the inner axles and secondary gear-boxes on the outer axles

Driving wheel diameter
3′ 7″

D6300*	D6309	D6318	D6326	D6334	D6342	D6350
D6301*	D6310	D6319	D6327	D6335	D6343	D6351
D6302*	D6311	D6320	D6328	D6336	D6344	D6352
D6303*	D6312	D6321	D6329	D6337	D6345	D6353
D6304*	D6313	D6322	D6330	D6338	D6346	D6354
D6305*	D6314	D6323	D6331	D6339	D6347	D6355
D6306	D6315	D6324	D6332	D6340	D6348	D6356
D6307	D6316	D6325	D6333	D6341	D6349	D6357
D6308	D6317					

Type 3 — Birmingham R.C. & W. Co. — Bo-Bo ◆

Introduced
1960

Engine
Sulzer 8-cyl 8LDA28 pressure-charged of 1,550 b.h.p. at 750 r.p.m. (continuous)

Weight
73 tons 8 cwt

Maximum tractive effort
45,000 lb

Total b.h.p.
1,550

Transmission
Electric. Four Crompton Parkinson 305 h.p. axle-hung nose-suspended traction motors

Driving wheel diameter
3′ 7″

*Built to Hastings line gauge

North British Type 2 1,000 b.h.p. diesel-hydraulic B-B No. D6302   [*A. Swain*

North British Type 2 1,100 b.h.p. diesel-hydraulic B-B No. D6339   [*P. J. Sharpe*

Birmingham R.C. & W. Co. Type 3 1,550 b.h.p. diesel-electric Bo-Bo No. D6571
[*N. E. Preedy*

D6500	D6515	D6529	D6543	D6557	D6571	D6585
D6501	D6516	D6530	D6544	D6558	D6572	D6586*
D6503	D6517	D6531	D6545	D6559	D6573	D6587*
D6504	D6518	D6532	D6546	D6560	D6574	D6588*
D6505	D6519	D6533	D6547	D6561	D6575	D6589*
D6506	D6520	D6534	D6548	D6562	D6576	D6590*
D6507	D6521	D6535	D6549	D6563	D6577	D6591*
D6508	D6522	D6536	D6550	D6564	D6578	D6592*
D6509	D6523	D6537	D6551	D6565	D6579	D6593*
D6510	D6524	D6538	D6552	D6566	D6580	D6594*
D6511	D6525	D6539	D6553	D6567	D6581	D6595*
D6512	D6526	D6540	D6554	D6568	D6582	D6596*
D6513	D6527	D6541	D6555	D6569	D6583	D6597*
D6514	D6528	D6542	D6556	D6570	D6584	

Type 3   English Electric   Co-Co

Introduced
1961

Total b.h.p.   ✱
1,750

Engine
English Electric 12-cyl 12CSVT of 1,750 b.h.p. at 850 r.p.m.

Transmission
Electric. Six English Electric axle-hung nose-suspended traction motors

Weight
108 tons

Driving wheel diameter
3' 7"

Maximum tractive effort
55,500 lb

D6700	D6722	D6744	D6766	D6788	D6810	D6832
D6701	D6723	D6745	D6767	D6789	D6811	D6833
D6702	D6724	D6746	D6768	D6790	D6812	D6834
D6703	D6725	D6747	D6769	D6791	D6813	D6835
D6704	D6726	D6748	D6770	D6792	D6814	D6836
D6705	D6727	D6749	D6771	D6793	D6815	D6837
D6706	D6728	D6750	D6772	D6794	D6816	D6838
D6707	D6729	D6751	D6773	D6795	D6817	D6839
D6708	D6730	D6752	D6774	D6796	D6818	D6840
D6709	D6731	D6753	D6775	D6797	D6819	D6841
D6710	D6732	D6754	D6776	D6798	D6820	D6842
D6711	D6733	D6755	D6777	D6799	D6821	D6843
D6712	D6734	D6756	D6778	D6800	D6822	D6844
D6713	D6735	D6757	D6779	D6801	D6823	D6845
D6714	D6736	D6758	D6780	D6802	D6824	D6846
D6715	D6737	D6759	D6781	D6803	D6825	D6847
D6716	D6738	D6760	D6782	D6804	D6826	D6848
D6717	D6739	D6761	D6783	D6805	D6827	D6849
D6718	D6740	D6762	D6784	D6806	D6828	D6850
D6719	D6741	D6763	D6785	D6807	D6829	D6851
D6720	D6742	D6764	D6786	D6808	D6830	D6852
D6721	D6743	D6765	D6787	D6809	D6831	D6853

D6854	D6875	D6896	D6917	D6938	D6959	D6980
D6855	D6876	D6897	D6918	D6939	D6960	D6981
D6856	D6877	D6898	D6919	D6940	D6961	D6982
D6857	D6878	D6899	D6920	D6941	D6962	D6983
D6858	D6879	D6900	D6921	D6942	D6963	D6984
D6859	D6880	D6901	D6922	D6943	D6964	D6985
D6860	D6881	D6902	D6923	D6944	D6965	D6986
D6861	D6882	D6903	D6924	D6945	D6966	D6987
D6862	D6883	D6904	D6925	D6946	D6967	D6988
D6863	D6884	D6905	D6926	D6947	D6968	D6989
D6864	D6885	D6906	D6927	D6948	D6969	D6990
D6865	D6886	D6907	D6928	D6949	D6970	D6991
D6866	D6887	D6908	D6929	D6950	D6971	D6992
D6867	D6888	D6909	D6930	D6951	D6972	D6993
D6868	D6889	D6910	D6931	D6952	D6973	D6994
D6869	D6890	D6911	D6932	D6953	D6974	D6995
D6870	D6891	D6912	D6933	D6954	D6975	D6996
D6871	D6892	D6913	D6934	D6955	D6976	D6997
D6872	D6893	D6914	D6935	D6956	D6977	D6998
D6873	D6894	D6915	D6936	D6957	D6978	D6999
D6874	D6895	D6916	D6937	D6958	D6979	

Type 3   Beyer Peacock (Hymek)   B-B

Introduced
1961

Total b.h.p.
1,700
1,350*

△

Engine
Bristol-Siddeley/Maybach MD870 of 1,700 b.h.p.
*Temporarily derated to 1,350 b.h.p.

Transmission
Hydraulic. Stone-Maybach Mekydro type 6184U

Weight
74 tons

Driving wheel diameter
3′ 9″

Maximum tractive effort
49,700 lb

D7000	D7015*	D7030	D7045*	D7059*	D7073*	D7087*
D7001*	D7016	D7031*	D7046	D7060	D7074	D7088
D7002	D7017*	D7032	D7047*	D7061*	D7075*	D7089
D7003*	D7018	D7033*	D7048	D7062	D7076	D7090
D7004	D7019*	D7034	D7049*	D7063*	D7077	D7091
D7005*	D7020	D7035*	D7050	D7064	D7078	D7092
D7006	D7021*	D7036	D7051*	D7065*	D7079	D7093
D7007*	D7022	D7037*	D7052	D7066	D7080	D7094
D7008	D7023*	D7038	D7053*	D7067*	D7081	D7095
D7009*	D7024	D7039*	D7054	D7068	D7082	D7096
D7010	D7025*	D7040	D7055*	D7069*	D7083*	D7097
D7011*	D7026	D7041*	D7056	D7070	D7084	D7098
D7012	D7027*	D7042	D7057*	D7071*	D7085*	D7099
D7013*	D7028	D7043*	D7058	D7072	D7086	D7100
D7014	D7029*	D7044				

English Electric Type 3 1,750 b.h.p. diesel-electric Co-Co No. D6715   [C. P. Boocock

English Electric Type 3 1,750 b.h.p. diesel-electric Co-Co No. D6819   [J. White

Beyer Peacock (Hymek) Type 3 1,700 b.h.p. diesel-hydraulic B-B No. D7002
[B. A. Haresnape

Type 2   British Railways   Bo-Bo

Class continued from D5299
                                                        *

D7500§	D7526§	D7552§	D7578§	D7603§	D7628§	D7653§
D7501§	D7527§	D7553§	D7579§	D7604§	D7629§	D7654§
D7502§	D7528§	D7554§	D7580§	D7605§	D7630§	D7655§
D7503§	D7529§	D7555§	D7581§	D7606§	D7631§	D7656§
D7504§	D7530§	D7556§	D7582§	D7607§	D7632§	D7657§
D7505§	D7531§	D7557§	D7583§	D7608§	D7633§	D7658§
D7506§	D7532§	D7558§	D7584§	D7609§	D7634§	D7659§
D7507§	D7533§	D7559§	D7585§	D7610§	D7635§	D7660§
D7508§	D7534§	D7560§	D7586§	D7611§	D7636§	D7661§
D7509§	D7535§	D7561§	D7587§	D7612§	D7637§	D7662§
D7510§	D7536§	D7562§	D7588§	D7613§	D7638§	D7663§
D7511§	D7537§	D7563§	D7589§	D7614§	D7639§	D7664§
D7512§	D7538§	D7564§	D7590§	D7615§	D7640§	D7665§
D7513§	D7539§	D7565§	D7591§	D7616§	D7641§	D7666§
D7514§	D7540§	D7566§	D7592§	D7617§	D7642§	D7667§
D7515§	D7541§	D7567§	D7593§	D7618§	D7643§	D7668§
D7516§	D7542§	D7568§	D7594§	D7619§	D7644§	D7669§
D7517§	D7543§	D7569§	D7595§	D7620§	D7645§	D7670§
D7518§	D7544§	D7570§	D7596§	D7621§	D7646§	D7671§
D7519§	D7545§	D7571§	D7597§	D7622§	D7647§	D7672§
D7520§	D7546§	D7572§	D7598§	D7623§	D7648§	D7673§
D7521§	D7547§	D7573§	D7599§	D7624§	D7649§	D7674§
D7522§	D7548§	D7574§	D7600§	D7625§	D7650§	D7675§
D7523§	D7549§	D7575§	D7601§	D7626§	D7651§	D7676§
D7524§	D7550§	D7576§	D7602§	D7627§	D7652§	D7677§
D7525§	D7551§	D7577§				

Type 1   English Electric   Bo-Bo

Introduced
1957

Total b.h.p.
1,000
                                                        *

Engine
English Electric 8 SVT Mk. II of 1,000
b.h.p. at 850 r.p.m. (continuous)

Transmission
Electric. Four axle-hung, nose-
suspended d.c. traction motors

Weight
72 tons

Driving wheel diameter
3′ 7″

Maximum tractive effort
42,000 lb

D8000	D8008	D8016	D8024	D8032	D8040	D8048
D8001	D8009	D8017	D8025	D8033	D8041	D8049
D8002	D8010	D8018	D8026	D8034	D8042	D8050
D8003	D8011	D8019	D8027	D8035	D8043	D8051
D8004	D8012	D8020	D8028	D8036	D8044	D8052
D8005	D8013	D8021	D8029	D8037	D8045	D8053
D8006	D8014	D8022	D8030	D8038	D8046	D8054
D8007	D8015	D8023	D8031	D8039	D8047	D8055

British Railways Type 2 1,250 b.h.p. diesel-electric Bo-Bo No. D7584   [N. E. Preedy

English Electric Type 1 1,000 b.h.p. diesel-electric Bo-Bo No. D8047   [C. P. Boocock

British Thomson-Houston Type 1 800 b.h.p. diesel-electric Bo-Bo No. D8236
    [P. J Sharpe

D8056	D8074	D8092	D8110	D8127	D8144	D8161
D8057	D8075	D8093	D8111	D8128	D8145	D8162
D8058	D8076	D8094	D8112	D8129	D8146	D8163
D8059	D8077	D8095	D8113	D8130	D8147	D8164
D8060	D8078	D8096	D8114	D8131	D8148	D8165
D8061	D8079	D8097	D8115	D8132	D8149	D8166
D8062	D8080	D8098	D8116	D8133	D8150	D8167
D8063	D8081	D8099	D8117	D8134	D8151	D8168
D8064	D8082	D8100	D8118	D8135	D8152	D8169
D8065	D8083	D8101	D8119	D8136	D8153	D8170
D8066	D8084	D8102	D8120	D8137	D8154	D8171
D8067	D8085	D8103	D8121	D8138	D8155	D8172
D8068	D8086	D8104	D8122	D8139	D8156	D8173
D8069	D8087	D8105	D8123	D8140	D8157	D8174
D8070	D8088	D8106	D8124	D8141	D8158	D8175
D8071	D8089	D8107	D8125	D8142	D8159	D8176
D8072	D8090	D8108	D8126	D8143	D8160	D8177
D8073	D8091	D8109				

Type 1   British   Bo-Bo
Thomson-Houston
*

Introduced
1957

Total b.h.p.
800

Engine
Paxman 16-cyl YHXL V-type, pressure charged, of 800 b.h.p. at 1,250 r.p.m.

Transmission
Electric Four B.T.H. nose-suspended traction motors with single reduction gear drive

Weight
68 tons

Driving wheel diameter
3′ 3½″

Maximum tractive effort
37,500 lb

D8200	D8207	D8214	D8220	D8226	D8232	D8238
D8201	D8208	D8215	D8221	D8227	D8233	D8239
D8202	D8209	D8216	D8222	D8228	D8234	D8240
D8203	D8210	D8217	D8223	D8229	D8235	D8241
D8204	D8211	D8218	D8224	D8230	D8236	D8242
D8205	D8212	D8219	D8225	D8231	D8237	D8243
D8206	D8213					

Type 1   North British   Bo-Bo
●

Introduced
1958

Total b.h.p.
800

Engine
Paxman 16-cyl 16YHXL of 800 b.h.p. at 1,250 r.p.m.

Transmission
Electric. Four G.E.C. axle-hung nose-suspended traction motors

Weight
68 tons

Driving wheel diameter
3′ 7″

Maximum tractive effort
42,000 lb

D8400	D8402	D8404	D8406	D8407	D8408	D8409
D8401	D8403	D8405				

Type I   Clayton   Bo-Bo

Introduced
1962

Engines
Two Paxman 6-cyl 6ZHXL of 450 b.h.p. at 1,500 r.p.m.

Weight
68 tons

Maximum tractive effort
40,000 lb

Total b.h.p.   ◆
900

Transmission
Electric. Four G.E.C. axle-hung nose-suspended traction motors
*Four Crompton Parkinson traction motors.

Driving wheel diameter
3′ 3½″

D8500	D8517	D8534	D8551	D8568	D8584	D8600*
D8501	D8518	D8535	D8552	D8569	D8585	D8601*
D8502	D8519	D8536	D8553	D8570	D8586	D8602*
D8503	D8520	D8537	D8554	D8571	D8587	D8603*
D8504	D8521	D8538	D8555	D8572	D8588*	D8604*
D8505	D8522	D8539	D8556	D8573	D8589*	D8605*
D8506	D8523	D8540	D8557	D8574	D8590*	D8606*
D8507	D8524	D8541	D8558	D8575	D8591*	D8607*
D8508	D8525	D8542	D8559	D8576	D8592*	D8608*
D8509	D8526	D8543	D8560	D8577	D8593*	D8609*
D8510	D8527	D8544	D8561	D8578	D8594*	D8610*
D8511	D8528	D8545	D8562	D8579	D8595*	D8611*
D8512	D8529	D8546	D8563	D8580	D8596*	D8612*
D8513	D8530	D8547	D8564	D8581	D8597*	D8613*
D8514	D8531	D8548	D8565	D8582	D8598*	D8614*
D8515	D8532	D8549	D8566	D8583	D8599*	D8615*
D8516	D8533	D8550	D8567			

Type 5   English-Electric   Co-Co
"Deltic"

Introduced
1961

Engines
Two 18-cyl Napier "Deltic" 18-25 of 1,650 b.h.p. at 1,500 r.p.m.

Weight
99 tons

Maximum tractive effort
50,000 lb

Total b.h.p.
3,300

Transmission
Electric. Six English Electric EE750 25G axle-hung nose-suspended traction motors

Driving wheel diameter
3′ 7″

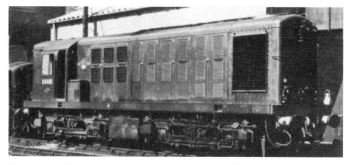

North British Type 1 800 b.h.p. diesel-electric Bo-Bo No. D8406   [K. L. Cook

Clayton Type 1 900 b.h.p. diesel-electric Bo-Bo No. D8559   [N. E. Preedy

Nameplate of English Electric Type 5 3,300 b.h.p. diesel-electric Co-Co No. D9000
Royal Scots Grey   [D. L. Percival

D9000	Royal Scots Grey
D9001	St. Paddy
D9002	The King's Own York-shire Light Infantry
D9003	Meld
D9004	Queen's Own Highlander
D9005	The Prince of Wales's Own Regiment of York-shire
D9006	
D9007	Pinza
D9008	The Green Howards
D9009	Alycidon
D9010	
D9011	The Royal Northum-berland Fusiliers
D9012	Crepello
D9013	The Black Watch
D9014	The Duke of Welling-ton's Regiment
D9015	Tulyar
D9016	Gordon Highlander
D9017	The Durham Light Infantry
D9018	Ballymoss
D9019	
D9020	Nimbus
D9021	Argyll and Sutherland Highlander

Type 1   British Railways   0-6-0

Introduced
1964

Engine
Paxman 6-cyl "Ventura" 6YJX of 650 b.h.p. at 1,500 r.p.m.

Weight
50 tons

Maximum tractive effort
30,910 lb

Total b.h.p.
650

Transmission
Hydraulic. Voith L217U

Driving wheel diameter
4′ 0″

D9500	D9508	D9516	D9524	D9532	D9540	D9548
D9501	D9509	D9517	D9525	D9533	D9541	D9549
D9502	D9510	D9518	D9526	D9534	D9542	D9550
D9503	D9511	D9519	D9527	D9535	D9543	D9551
D9504	D9512	D9520	D9528	D9536	D9544	D9552
D9505	D9513	D9521	D9529	D9537	D9545	D9553
D9506	D9514	D9522	D9530	D9538	D9546	D9554
D9507	D9515	D9523	D9531	D9539	D9547	D9555

Type 3   L.M.S.   Co-Co

Introduced
1947

Engine
English Electric 16-cyl of 1,600 b.h.p. at 750 r.p.m. (continuous rating)

Weight
127 tons 13 cwt

Maximum tractive effort
41,400 lb

10001

Total b.h.p.   ◆
1,600

Transmission
Electric. Six nose-suspended motors single reduction gear drive

Driving wheel diameter
3′ 6″

English Electric Type 5 3,300 b.h.p. diesel-electric Co-Co No. D9011 *The Royal Northumberland Fusiliers* *[P. J. Sharpe*

British Railways Type 1 650 b.h.p. diesel-hydraulic 0-6-0 No. D9500 *[British Railways*

L.M.S. 350 b.h.p. diesel-electric 0-6-0 No. 12032 *[P. J. Sharpe*

Shunter   L.M.S.   0-6-0

Introduced
1939

Engine
English Electric 6-cyl of 350 b.h.p.

Weight
54 tons 16 cwt

Maximum tractive effort
33,000 lb

Total b.h.p.
350

Transmission
Electric. Single motor, jackshaft drive

Driving wheel diameter
4′ 3″

12003	12008	12013	12017	12021	12025	12029
12004	12009	12014	12018	12022	12026	12030
12005	12010	12015	12019	12023	12027	12031
12006	12011	12016	12020	12024	12028	12032
12007	12012					

Shunter   L.M.S. and   0-6-0
British Railways

Introduced
1945

Engine
English Electric 6-cyl of 350 b.h.p.

Weight
47 tons 5 cwt

Maximum tractive effort
35,000 lb

Total b.h.p.
350

Transmission
Electric. Two nose-suspended motors, double reduction gear drive

Driving wheel diameter
4′ 0½″

12033	12049	12064	12079	12094	12109	12124
12034	12050	12065	12080	12095	12110	12125
12035	12051	12066	12081	12096	12111	12126
12036	12052	12067	12082	12097	12112	12127
12037	12053	12068	12083	12098	12113	12128
12038	12054	12069	12084	12099	12114	12129
12039	12055	12070	12085	12100	12115	12130
12040	12056	12071	12086	12101	12116	12131
12041	12057	12072	12087	12102	12117	12132
12042	12058	12073	12088	12103	12118	12133
12043	12059	12074	12089	12104	12119	12134
12044	12060	12075	12090	12105	12120	12135
12045	12061	12076	12091	12106	12121	12136
12046	12062	12077	12092	12107	12122	12137
12047	12063	12078	12093	12108	12123	12138
12048						

Shunter   L.N.E.R.   0-6-0

Introduced
1944

Engine
English Electric 6-cyl of 350 b.h.p.

Weight
50 tons

Maximum tractive effort
32,000 lb

Total b.h.p.
350

Transmission
Electric. Two nose-suspended motors, double reduction gear drive

Driving wheel diameter
4' 0"

15000   15001   15002   15003

Shunter   English Electric   0-6-0

Introduced
1936

Engine
English Electric 6-cyl of 350 b.h.p.

Weight
51 tons 10 cwt

Maximum tractive effort
30,000 lb

Total b.h.p.
350

Transmission
Electric. Two nose-suspended motors, single reduction gear drive

Driving wheel diameter
4' 1"

15100

Shunter   British Railways   0-6-0

Introduced
1948

Engine
English Electric 6-cyl of 350 b.h.p.

Weight
50 tons

Maximum tractive effort
33,500 lb

Total b.h.p.
350

Transmission
Electric. Two nose-suspended motors, double reduction gear drive

Driving wheel diameter
4' 0½"

15101   15102   15103   15104   15105   15106

L.M.S./British Railways 350 b.h.p. diesel-electric 0-6-0 No. 12113   [R. E. Vincent

S.R. 350 b.h.p. diesel-electric 0-6-0 No. 15201   [R. A. Panting

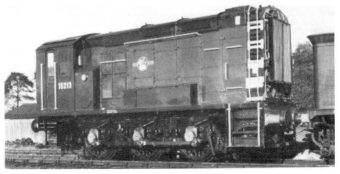

British Railways 350 b.h.p. diesel-electric 0-6-0 No. 15213   [G. W. Morrison

Shunter   S.R.   0-6-0

Introduced
1937

Engine
English Electric 6-cyl of 350 b.h.p.

Weight
55 tons 5 cwt

Maximum tractive effort
30,000 lb

Total b.h.p.
350

Transmission
Electric. Two nose-suspended motors, single reduction gear drive

Driving wheel diameter
4′ 6″

15201   15202   15203

Shunter   British Railways   0-6-0

Introduced
1949

Engine
English Electric 6-cyl of 350 b.h.p.

Weight
45 tons

Maximum tractive effort
24,000 lb

Total b.h.p.
350

Transmission
Electric. Two nose-suspended motors, double reduction gear drive

Driving wheel diameter
4′ 6″

15211	15215	15219	15223	15227	15231	15234
15212	15216	15220	15224	15228	15232	15235
15213	15217	15221	15225	15229	15233	15236
15214	15218	15222	15226	15230		

LOCOMOTIVES ON TRIAL

British Railways are providing facilities for road tests of the following seven locomotives, which remain the property of the manufacturers and are not included in B.R. stock.

Shunter   English Electric   0-6-0

Introduced
1957

Engine
English Electric 6RKT of 500 b.h.p. at 750 r.p.m.

Weight
48 tons

Maximum tractive effort
33,000 lb

Total b.h.p.
500

Transmission
Electric. One English Electric traction motor coupled to double-reduction gear box final drive

Driving wheel diameter
4′ 0″

D0226

Shunter   English Electric   0-6-0

Introduced
1957

Engine
English Electric 6RKT of 500 b.h.p. at 750 r.p.m.

Weight
48 tons

Maximum tractive effort
33,000 lb

D0227

Total b.h.p.
500

Transmission
Hydraulic. Lysholm-Smith torque-converter and three-speed reduction gear to final drive

Driving wheel diameter
4' 0"

Type 4   Birmingham R.C. & W. Co.   Co-Co

Introduced
1962

Engine
Sulzer 12-cyl 12LDA28-C, inter-cooled, of 2,750 b.h.p. at 800 r.p.m.

Weight
114 tons

Maximum tractive effort
55,000 lb

D0260 *Lion*

Total b.h.p.
2,750

Transmission
Electric. Six A.E.I. axle-hung, nose-suspended traction motors

Driving wheel diameter
3' 9"

Type 4   Brush   Co-Co

Introduced
1961

Engines
Two Maybach MD655 V-type of 1,440 b.h.p. at 1,500 r.p.m.

Weight
115 tons

Maximum tractive effort
60,000 lb

D0280 *Falcon*

Total b.h.p.
2,700

Transmission
Electric. Six Brush traction motors

Driving wheel diameter
3' 7"

Type 4   English Electric   Co-Co

Introduced
1962

Engine
English Electric 16-cyl 16CSVT, after-cooled, of 2,700 b.h.p.

Weight
105 tons

Maximum tractive effort
50,000 lb

Total b.h.p.
2,700

Transmission
Electric

Driving wheel diameter
3′ 6″

DP2

Gas Turbine   English Electric   4-6-0

Introduced
1961

Engine
English Electric gas turbine of 2,750 b.h.p. at 9,000 r.p.m.

Weight
Locomotive: 79 tons 16 cwt
Tender: 44 tons

Maximum tractive effort
38,000 lb

Total b.h.p.
2,750

Transmission
Mechanical. Gearbox and flexible drive to coupled axles

Driving wheel diameter
5′ 9″

GT3

Shunter   Yorkshire Engine Co.   0-8-0

Introduced
1961

Engines
2 Rolls-Royce C8SFL of 311 b.h.p. at 1,800 r.p.m.

Weight
58 tons

Maximum tractive effort
45,000 lb

Total b.h.p.
600

Transmission
Hydraulic

Driving wheel diameter
3′ 9″

Taurus

Shunter — Hibberd & Co. — 0-4-0

Introduced
1950

Engine
English National 4-cyl Gas type DA4
of 52 b.h.p. at 1,250 r.p.m.

Weight
11 tons

Maximum tractive effort

Total b.h.p.
52

Transmission
Mechanical. Spur-type three-speed
gearbox with roller chains

Driving wheel diameter

(Original number in brackets)

52 (11104)

Shunter — Ruston & Hornsby — 0-4-0

Introduced
1955

Engine
Ruston & Hornsby Mark 4V vertical
4-cyl of 88 b.h.p.

Weight
17 tons

Maximum tractive effort
9,500 lb

Total b.h.p.
88

Transmission
Mechanical

Driving wheel diameter
3′ 0″

56

Shunter — Barclay — 0-4-0

Introduced
1958

Engine

Weight

Maximum tractive effort

Total b.h.p.
150

Transmission
Mechanical

Driving wheel diameter

81   82   83

Shunter   Ruston & Hornsby   0-4-0

Introduced
1959

Engine

Weight

Maximum tractive effort

Total b.h.p.
88

Transmission
Mechanical

Driving wheel diameter

84   85   87

Shunter   Hunslet   0-6-0

Introduced
1955

Engine
Gardner 8L3 of 204 b.h.p. at 1,200 r.p.m.

Weight
30 tons

Maximum tractive effort
14,500 lb

(Original number in brackets)

Total b.h.p.
204

Transmission
Mechanical. Hunslet patent friction clutch. Hunslet four-speed gearbox incorporating reverse and final drive gears

Driving wheel diameter
3′ 9″

88 (D2612)   89 (D2615)

Shunter   British Railways   0-6-0

Introduced
1958

Engine
Gardner 8L3 of 204 b.h.p. at 1,200 r.p.m.

Weight
30 tons 4 cwt

Maximum tractive effort
15,000 lb

Total b.h.p.
200

Transmission
Mechanical. Wilson-Drewry Director air-operated epicyclic gearbox. R.F. 11 spiral bevel reverse/final drive unit

Driving wheel diameter
3′ 7″

91   92

Above: Ruston & Hornsby 88 b.h.p. diesel-mechanical 0-4-0 No. 84 [*C. Symes*

Right: John Fowler & Co. 150 b.h.p. diesel-mechanical 0-4-0 No. ED6 [*J. E. Wilkinson*

Below: Ruston & Hornsby 165 b.h.p. diesel-electric 0-6-0 No. PWM 653 [*J. A. Coiley*

Shunter   John Fowler & Co.   0-4-0

Introduced
1936

Engine
Fowler 4C vertical of 150 b.h.p. at
1,000 r.p.m. (1 hr rating)

Weight
29 tons

Maximum tractive effort
15,000 lb

Total b.h.p.
150

Transmission
Mechanical. Four-speed gearbox

Driving wheel diameter
3′ 3″

ED2   ED3   ED5   ED6

Shunter   Ruston & Hornsby   0-4-0

Introduced
1958

Engine
Ruston 4YCL

Weight
8 tons 4 cwt

Maximum tractive effort
4,200 lb

Total b.h.p.

Transmission
Mechanical. Chain drive

Driving wheel diameter
2′ 6″

Gauge
3′ 0″

ED10

Shunter   Ruston & Hornsby   0-4-0

Introduced
1958

Engine

Weight
3 tons 10 cwt

Maximum tractive effort
1,890 lb

Total b.h.p.
20

Transmission
Mechanical

Driving wheel diameter

Gauge
1′ 6″

ZM32

Shunter   Ruston & Hornsby   0-4-0

Introduced
1946

Engine
Ruston 4VRH

Weight
7 tons 10 cwt

Maximum tractive effort
3,480 lb

Total b.h.p.
48

Transmission
Mechanical. Chain drive

Driving wheel diameter
2' 6"

This locomotive was supplied to the Bristol Aviation Co. in 1946 and was later purchased by British Railways.

DS1169

Shunter   Drewry   0-6-0

Introduced
1947

Engine
Gardner 8L3 of 204 b.h.p.

Weight
24 tons 15 cwt

Maximum tractive effort
16,850 lb

Total b.h.p.
204

Transmission
Mechanical. Five-speed gearbox

Driving wheel diameter
3' 3"

DS1173

WESTERN REGION

Shunter   Ruston & Hornsby   0-4-0

Introduced
1957

Engine
Ruston & Hornsby 4-cyl of 88 b.h.p.

Weight
17 tons

Maximum tractive effort
9,500 lb

Total b.h.p.
88

Transmission
Mechanical. Chain driven from gearbox

Driving wheel diameter
3' 0"

20

Shunter   Ruston & Hornsby   0-6-0

Introduced
1953

Engine
Ruston & Hornsby 6-cyl of 165 b.h.p.

Weight
30 tons

Maximum tractive effort
17,000 lb

Total b.h.p.
165

Transmission
Electric. One B.T.H. nose-suspended traction motor

Driving wheel diameter
3′ 2½″

PWM650   PWM651   PWM652   PWM653   PWM654

EASTERN REGION DIESEL
LOCOMOTIVE CLASSIFICATION

Horse-power	Description	Locomotive Nos.	Code
153	Hunslet/Gardner	D2950–2	1/15
153	Barclay/Gardner	D2953–6	1/12
165	Ruston & Hornsby	D2957–8	1/16
170	Yorkshire Engine Co.	D2850–69	1/17
200	N.B. Loco. Co./Paxman ...	D2700–7	2/4A
200	Brush/Petter	D2999	2/2
204	B.R./Gardner	D2000–2199, 2372–99	2/1
204	Drewry/Gardner (3′ 3″ wheel) ...	D2200–14	2/13A
204	Drewry/Gardner (3′ 6″ wheel) ...	D2215–73	2/13
204	Drewry/Gardner (3′ 7″ wheel) ...	D2274–2340	2/13
204	Barclay/Gardner (4-speed) ...	D2400–9	2/12A
204	Barclay/Gardner (5-speed) ...	D2410–44	2/12
204	Hudswell-Clarke/Gardner ...	D2500–19	2/14
204	Hunslet/Gardner (3′ 4″ wheel) ...	D2550–73	2/15A
204	Hunslet/Gardner (3′ 9″ wheel) ...	D2574–D2618 ...	2/15
225	N.B. Loco. Co./M.A.N. ...	D2708–80	2/4
330	N.B. Loco. Co./M.A.N. ...	D2900–13	3/4
350	B.R./English Electric ...	D3000–3116/27–36/67 –3438/54–72, 3503– 3611/52-64/72–3718/ 22–4048	3/1
350	B.R./Crossley	D3117–26	3/1B
350	B.R./Blackstone/G.E.C. ...	D3137–51, 3439–53/ 73–3502, 3612–51 4049–94	3/1C
350	B.R./Blackstone/B.T.H. ...	D3152–66	3/1D
350	B.R./E.E. (max. speed 27 m.p.h.)	D3665–71, 3719–21	3/1A
350	L.M.S./English Electric (4′ 3″ wheel)	12003–32	3/8

Horse-power	Description	Locomotive Nos.	Code
350	L.M.S./English Electric (4′ 0½″ wheel)	12033–12138 ...	3/8A
350	L.N.E./English Electric	15000–3	3/10
350	G.W./English Electric (4′ 1″ wheel)	15100	3/11A
350	G.W./English Electric (4′0½″ wheel)	15101–6	3/11
350	S.R./English Electric	15201–3	3/9A
350	S.R./English Electric	15211–36 ...	3/9
800	B.T.H./Paxman	D8200–43	8/5
800	N.B. Loco. Co./Paxman	D8400–9	8/4
900	Clayton/Paxman	D8500–8615 ...	9/18
1,000	N.B. Loco. Co./M.A.N./G.E.C. ...	D6100–37 ...	10/4
1,000	N.B. Loco. Co./M.A.N./Voith ...	D6300–5 ...	10/4A
1,000	English Electric	D8000–8127 ...	10/3
1,100	English Electric/Napier	D5900–9 ...	11/3
1,100	N.B. Loco. Co./M.A.N./G.E.C. ...	D6138–57 ...	11/4
1,100	N.B. Loco. Co./M.A.N./Voith ...	D6306–57 ...	11/4A
1,160	B.R./Sulzer	D5000–48 ...	11/1
1,160	B.R./Sulzer	D5049–5150 ...	11/1A
1,160	Birmingham/Sulzer	D5300–46 ...	11/6
1,200	Metro. Vickers/Crossley	D5700–19 ...	12/5
1,250	Brush/Mirrlees	D5500–19 ...	12/2
1,250	Birmingham/Sulzer	D5347–5415 ...	12/6
1,250	B.R./Sulzer	D5151–5299 ...	12/1
1,365	Brush/Mirrlees	D5520–44/6–5654/ 71–99, 5800–62 ...	13/2
1,550	Birmingham/Sulzer	D6500–85 ...	15/6
1,550	Birmingham/Sulzer	D6586–97 ...	15/6A
1,600	L.M.S./English Electric	10001 ...	16/8
1,600	Brush/Mirrlees	D5545, 5655–70 ...	16/2
1,700	Beyer Peacock/Maybach	D7000–7100 ...	17/7
1,750	English Electric	D6700–6937 ...	17/3
2,000	B.R./Maybach/Mekydro	D800–2	20/1
2,000	English Electric	D200–399 ...	20/3
2,000	N.B. Loco. Co./M.A.N./Voith ...	D600–4 ...	20/4
2,200	B.R./Maybach/Mekydro	D803–29/31/2/66–70	22/1
2,200	N.B. Loco. Co.	D833–65 ...	22/4
2,300	B.R./Sulzer	D1–10 ...	23/1
2,500	B.R./Sulzer	D11–137 ...	25/1
2,500	B.R./Sulzer/Brush	D138–93 ...	25/1A
2,700	B.R./Maybach/Voith	D1000–73 ...	27/1
2,750	Brush/Sulzer	D1500–1861 ...	27/2
3,300	English Electric/Napier Deltic ...	D9000–21	33/3

B.R. DIESEL MULTIPLE-UNITS

UNLESS otherwise stated, all multiple-unit trains are gang-wayed within each set, with guard's and luggage compartment at the inner end of motor brake coaches, and seating is in open saloons with centre and/or end doors. The letter (L) in the headings indicates an open vehicle fitted with toilet facilities; (K) indicates a side corridor vehicle with toilet. Two standard lengths of underframe are in use, namely 56 ft. 11 in. and 63 ft. 5 in. but the actual body lengths vary by a few inches for the same type of underframe. The dimensions shown are the length over body and the overall width.

Several of the types listed are sub-divided by reason of detail or mechanical differences. For example, a certain number of cars in a class may have different seating arrangement or a different make of engine but are otherwise similar to the main batch. Such differences are noted in the heading to the class and given a reference mark by which the relevant dimensions or details and the cars concerned can be identified. The type of set in which each class is formed on delivery, together with the principal manufacturer, is shown at the head of the details for that class, although it should be noted that changes may occur owing to varying operating conditions, even to the extent of coupling different makes of car in the same set or running power cars without intermediate trailers. Most railcars are fitted with a standard Mechanical transmission of a cardan shaft and freewheel to a four-speed epicyclic gearbox, and a further cardan shaft to the final drive. Where a non-standard transmission is employed, full details are shown under the relevant heading. Cars are listed in numerical order by type and not by set formation.

COUPLING CODES

Although several multiple-unit diesel sets can be coupled together and driven by one man in the leading cab, for various reasons it is not possible for all types of diesel unit to work together. In order to distinguish cars that can run together, all have painted at each end above the buffers a colour code symbol. A miniature symbol also appears on the plug socket covers. Only units bearing the same symbol may be coupled together.

* ✱ **ORANGE STAR**   ● **WHITE CIRCLE**

* ◆ **YELLOW DIAMOND**   ■ **BLUE SQUARE**

Derby Works, B.R. (2)

MOTOR BRAKE SECOND ■

Engines
Two B.U.T. (Leyland) 6-cyl. horizontal type of 230 b.h.p.
*Two Rolls-Royce 8-cyl. horizontal type of 238 b.h.p.
†Two B.U.T. (Leyland) 6-cyl. horizontal type of 230 b.h.p.

Transmission
Mechanical. Standard
*Hydraulic. Twin-disc Torque converter
†Mechanical. Standard. Fitted with Self Changing Gears Ltd. automatic four-speed gearbox.

Body: 64′ 6″ × 9′ 3″

Weight: 35 tons 10 cwt (37 tons 10 cwt†

Seats: 2nd, 62

E50000*	E50009	E50018	E50026	E50035	E50043
E50001	E50010	E50019	E50027	E50036	E50044
E50002	E50011	E50020	E50029	E50037	E50045
E50003	E50012	E50021	E50030	E50038	E50046
E50004	E50013	E50022	E50031	E50039	E50047
E50005	E50014	E50023	E50032	E50040	E50048
E50006	E50015	E50024	E50033	E50041	E50049†
E50007	E50016	E50025	E50034	E50042	
E50008	E50017				

Derby Works, B.R. (3 Suburban)

MOTOR BRAKE SECOND ■

Engines
Two B.U.T. (Leyland) 6-cyl. horizontal type of 150 b.h.p.

Transmission
Mechanical. Standard

Body: 64′ 0″ × 9′ 3″. Non-gangwayed, side doors to each seating bay

Weight: 35 tons 10 cwt   **Seats:** 2nd, 65

W50050	W50057	W50064	W50071	W50078	W50085
W50051	W50058	W50065	W50072	W50079	W50086
W50052	W50059	W50066	W50073	W50080	W50087
W50053	W50060	W50067	W50074	W50081	W50088
W50054	W50061	W50068	W50075	W50082	W50089
W50055	W50062	W50069	W50076	W50083	W50090
W50056	W50063	W50070	W50077	W50084	W50091

Derby Works, B.R. (3 Suburban)

MOTOR SECOND ■

Engines
Two B.U.T. (Leyland) 6-cyl. horizontal type of 150 b.h.p.

Transmission
Mechanical. Standard

Body: 64′ 0″ × 9′ 3″. Non-gangwayed, side doors to each seating bay

Weight: 35 tons 10 cwt   **Seats:** 2nd, 95

[M. Mensing]

Derby three-car suburban unit passing over Aynho troughs

W50092	W50099	W50106	W50113	W50120	W50128
W50093	W50100	W50107	W50114	W50121	W50129
W50094	W50101	W50108	W50115	W50122	W50130
W50095	W50102	W50109	W50116	W50123	W50131
W50096	W50103	W50110	W50117	W50124	W50132
W50097	W50104	W50111	W50118	W50126	W50133
W50098	W50105	W50112	W50119	W50127	

Metropolitan-Cammell (2)
MOTOR BRAKE SECOND ■

Engines
Two Rolls-Royce 6-cyl. horizontal type of 180 b.h.p.
*Two Rolls-Royce 6-cyl. type super-charged to 230 b.h.p.

Transmission
Mechanical. Standard

Body: 57' 0" × 9' 3"   **Weight:** 33 tons   **Seats: 2nd, 52**

M50134	M50135	M50136*	M50137

Metropolitan-Cammell (4)
MOTOR COMPOSITE (L) ■

Engines
Two B.U.T. (A.E.C.) 6-cyl. horizontal type of 150 b.h.p.

Transmission
Mechanical. Standard

Body: 57' 0" × 9' 3"   **Weight:** 32 tons   **Seats: 1st, 12; 2nd, 45**

E50138	E50141	E50144	E50146	E50148	E50150
E50139	E50142	E50145	E50147	E50149	E50151
E50140	E50143				

Metropolitan-Cammell (2)
MOTOR BRAKE SECOND ■

Engines
Two B.U.T. (A.E.C.) 6-cyl. horizontal type of 150 b.h.p.

Transmission
Mechanical. Standard

Body: 57' 0" × 9' 3"   **Weight:** 32 tons   **Seats: 2nd, 52**

E50152	E50153	E50154	E50155	E50156	E50157

Metropolitan-Cammell (2)
MOTOR COMPOSITE (L) ■

Engines
Two B.U.T. (A.E.C.) 6-cyl. horizontal type of 150 b.h.p.

Transmission
Mechanical. Standard

Body: 57' 0" × 9' 3"   **Weight:** 32 tons   **Seats: 1st, 12; 2nd, 53**

E50158	E50159	E50160	E50161	E50162	E50163

Metropolitan-Cammell (2)

MOTOR BRAKE SECOND ■

For details see E50152-7

E50164	E50165	E50166	E50167

Metropolitan-Cammell (2)

MOTOR COMPOSITE (L) ■

For details see E50158-63

E50168	E50169	E50170	E50171

Metropolitan-Cammell (4)

MOTOR COMPOSITE (L) ■

For details see E50158-63

E50172	E50178	E50182	E50186	E50190	E50194
E50174	E50179	E50183	E50187	E50191	E50195
E50175	E50180	E50184	E50188	E50192	E50196
E50176	E50181	E50185	E50189	E50193	E50197
E50177					

Metropolitan-Cammell (2)

MOTOR BRAKE SECOND ■

For details see E50152-7

E50198	E50204	E50210	E50216	E50222	E50228
E50199	E50205	E50211	E50217	E50223	E50229
E50200	E50206	E50212	E50218	E50224	E50230
E50201	E50207	E50213	E50219	E50225	E50231
E50202	E50208	E50214	E50220	E50226	E50232
E50203	E50209	E50215	E50221	E50227	E50233

Metropolitan-Cammell (4)

MOTOR COMPOSITE (L) ■

For details see E50138-51

E50234	E50236	E50238	E50240	E50242	E50244
E50235	E50237	E50239	E50241	E50243	E50245

Metropolitan-Cammell (2)

MOTOR BRAKE SECOND ■

Engines
Two B.U.T. (A.E.C.) 6-cyl. horizontal
type of 150 b.h.p.

Transmission
Mechanical. Standard

Body: 57′ 0″ × 9′ 3″   **Weight:** 32 tons   **Seats: 2nd,** 44

E50246	E50247	E50248

Cravens (4)

MOTOR BRAKE SECOND ■

Engines
Two B.U.T. (A.E.C.) 6-cyl. horizontal
type of 150 b.h.p.

Transmission
Mechanical. Standard

Body: 57′ 6″ × 9′ 2″   **Weight:** 30 tons 10 cwt   **Seats: 2nd,** 52

E50249

Metropolitan-Cammell (2)

MOTOR BRAKE SECOND ■

Engines
Two B.U.T. (A.E.C.) 6-cyl. horizontal
type of 150 b.h.p.

Transmission
Mechanical. Standard

Body: 57′ 0″ × 9′ 3″   **Weight:** 32 tons   **Seats: 2nd,** 52

E50250	E50252	E50254	E50256	E50258	E50259
E50251	E50253	E50255	E50257		

Metropolitan-Cammell (2)

MOTOR COMPOSITE (L) ■

Engines
Two B.U.T. (A.E.C.) 6-cyl. horizontal
type of 150 b.h.p.

Transmission
Mechanical. Standard

Body: 57′ 0″ × 9′ 3″   **Weight:** 32 tons   **Seats: 1st,** 12; **2nd,** 53

E50260	E50262	E50264	E50266	E50268	E50269
E50261	E50263	E50265	E50267		

Metropolitan-Cammell (3)

MOTOR COMPOSITE (L) ■

Engines
Two Rolls-Royce 6-cyl. horizontal
type of 180 b.h.p.

Transmission
Mechanical. Standard

Body: 57′ 0″ × 9′ 3″   **Weight:** 33 tons   **Seats: 1st,** 12; **2nd,** 53

E50270	E50272	E50274	E50276	E50278	E50279
E50271	E50273	E50275	E50277		

Metropolitan-Cammell (3)
MOTOR BRAKE SECOND ■

Engines
Two Rolls-Royce 6-cyl. horizontal
type of 180 b.h.p.

Transmission
Mechanical. Standard

Body: 57′ 0″ × 9′ 3″   **Weight:** 33 tons   **Seats: 2nd,** 52

E50280	E50283	E50285	E50287	E50289	E50291
E50281	E50284	E50286	E50288	E50290	E50292
E50282					

Metropolitan-Cammell (2)
MOTOR BRAKE SECOND ■

Engines
Two B.U.T. (A.E.C.) 6-cyl. horizontal
type of 150 b.h.p.

Transmission
Mechanical. Standard

Body: 57′ 0″ × 9′ 3″   **Weight:** 32 tons   **Seats: 2nd,** 52

E50293	E50294	E50295	E50296

Metropolitan-Cammell (3)
MOTOR BRAKE SECOND ■

Engines
Two B.U.T. 6-cyl. horizontal type of
150 b.h.p.

Transmission
Mechanical. Standard

Body: 57′ 0″ × 9′ 3″   **Weight:** 31 tons 10 cwt   **Seats: 2nd,** 52

M50303	M50306	M50309	M50312	M50315	M50318
M50304	M50307	M50310	M50313	M50316	M50319
M50305	M50308	M50311	M50314	M50317	M50320

Metropolitan-Cammell (3)
MOTOR COMPOSITE (L) ■

Engines
Two B.U.T. 6-cyl. horizontal type of
150 b.h.p.

Transmission
Mechanical. Standard

Body: 57′ 0″ × 9′ 3″   **Weight:** 32 tons   **Seats: 1st,** 12; **2nd,** 53

M50321	M50324	M50327	M50330	M50333	M50336
M50322	M50325	M50328	M50331	M50334	M50337
M50323	M50326	M50329	M50332	M50335	M50338

Gloucester R.C. & W. Co. (2)
MOTOR BRAKE SECOND ■

Engines
Two B.U.T. (A.E.C.) 6-cyl. horizontal
type of 150 b.h.p.

Transmission
Mechanical. Standard
* Fitted with C.A.V. Ltd. automatic
gear change equipment

Body: 57′ 6″ × 9′ 3″   **Weight:** 30 tons 5 cwt   **Seats: 2nd,** 52

SC50339	SC50343	SC50347	M50350	M50353	M50356
SC50340	SC50344	M50348	M50351	M50354	M50357
SC50341	SC50345	M50349	M50352	M50355	M50358*
SC50342	SC50346				

Cravens (2)

MOTOR BRAKE SECOND ■

Engines
Two B.U.T. (Leyland) (A.E.C.*) 6-cyl. horizontal type of 150 b.h.p.

Transmission
Mechanical. Standard

Body: 57′ 6″ × 9′ 2″   **Weight:** 29 tons   **Seats:** 2nd, 52

E50359	E50365	E50371*	E50377*	E50383*	E50389*
E50360	E50366	E50372*	E50378*	E50384*	M50390*
E50361	E50367	E50373*	E50379*	E50385*	M50391*
E50362	E50368	E50374*	E50380*	E50386*	M50392*
E50363	E50369	E50375*	E50381*	E50387*	M50393*
E50364	E50370	E50376*	E50382*	E50388*	M50394*

Park Royal Vehicles (2)

MOTOR BRAKE SECOND ■

Engines
Two B.U.T. (A.E.C.) 6-cyl. horizontal type of 150 b.h.p.

Transmission
Mechanical. Standard

Body: 57′ 6″ × 9′ 3″   **Weight:** 33 tons 8 cwt   **Seats:** 2nd, 52

M50395	M50399	M50403	M50406	M50409	M50412
M50396	M50400	M50404	M50407	M50410	M50413
M50397	M50401	M50405	M50408	M50411	M50414
M50398	M50402				

D. Wickham & Co. (2)

MOTOR BRAKE SECOND ■

Engines
Two B.U.T. (Leyland) 6-cyl. horizontal type of 150 b.h.p.

Transmission
Mechanical. Standard

Body: 57′ 0″ × 9′ 3″   **Weight:** 27 tons 10 cwt   **Seats:** 2nd, 59

E50416	E50417	E50418

Birmingham R. C. & W. Co. (3)

MOTOR BRAKE SECOND ■

Engines
Two B.U.T. (Leyland) 6-cyl. horizontal type of 150 b.h.p.

Transmission
Mechanical. Standard

Body: 57′ 6″ × 9′ 3″   **Weight:** 31 tons   **Seats:** 2nd, 52

M50420	M50421	M50422	M50423

Birmingham R. C. & W. Co. (3)

MOTOR COMPOSITE (L) ∎

Engines
Two B.U.T. (Leyland) 6-cyl. horizontal type of 150 b.h.p.

Transmission
Mechanical. Standard

Body: 57′ 6″ × 9′ 3″   **Weight:** 31 tons   **Seats:** 1st, 12; 2nd, 54

M50424	M50425	M50426	M50427

Birmingham R. C. & W. Co. (3)

MOTOR BRAKE SECOND ∎

For details see M50420-3

M50428	M50437	M50446	M50455	M50464	M50472
M50429	M50438	M50447	M50456	M50465	M50473
M50430	M50439	M50448	M50457	M50466	M50474
M50431	M50440	M50449	M50458	M50467	M50475
M50432	M50441	M50450	M50459	M50468	M50476
M50433	M50442	M50451	M50460	M50469	M50477
M50434	M50443	M50452	M50461	M50470	M50478
M50435	M50444	M50453	M50462	M50471	M50479
M50436	M50445	M50454	M50463		

Birmingham R. C. & W. Co. (3)

MOTOR COMPOSITE (L) ∎

For details see M50424-7

M50480	M50489	M50498	M50507	M50516	M50524
M50481	M50490	M50499	M50508	M50517	M50525
M50482	M50491	M50500	M50509	M50518	M50526
M50483	M50492	M50501	M50510	M50519	M50527
M50484	M50493	M50502	M50511	M50520	M50528
M50485	M50494	M50503	M50512	M50521	M50529
M50486	M50495	M50504	M50514	N50522	M50530
M50487	M50496	M50505	M50515	M50523	M50531
M50488	M50497	M50506			

Birmimgham R. C. & W. Co. (2)

MOTOR BRAKE SECOND ∎

Engines
Two B.U.T. (Leyland) 6-cyl. horizontal type of 150 b.h.p.

Transmission
Mechanical. Standard

Body: 57′ 6″ × 9′ 3″   **Weight:** 31 tons   **Seats:** 2nd, 52

M50532	M50534	M50536	M50538	M50540	M50541
M50533	M50535	M50537	M50539		

Birmingham R. C. & W. Co. (4)

MOTOR COMPOSITE (L) ■

Engines
Two B.U.T. (Leyland) 6-cyl. horizontal type of 150 b.h.p.

Transmission
Mechanical. Standard

Body: 57′ 6″ × 9′ 3″   **Weight:** 31 tons   **Seats:** 1st, 12; 2nd, 51

E50542	E50551	E50560	E50569	E50578	E50586
E50543	E50552	E50561	E50570	E50579	E50587
E50544	E50553	E50562	E50571	E50580	E50588
E50545	E50554	E50563	E50572	E50581	E50589
E50546	E50555	E50564	E50573	E50582	E50590
E50547	E50556	E50565	E50574	E50583	E50591
E50548	E50557	E50566	E50575	E50584	E50592
E50549	E50558	E50567	E50576	E50585	E50593
E50550	E50559	E50568	E50577		

Birmingham R. C. & W. Co. (2)

MOTOR BRAKE SECOND ■

Engines
Two B.U.T. (Leyland) 6-cyl. horizontal type of 160 b.h.p.

Transmission
Mechanical. Standard

Body: 57′ 6″ × 9′ 3″   **Weight:** 31 tons   **Seats:** 2nd, 52

E50594	E50595	E50596	E50597	E50598

Derby Works, B.R. (2 or 3*)

MOTOR BRAKE SECOND ■

Engines
Two B.U.T. (Leyland) 6-cyl. horizontal type of 150 b.h.p.

Transmission
Mechanical. Standard

Body: 57′ 6″ × 9′ 2″   **Weight:** 28 tons 10 cwt   **Seats:** 2nd, 52

E50599	E50605	E50610	E50615	E50620*	M50625
E50600	E50606	E50611	E50616	E50621*	M50626
E50601	E50607	E50612	E50617	E50622*	M50627
E50602	E50608	E50613	E50618	E50623*	M50628
E50603	E50609	E50614	E50619	E50624*	M50629
E50604					

Derby Works, B.R. (3* or 4)
MOTOR COMPOSITE (L) ∎

Engines
Two B.U.T. (Leyland) 6-cyl. horizontal type of 150 b.h.p.

Transmission
Mechanical. Standard

Body: 57′ 6″ × 9′ 2″ **Weight:** 28 tons **Seats: 1st,** 12; **2nd,** 50

E50630	E50633	E50636	E50639	E50642*	E50645*
E50631	E50634	E50637	E50640	E50643*	E50646*
E50632	E50635	E50638	E50641	E50644*	

Swindon Works, B.R. (3 Cross Country)
MOTOR SECOND (L) ∎

Engines
Two B.U.T. (A.E.C.) 6-cyl. horizontal type of 150 b.h.p.

Transmission
Mechanical. Standard

Body: 64′ 6″ × 9′ 3″ **Weight:** 36 tons 10 cwt **Seats: 2nd,** 68

W50647	W50656	W50664	W50672	W50680	W50688
W50648	W50657	W50665	W50673	W50681	W50689
W50649	W50658	W50666	W50674	W50682	W50690
W50650	W50659	W50667	W50675	W50683	W50691
W50651	W50660	W50668	W50676	W50684	W50692
W50652	W50661	W50669	W50677	W50685	W50693
W50653	W50662	W50670	W50678	W50686	W50694
W50654	W50663	W50671	W50679	W50687	W50695
W50655					

Swindon Works, B.R. (3 Cross Country)
MOTOR BRAKE COMPOSITE ∎

Engines
Two B.U.T. (A.E.C.) 6-cyl. horizontal type of 150 b.h.p.

Transmission
Mechanical. Standard

Body: 64′ 6″ × 9′ 3″ **Weight:** 36 tons **Seats: 1st,** 18; **2nd,** 16

W50696	W50705	W50713	W50721	W50729	W50737
W50697	W50706	W50714	W50722	W50730	W50738
W50698	W50707	W50715	W50723	W50731	W50739
W50699	W50708	W50716	W50724	W50732	W50740
W50700	W50709	W50717	W50725	W50733	W50741
W50701	W50710	W50718	W50726	W50734	W50742
W50702	W50711	W50719	W50727	W50735	W50743
W50703	W50712	W50720	W50728	W50736	W50744
W50704					

Derby twin unit with motor brake second No. M50628 leading   [*M. Mensing*

Swindon three-car Cross-country unit on a Kingham–Worcester working [*M. Mensing*

Metropolitan-Cammell (3)
MOTOR COMPOSITE (L) ■

Engines
Two Rolls-Royce 6-cyl. horizontal type of 180 b h.p.

Transmission
Mechanical. Standard

Body: 57' 0" × 9' 3" **Weight:** 32 tons **Seats:** 1st, 12; 2nd, 53

E50745	E50746	E50747

Metropolitan-Cammell (4)
MOTOR COMPOSITE (L) ■

Engines
Two B.U.T. (A.E.C.) 6-cyl. horizontal type of 150 b.h.p.

Transmission
Mechanical. Standard

Body: 57' 0" × 9' 3" **Weight:** 32 tons **Seats:** 1st, 12; 2nd, 53

E50748	E50749	E50750	E50751

Cravens (3)
MOTOR BRAKE SECOND ■

Engines
Two B.U.T. (Leyland) 6-cyl. horizontal type of 150 b.h.p.

Transmission
Mechanical. Standard

Body: 57' 6" × 9' 2" **Weight:** 30 tons **Seats:** 2nd, 52

M50752	M50756	M50759	M50762	M50765	M50768
M50753	M50757	M50760	M50763	M50766	M50769
M50754	M50758	M50761	M50764	M50767	M50770
M50755					

Cravens (2)
MOTOR BRAKE SECOND ■

Engines
Two B.U.T. (A.E.C.) 6-cyl. horizontal type of 150 b.h.p.

Transmission
Mechanical. Standard

Body: 57' 6" × 9' 2" **Weight:** 30 tons **Seats:** 2nd, 52

M50771	M50774	M50776	M50778	M50780	M50782
M50772	M50775	M50777	M50779	M50781	M50784
M50773					

Cravens (3)
MOTOR COMPOSITE (L) ■

Engines
Two B.U.T. (Leyland) 6-cyl. horizontal type of 150 b.h.p.

Transmission
Mechanical. Standard

Body: 57' 6" × 9' 2" **Weight:** 30 tons **Seats:** 1st, 12; 2nd, 51

M50785   M50789   M50792   M50795   M50798   M50801
M50786   M50790   M50793   M50796   M50799   M50802
M50787   M50791   M50794   M50797   M50800   M50803
M50788

Cravens (2)

MOTOR COMPOSITE (L) ∎

Engines
Two B.U.T. (A.E.C.) 6-cyl. horizontal
type of 150 b.h.p.

Transmission
Mechanical. Standard

Body: 57′ 6″ × 9′ 2″   **Weight:** 30 tons   **Seats:** 1st, 12; 2nd, 51

M50804   M50807   M50810   M50812   M50814   M50816
M50805   M50809   M50811   M50813   M50815   M50817
M50806

Derby Works, B.R. (3 Suburban)

MOTOR BRAKE SECOND ∎

For details see W50050-91

W50818   W50827   W50836   W50845   W50854   W50863
W50819   W50828   W50837   W50846   W50855   W50864
W50820   W50829   W50838   W50847   W50856   W50865
W50821   W50830   W50839   W50848   W50857   W50866
W50822   W50831   W50840   W50849   W50858   W50867
W50823   W50832   W50841   W50850   W50859   W50868
W50824   W50833   W50842   W50851   W50860   W50869
W50825   W50834   W50843   W50852   W50861   W50870
W50826   W50835   W50844   W50853   W50862

Derby Works, B.R. (3 Suburban)

MOTOR SECOND ∎

For details see W50092-50133

W50871   W50880   W50889   W50898   W50907   W50916
W50872   W50881   W50890   W50899   W50908   W50917
W50873   W50882   W50891   W50900   W50909   W50918
W50874   W50883   W50892   W50901   W50910   W50919
W50875   W50884   W50893   W50902   W50911   W50920
W50876   W50885   W50894   W50903   W50912   W50921
W50877   W50886   W50895   W50904   W50913   W50922
W50878   W50887   W50896   W50905   W50914   W50923
W50879   W50888   W50897   W50906   W50915

Derby Works, B.R. (2)

MOTOR BRAKE SECOND ■

Engines
Two B.U.T. (A.E.C.) 6-cyl. horizontal type of 150 b.h.p.

Transmission
Mechanical. Standard

Body: 57′ 6″ × 9′ 2″   **Weight:** 28 tons 10 cwt   **Seats: 2nd,** 52

M50924	M50926	M50928	M50930	M50932	M50934
M50925	M50927	M50929	M50931	M50933	M50935

Swindon Works, B.R. (6 Inter-City)

MOTOR SECOND (L) ●

Engines
Two B.U.T. 6-cyl. horizontal type of 150 b.h.p.

Transmission
Mechanical. Standard

Body: 64′ × 6″ × 9′ 3″. Gangwayed both ends, side driving compartment at one end

Weight: 38 tons   **Seats: 2nd,** 64

SC50936

Derby Works, B.R. (2)

MOTOR BRAKE SECOND ■

Engines
Two B.U.T. (Leyland) 6-cyl. horizontal type of 150 b.h.p.

Transmission
Mechanical. Standard

Body: 57′ 6″ × 9′ 2″   **Weight:** 28 tons 10 cwt   **Seats: 2nd,** 52

M50938	M50947	M50956	M50964	M50972	M50980
M50939	M50948	M50957	M50965	M50973	M50981
M50940	M50949	M50958	M50966	M50974	M50982
M50941	M50950	M50959	M50967	M50975	M50983
M50942	M50951	M50960	M50968	M50976	M50984
M50943	M50952	M50961	M50969	M50977	M50985
M50944	M50953	M50962	M50970	M50978	M50986
M50945	M50954	M50963	M50971	M50979	M50987
M50946	M50955				

Derby Works, B.R. (3 Suburban)

MOTOR SECOND ✳

Engines
Two Rolls-Royce horizontal type of 238 b.h.p.

Transmission
Hydraulic. Twin-disc torque converter

Body: 64′ 0″ × 9′ 3″. Non-gangwayed, side doors to each seating bay

Weight: 39 tons 10 cwt   **Seats: 2nd,** 95

E50988	E50992	E50996	E50999	E51002	E51005
E50989	E50993	E50997	E51000	E51003	E51006
E50990	E50994	E50998	E51001	E51004	E51007
E50991	E50995				

Swindon Works, B.R.   (6 Inter-City)

MOTOR SECOND (L) ●

Engines
Two B.U.T. 6-cyl. horizontal type of 150 b.h.p.

Transmission
Mechanical. Standard

Body: 64' 6" × 9' 3". Gangwayed both ends, side driving compartment at one end

Weight: 38 tons   **Seats: 2nd,** 64

SC51008	SC51012	SC51016	SC51020	SC51024	SC51027
SC51009	SC51013	SC51017	SC51021	SC51025	SC51028
SC51010	SC51014	SC51018	SC51022	SC51026	SC51029
SC51011	SC51015	SC51019	SC51023		

Swindon Works, B.R.   (3 or 6 Inter-City)

MOTOR BRAKE SECOND (L) ●

Engines
Two B.U.T. (A.E.C.) 6-cyl. horizontal type of 150 b.h.p.

Transmission
Mechanical. Standard

Body: 64' 6" × 9' 3"   **Weight:** 38 tons   **Seats: 2nd,** 52

SC51030	SC51034	SC51038	SC51042	SC51046	SC51049
SC51031	SC51035	SC51039	SC51043	SC51047	SC51050
SC51032	SC51036	SC51040	SC51044	SC51048	SC51051
SC51033	SC51037	SC51041	SC51045		

Gloucester R. C. & W. Co.   (3 Cross Country)

MOTOR BRAKE COMPOSITE ■

Engines
Two B.U.T. 6-cyl. horizontal type of 150 b.h.p

Transmission
Mechanical. Standard

Body: 64' 6" × 9' 3"   **Weight:** 36 tons 19 cwt   **Seats: 1st,** 18; **2nd,** 16

W51052	W51057	W51062	W51067	W51072	W51076
W51053	W51058	W51063	W51068	W51073	W51077
W51054	W51059	W51064	W51069	W51074	W51078
W51055	W51060	W51065	W51070	W51075	W51079
W51056	W51061	W51066	W51071		

Above: Swindon three-car Inter-city unit

[*P. J. Sharpe*]

Left: Gloucester three-car Cross-country unit with motor second No. W51099 leading

[*M. Mensing*]

Below: Two Metro-Cammell twin units. The leading car is motor brake second No. M51190

[*M. Mensing*]

Gloucester R. C. & W. Co.

(3 Cross Country)

MOTOR SECOND (L)

■

Engines
Two B.U.T. 6-cyl. horizontal type of 150 b.h.p.

Transmission
Mechanical. Standard

Body: 64′ 6″ × 9′ 3″   **Weight:** 37 tons 10 cwt   **Seats:** 2nd, 68

W51080	W51085	W51090	W51095	W51100	W51104
W51081	W51086	W51091	W51096	W51101	W51105
W51082	W51087	W51092	W51097	W51102	W51106
W51083	W51088	W51093	W51098	W51103	W51107
W51084	W51089	W51094	W51099		

Gloucester R. C. & W. Co.

(2)

MOTOR BRAKE SECOND

■

For details see SC50339-M50357

SC51108	SC51112	SC51116	SC51119	SC51122	SC51125
SC51109	SC51113	SC51117	SC51120	SC51123	SC51126
SC51110	SC51114	SC51118	SC51121	SC51124	SC51127
SC51111	SC51115				

Derby Works, B.R.

(3 Suburban)

MOTOR BRAKE SECOND

■

For details see W50050-91

W51128	W51131	W51133	W51135	W51137	W51139
W51129	W51132	W51134	W51136	W51138	W51140
W51130					

Derby Works, B.R.

(3 Suburban)

MOTOR SECOND

■

For details see W50092-50133

W51141	W51144	W51146	W51148	W51150	W51152
W51142	W51145	W51147	W51149	W51151	W51153
W51143					

Derby Works, B.R.

(3 Suburban)

MOTOR BRAKE SECOND

✱

Engines
Two Rolls-Royce horizontal type of 238 b.h.p.

Transmission
Hydraulic. Twin-disc torque converter

Body: 64′ 0″ × 9′ 3″. Non-gangwayed, side doors to each seating bay

Weight: 39 tons 10 cwt   **Seats:** 2nd, 65

E51154	E51158	E51162	E51165	E51168	E51171
E51155	E51159	E51163	E51166	E51169	E51172
E51156	E51160	E51164	E51167	E51170	E51173
E51157	E51161				

Metropolitan-Cammell (2)

MOTOR BRAKE SECOND ∎

Engines
Two B.U.T. (A.E.C.) 6-cyl. horizontal
type of 150 b.h.p.

Transmission
Mechanical. Standard

Body: 57: 0″ × 9′ 3″   **Weight:** 32 tons   **Seats: 2nd,** 52

M51174	M51188	M51202	E51215	SC51228	SC51241
M51175	M51189	M51203	E51216	SC51229	SC51242
M51176	M51190	E51204	E51217	SC51230	SC51243
M51177	M51191	E51205	E51218	SC51231	SC51244
M51178	M51192	E51206	E51219	SC51232	SC51245
M51179	M51193	E51207	E51220	SC51233	SC51246
M51180	M51194	E51208	E51221	SC51234	SC51247
M51181	M51195	E51209	E51222	SC51235	SC51248
M51182	M51196	E51210	E51223	SC51236	SC51249
M51183	M51197	E51211	SC51224	SC51237	SC51250
M51184	M51198	E51212	SC51225	SC51238	SC51251
M51185	M51199	E51213	SC51226	SC51239	SC51252
M51186	M51200	E51214	SC51227	SC51240	SC51253
M51187	M51201				

Cravens (2)

MOTOR BRAKE SECOND ∎

Engines
Two B.U.T. (A.E.C.) 6-cyl. horizontal
type of 150 b.h.p.

Transmission
Mechanical. Standard

Body: 57′ 6″ × 9′ 2″   **Weight:** 30 tons   **Seats: 2nd,** 52

E51254	E51262	E51270	E51278	E51286	E51294
E51255	E51263	E51271	E51279	E51287	E51295
E51256	E51264	E51272	E51280	E51288	E51296
E51257	E51265	E51273	E51281	E51289	E51297
E51258	E51266	E51274	E51282	E51290	E51298
E51259	E51267	E51275	E51283	E51291	E51299
E51260	E51268	E51276	E51284	E51292	E51300
E51261	E51269	E51277	E51285	E51293	E51301

Birmingham R. C. & W. Co. (3 Suburban)

MOTOR BRAKE SECOND ∎

Engines

Transmission
Mechanical. Standard

Body: 64′ 0″ × 9′ 3″. Non-gangwayed, side doors to each seating bay

Weight: 36 tons   **Seats: 2nd,** 65

W51302	W51305	W51308	W51311	W51313	W51315
W51303	W51306	W51309	W51312	W51314	W51316
W51304	W51307	W51310			

Birmingham R. C. & W. Co.   (3 Suburban)

MOTOR SECOND ■

Engines   **Transmission**
Mechanical. Standard
Body: 64′ 0″ × 9′ 3″. Non-gangwayed, side doors to each seating bay

Weight: 36 tons   **Seats: 2nd,** 91

W51317	W51320	W51323	W51326	W51328	W51330
W51318	W51321	W51324	W51327	W51329	W51331
W51319	W51322	W51325			

Pressed Steel Co.   (3 Suburban)

MOTOR BRAKE SECOND ■

Engines   **Transmission**
Two B.U.T. (Leyland) 6-cyl. horizon-   Mechanical. Standard
tal type of 150 b.h.p.
Body: 64′ 0″ × 9′ 3″. Non-gangwayed, side doors to each seating bay

Weight: 36 tons   **Seats: 2nd,** 65

W51332	W51339	W51346	W51353	W51360	W51367
W51333	W51340	W51347	W51354	W51361	W51368
W51334	W51341	W51348	W51355	W51362	W51369
W51335	W51342	W51349	W51356	W51363	W51370
W51336	W51343	W51350	W51357	W51364	W51371
W51337	W51344	W51351	W51358	W51365	W51372
W51338	W51345	W51352	W51359	W51366	W51373

Pressed Steel Co.   (3 Suburban)

MOTOR SECOND ■

Engines   **Transmission**
Two B.U.T. (Leyland) 6-cyl. horizon-   Mechanical. Standard
tal type of 150 b.h.p.
Body: 64′ 0″ × 9′ 3″. Non-gangwayed, side doors to each seating bay

Weight: 36 tons   **Seats: 2nd,** 91

W51374	W51381	W51388	W51395	W51402	W51409
W51375	W51382	W51389	W51396	W51403	W51410
W51376	W51383	W51390	W51397	W51404	W51411
W51377	W51384	W51391	W51398	W51405	W51412
W51378	W51385	W51392	W51399	W51406	W51413
W51379	W51386	W51393	W51400	W51407	W51414
W51380	W51387	W51394	W51401	W51408	W51415

Derby Works, B.R. (2)

MOTOR BRAKE SECOND ■

Engines
Two B.U.T. (A.E.C.) 6-cyl. horizontal type of 150 b.h.p.

Transmission
Mechanical. Standard

Body: 57′ 6″ × 9′ 2″   **Weight:** 29 tons   **Seats: 2nd,** 52

M51416	M51418	M51420	M51422	M51423	M51424
M51417	M51419	M51421			

Metropolitan-Cammell (2)

MOTOR BRAKE SECOND ■

Engines
Two B.U.T. (Leyland) 6-cyl. horizontal type of 150 b.h.p.

Transmission
Mechanical. Standard

Body: 57′ 0″ × 9′ 3″   **Weight:** 32 tons   **Seats: 2nd,** 52

E51425	E51427	E51429	E51431	E51433	E51434
E51426	E51428	E51430	E51432		

Metropolitan-Cammell (3 or 4*)

MOTOR BRAKE SECOND ■

Engines
Two B.U.T. (Leyland) 6-cyl. horizontal type of 150 b.h.p.

Transmission
Mechanical. Standard

Body: 57′ 0″ × 9′ 3″   **Weight:** 32 tons   **Seats: 2nd,** 52

E51435*	E51441*	SC51447	SC51453	SC51459	SC51465
E51436*	E51442*	SC51448	SC51454	SC51460	SC51466
E51437*	E51443*	SC51449	SC51455	SC51461	SC51467
E51438*	E51444*	SC51450	SC51456	SC51462	SC51468
E51439*	SC51445	SC51451	SC51457	SC51463	SC51469
E51440*	SC51446	SC51452	SC51458	SC51464	SC51470

Cravens (2)

MOTOR BRAKE SECOND ■

Engines
Two B.U.T. (A.E.C.) 6-cyl. horizontal type of 150 b.h.p.

Transmission
Mechanical. Standard

Body: 57′ 6″ × 9′ 2″   **Weight:** 30 tons 10 cwt   **Seats: 2nd,** 52

E51471	SC51475	SC51479	SC51483	SC51487	SC51491
E51472	SC51476	SC51480	SC51484	SC51488	SC51492
SC51473	SC51477	SC51481	SC51485	SC51489	SC51493
SC51474	SC51478	SC51482	SC51486	SC51490	SC51494

Metropolitan-Cammell (2)
MOTOR COMPOSITE (L) ■

Engines
Two B.U.T. (Leyland) 6-cyl. horizontal type of 150 b.h.p.

Transmission
Mechanical. Standard

Body: 57′ 0″ × 9′ 3″   **Weight:** 32 tons   **Seats:** 1st, 12; 2nd, 53

E51495	E51497	E51499	E51501	E51503	E51504
E51496	E51498	E51500	E51502		

Metropolitan-Cammell (3 or 4*)
MOTOR COMPOSITE (L) ■

Engines
Two B.U.T. (Leyland) 6-cyl. horizontal type of 150 b.h.p.

Transmission
Mechanical. Standard

Body: 57′ 0″ × 9′ 3″   **Weight:** 32 tons   **Seats:** 1st, 12; 2nd, 53

E51505*	E51511*	SC51517	SC51523	SC51529	SC51535
E51506*	E51512*	SC51518	SC51524	SC51530	SC51536
E51507*	E51513*	SC51519	SC51525	SC51531	SC51537
E51508*	E51514*	SC51520	SC51526	SC51532	SC51538
E51509*	SC51515	SC51521	SC51527	SC51533	SC51539
E51510*	SC51516	SC51522	SC51528	SC51534	SC51540

Metropolitan-Cammell (3)
MOTOR BRAKE SECOND ■

For details see E51435-SC51470

E51541	E51543	E51544	E51545	E51546	E51547
E51542					

Metropolitan-Cammell (2)
MOTOR BRAKE SECOND ■

Engines
Two B.U.T. (A.E.C.) 6-cyl. horizontal type of 150 b.h.p.

Transmission
Mechanical. Standard

Body: 57′ 0″ × 9′ 3″   **Weight:** 31 tons 10 cwt   **Seats: 2nd, 52**

E51548	E51549	E51550

Metropolitan-Cammell (3)
MOTOR COMPOSITE (L) ■

For details see E51505-SC51540

E51551	E51553	E51554	E51555	E51556	E51557
E51552					

Metropolitan-Cammell (2)
MOTOR COMPOSITE (L) ■

Engines
Two B.U.T. (A.E.C.) 6-cyl. horizontal
type of 150 b.h.p.

Transmission
Mechanical. Standard

Body: 57′ 0″ × 9′ 3″   **Weight:** 31 tons 10 cwt   **Seats:** 1st, 12; 2nd, 53

E51558   E51559   E51560

Derby Works, B.R. (2)
MOTOR COMPOSITE (L) ■

Engines
Two B.U.T. (A.E.C.) 6-cyl. horizontal
type of 150 b.h.p.

Transmission
Mechanical. Standard

Body: 57′ 6″ × 9′ 2″   **Weight:** 27 tons   **Seats:** 1st, 12; 2nd, 53

| M51561 | M51563 | M51565 | M51567 | M51569 | M51571 |
| M51562 | M51564 | M51566 | M51568 | M51570 | M51572 |

Swindon Works, B.R. (3 Cross Country)
MOTOR BRAKE COMPOSITE (L) ■

Engines
Two B.U.T. 6-cyl. horizontal type of
150 b.h.p.

Transmission
Mechanical. Standard

Body: 64′ 6″ × 9′ 3″   **Weight:** 36 tons 7 cwt   **Seats:** 1st, 18; 2nd, 16

| W51573 | W51575 | W51577 | W51579 | W51580 | W51581 |
| W51574 | W51576 | W51578 | | | |

Swindon Works, B.R. (3 Cross Country)
MOTOR SECOND (L) ■

Engines
Two B.U.T. 6-cyl. horizontal type of
150 b.h.p.

Transmission
Mechanical. Standard

Body: 64′ 6″ × 9′ 3″   **Weight:** 36 tons 10 cwt   **Seats:** 2nd, 68

| W51582 | W51584 | W51586 | W51588 | W51589 | W51590 |
| W51583 | W51585 | W51587 | | | |

Derby Works, B.R. (4 Suburban)
MOTOR BRAKE SECOND ■

Engines
Two Rolls-Royce 8-cyl. horizontal
type of 238 b.h.p.

Transmission
Hydraulic. Torque converter

Body: 64′ 0″ × 9′ 3″. Non-gangwayed, side doors to each seating bay

Weight: 40 tons   **Seats:** 2nd, 76

Two Western Region Pressed Steel three-car suburban units on a Paddington–Oxford working. The rear car is motor brake second No. W51351 [B. Stephenson

London Midland Region St. Pancras area Derby four-car suburban unit. The leading car is motor brake second No. M51613 [B. Stephenson

M51591	M51601	M51612	M51622	M51632	M51642
M51592	M51602	M51613	M51623	M51633	M51643
M51593	M51603	M51614	M51624	M51634	M51644
M51594	M51604	M51615	M51625	M51635	M51645
M51595	M51605	M51616	M51626	M51636	M51646
M51596	M51606	M51617	M51627	M51637	M51647
M51597	M51607	M51618	M51628	M51638	M51648
M51598	M51608	M51619	M51629	M51639	M51649
M51599	M51610	M51620	M51630	M51640	M51650
M51600	M51611	M51621	M51631	M51641	

Derby Works, B.R. (4 Suburban)

MOTOR BRAKE SECOND ■

Engines
Two B.U.T. (Leyland) 6-cyl. horizontal type of 230 b.h.p.

Transmission
Mechanical. Standard

Body: 64′ 0″ × 9′ 3″. Non-gangwayed, side doors to each seating bay

Weight: 38 tons   **Seats: 2nd, 78**

M51651	M51656	M51661	M51666	M51671	M51676
M51652	M51657	M51662	M51667	M51672	M51677
M51653	M51658	M51663	M51668	M51673	M51678
M51654	M51659	M51664	M51669	M51674	M51679
M51655	M51660	M51665	M51670	M51675	M51680

Cravens (2)

MOTOR BRAKE SECOND ■

Engine
One Rolls-Royce 8-cyl. horizontal type of 238 b.h.p.

Transmission
Mechanical. Standard

Body: 57′ 6″ × 9′ 2″   **Weight:** 29 tons 10 cwt   **Seats: 2nd, 52**

M51681	M51686	M51690	M51694	M51698	M51702
M51682	M51687	M51691	M51695	M51699	M51703
M51683	M51688	M51692	M51696	M51700	M51704
M51684	M51689	M51693	M51697	M51701	M51705
M51685					

Cravens (2)

MOTOR COMPOSITE (L) ■

Engine
One Rolls-Royce 8-cyl. horizontal type of 238 b.h.p.

Transmission
Mechanical. Standard

Body: 57′ 6″ × 9′ 2″   **Weight:** 29 tons   **Seats: 1st, 12; 2nd, 51**

M51706	M51711	M51715	M51719	M51723	M51727
M51707	M51712	M51716	M51720	M51724	M51728
M51708	M51713	M51717	M51721	M51725	M51729
M51709	M51714	M51718	M51722	M51726	M51730
M51710					

Cravens (2)

MOTOR BRAKE SECOND ◾

Engine
One Rolls-Royce 8-cyl. horizontal type of 238 b.h.p.

Transmission
Hydraulic. Torque converter

Body: 57′ 6″ × 9′ 2″   **Weight:** 29 tons 10 cwt   **Seats:** 2nd, 52

M51731	M51736	M51740	M51744	M51748	M51752
M51732	M51737	M51741	M51745	M51749	M51753
M51733	M51738	M51742	M51746	M51750	M51754
M51734	M51739	M51743	M51747	M51751	M51755
M51735					

Cravens (2)

MOTOR COMPOSITE (L) ◾

Engine
One Rolls-Royce 8-cyl. horizontal type of 238 b.h.p.

Transmission
Hydraulic. Torque converter

Body: 57′ 6″ × 9′ 2″   **Weight:** 29 tons   **Seats:** 1st, 12; 2nd, 51

M51756	M51760	M51764	M51768	M51773	M51777
M51757	M51761	M51765	M51769	M51774	M51778
M51758	M51762	M51766	M51771	M51775	M51779
M51759	M51763	M51767	M51772	M51776	

Swindon Works, B.R. (3 Cross Country)

MOTOR BRAKE COMPOSITE ◾

Engines
Two B.U.T. 6-cyl. horizontal type of 150 b.h.p.

Transmission
Mechanical. Standard

Body: 64′ 6″ × 9′ 3″   **Weight:** 36 tons 7 cwt   **Seats:** 1st, 18; 2nd, 16

SC51781	SC51783	SC51784	SC51785	SC51786	SC51787
SC51782					

Swindon Works, B.R. (3 Cross Country)

MOTOR SECOND (L) ◾

Engines
Two B.U.T. 6-cyl horizontal type of 150 b.h.p.

Transmission
Mechanical. Standard

Body: 64′ 6″ × 9′ 3″   **Weight:** 36 tons 10 cwt   **Seats:** 2nd, 68

SC51788	SC51790	SC51791	SC51792	SC51793	SC51794
SC51789					

Metropolitan-Cammell (3)
MOTOR BRAKE SECOND ■

Engines
Two B.U.T. (A.E.C.) b-cyl. horizontal type of 150 b.h.p.

Transmission
Mechanical. Standard

Body: 57′ 0″ × 9′ 3″   **Weight:** 32 tons   **Seats:** 2nd, 52

SC51795	SC51797	SC51798	SC51799	SC51800	SC51801
SC51796					

Metropolitan-Cammell (3)
MOTOR COMPOSITE (L) ■

Engines
Two B.U.T. (A.E.C.) 6-cyl. horizontal type of 150 b.h.p.

Transmission
Mechanical. Standard

Body: 57′ 0″ × 9′ 3″   **Weight:** 32 tons   **Seats:** 1st, 12; 2nd, 53

SC51802	SC51804	SC51805	SC51806	SC51807	SC51808
SC51803					

Birmingham R. C. & W. Co. (3)
MOTOR BRAKE COMPOSITE ■

Engines
Two Rolls-Royce Series 130D of 180 b.h.p.

Transmission
Mechanical. Standard

Body: 57′ 6″ × 9′ 3″   **Weight:** 32 tons   **Seats:** 1st, 12; 2nd, 33

E51809	E51813	E51816	E51819	E51823	E51826
E51810	E51814	E51817	E51820	E51824	E51827
E51811	E51815	E51818	E51822	E51825	E51828
E51812					

Birmingham R. C. & W. Co. (3)
MOTOR COMPOSITE (L) ■

Engines
Two Rolls-Royce Series 130D of 180 b.h.p.

Transmission
Mechanical. Standard

Body: 57′ 6″ × 9′ 3″   **Weight:** 31 tons 10 cwt   **Seats:** 1st, 12; 2nd, 54

E51829	E51833	E51836	E51840	E51843	E51846
E51830	E51834	E51838	E51841	E51844	E51847
E51831	E51835	E51839	E51842	E51845	E51848
E51832					

Derby Works, B.R. (4 Suburban)

MOTOR BRAKE SECOND ■

Engines
Two B.U.T. 6-cyl. horizontal type of
230 b.h.p.

Transmission
Mechanical. Standard

Body: 64′ 0″ × 9′ 3″. Non-gangwayed, side doors to each seating bay

Weight: 38 tons   **Seats: 2nd,** 78

M51849	M51858	M51867	M51876	M51885	M51893
M51850	M51859	M51868	M51877	M51886	M51894
M51851	M51860	M51869	M51878	M51887	M51895
M51852	M51861	M51870	M51879	M51888	M51896
M51853	M51862	M51871	M51880	M51889	M51897
M51854	M51863	M51872	M51881	M51890	M51898
M51855	M51864	M51873	M51882	M51891	M51899
M51856	M51865	M51874	M51883	M51892	M51900
M51857	M51866	M51875	M51884		

Derby Works, B.R. (2)

MOTOR BRAKE SECOND ■

Engines
Two B.U.T. (A.E.C.) 6-cyl. horizontal
type of 150 b.h.p.

Transmission
Mechanical. Standard

Body: 57′ 6″ × 9′ 2″   **Weight:** 28 tons 10 cwt   **Seats: 2nd,** 52

M51901	M51910	M51919	M51927	M51935	M51943
M51902	M51911	M51920	M51928	M51936	M51944
M51903	M51912	M51921	M51929	M51937	M51945
M51904	M51913	M51922	M51930	M51938	M51946
M51905	M51914	M51923	M51931	M51939	M51947
M51906	M51915	M51924	M51932	M51940	M51948
M51907	M51916	M51925	M51933	M51941	M51949
M51908	M51917	M51926	M51934	M51942	M51950
M51909	M51918				

Swindon Works, B.R. (6 Trans-Pennine)

MOTOR COMPOSITE ■

Engines
Two B.U.T. (Leyland) 6-cyl. horizontal type of 230 b.h.p.

Transmission
Mechanical. Standard

Body: 64′ 6″ × 9′ 3″   **Weight:**   **Seats: 1st,** 21; **2nd,** 36

E51951	E51954	E51957	E51960	E51963	E51966
E51952	E51955	E51958	E51961	E51964	E51967
E51953	E51956	E51959	E51962	E51965	

Swindon-built six-car Trans-Pennine unit, temporarily running as a five-car unit, near Marsden

[J. S. Whiteley]

Swindon Works, B.R.

MOTOR BRAKE SECOND (K) ■

(non-driving)

Engines
Two B.U.T. (Leyland) 6-cyl. horizontal type of 230 b.h.p.

Transmission
Mechanical. Standard

Body: 64' 6" × 9' 3"   **Weight:**   **Seats: 2nd,** 48

E51968	E51971	E51974	E51977	E51980	E51983
E51969	E51972	E51975	E51978	E51981	E51984
E51970	E51973	E51976	E51979	E51982	

Derby Works, B.R. (3)

MOTOR BRAKE SECOND ■

Engines
Two B.U.T. 6-cyl. horizontal type of 150 b.h.p.

Transmission
Mechanical. Standard

Body: 58' 1" × 9' 3"   **Weight:** 34 tons 10 cwt   **Seats: 2nd,** 52

SC51985	SC51990	SC51995	SC51999	SC52003	SC52007
SC51986	SC51991	SC51996	SC52000	SC52004	SC52008
SC51987	SC51992	SC51997	SC52001	SC52005	SC52009
SC51988	SC51993	SC51998	SC52002	SC52006	SC52010
SC51989	SC51994				

Derby Works, B.R. (3)

MOTOR COMPOSITE (L) ■

Engines
Two B.U.T. 6-cyl. horizontal type of 150 b.h.p.

Transmission
Mechanical. Standard

Body: 58' 1" × 9' 3"   **Weight:** 35 tons   **Seats: 1st,** 12; **2nd,** 53

SC52011	SC52016	SC52021	SC52025	SC52029	SC52033
SC52012	SC52017	SC52022	SC52026	SC52030	SC52034
SC52013	SC52018	SC52023	SC52027	SC52031	SC52035
SC52014	SC52019	SC52024	SC52028	SC52032	SC52036
SC52015	SC52020				

Derby Works, B.R. (2)

MOTOR COMPOSITE (L) ■

Engines
Two B.U.T. 6-cyl. horizontal type of 150 b.h.p.

Transmission
Mechanical. Standard

Body: 57' 6" × 9' 2"   **Weight:** 28 tons   **Seats: 1st,** 12; **2nd,** 53

M52037	M52042	M52047	M52052	M52057	M52062
M52038	M52043	M52048	M52053	M52058	M52063
M52039	M52044	M52049	M52054	M52059	M52064
M52040	M52045	M52050	M52055	M52060	M52065
M52041	M52046	M52051	M52056	M52061	

Birmingham R. C. & W. Co. (3)
MOTOR BRAKE COMPOSITE ∎

Engines
Two Rolls-Royce Series 130D of 180 b.h.p.

Transmission
Mechanical. Standard

Body: 57′ 6″ × 9′ 3″   **Weight:** 32 tons   **Seats:** 1st, 12; 2nd, 33

M52066	M52068	M52070	M52072	M52074	M52075
M52067	M52069	M52071	M52073		

Birmingham R. C. & W. Co. (3)
MOTOR COMPOSITE (L) ∎

Engines
Two Rolls-Royce Series 130D of 180 b.h.p.

Transmission
Mechanical. Standard

Body: 57′ 6″ × 9′ 3″   **Weight:** 31 tons 10 cwt   **Seats:** 1st, 12; 2nd, 54

M52076	M52078	M52080	M52082	M52084	M52085
M52077	M52079	M52081	M52083		

Swindon Works, B.R. (4 Inter-City)
MOTOR BRAKE SECOND (L) ∎

Engines
Two B.U.T. (Leyland) 6-cyl. horizontal type of 230 b.h.p.

Transmission
Mechanical. Standard

Body: 64′ 11½″ × 9′ 3″   **Weight:**   **Seats:** 2nd, 32

W52086	W52088	W52090	W52092	W52094	W52095
W52087	W52089	W52091	W52093		

Swindon Works, B.R. (4 Inter-City)
MOTOR SECOND (K) ∎

Engines
Two B.U.T. (Leyland) 6-cyl. horizontal type of 230 b.h.p.

Transmission
Mechanical. Standard

Body: 64′ 11½″ × 9′ 3″   **Weight:**   **Seats:** 2nd, 56

W52096	W52098	W52100	W52102	W52104	W52105
W52097	W52099	W52101	W52103		

Birmingham R.C. & W. Co. three-car unit on a Harrogate-Liverpool working

[J. D. Benson

Swindon four-car Inter-city unit. The leading car is motor second No. W52105

[C. Symes

Gloucester R. C. & W. Co. (1)

MOTOR BRAKE SECOND ■

Engines
Two B.U.T. (A.E.C.) 6-cyl. horizontal type of 150 b.h.p.

Transmission
Mechanical. Standard

Body: 64′ 6″ × 9′ 3″. Non-gangwayed, side doors to each seating bay

Weight: 35 tons   **Seats: 2nd,** 65

W55000	W55004	W55008	W55011	W55014	W55017
W55001	W55005	W55009	W55012	W55015	W55018
W55002	W55006	W55010	W55013	W55016	W55019
W55003	W55007				

Pressed Steel Co. (1)

MOTOR BRAKE SECOND ■

Engines
Two B.U.T. 6-cyl. horizontal type of 150 b.h.p.

Transmission
Mechanical. Standard

Body: 64′ 6″ × 9′ 3″. Non-gangwayed, side doors to each seating bay

Weight: 37 tons   **Seats: 2nd,** 65

W55020	W55023	W55026	W55029	W55032	W55034
W55021	W55024	W55027	W55030	W55033	W55035
W55022	W55025	W55028	W55031		

Gloucester R. C. & W. Co. (1)

MOTOR PARCELS VAN ■

Engines
Two B.U.T. (A.E.C.) 6-cyl. horizontal type of 230 b.h.p.

Transmission
Mechanical. Standard

Body: 64′ 6″ × 9′ 3″ (Non-gangwayed*)   **Weight:** 41 tons (40 tons*)

M55987*	M55989*	W55991	W55993	W55995	W55996
M55988*	M55990*	W55992	W55994		

Cravens (1)

MOTOR PARCELS VAN ◆

Engines
Two B.U.T. (A.E.C.) 6-cyl. horizontal type of 150 b.h.p.

Transmission
Mechanical. Standard

Body: 57′ 6″ × 9′ 3″. Non-gangwayed   **Weight:** 30 tons

M55997	M55998	M55999

Right: Gloucester R.C. & W. Co. single-unit motor brake second No. W55008 [*M. Mensing*

Centre: Pressed Steel single-unit motor brake second No. W55030 [*C. P Boocock*

Bottom: Gloucester R.C. & W. Co. motor parcels van No. W55992 [*B. Stephenson*

Derby Works, B.R. (2)
DRIVING TRAILER COMPOSITE (L) ■
Body: 64′ 6″ × 9′ 3″   **Weight:** 29 tons (31 tons*)   **Seats:** 1st, 12; 2nd, 62

E56000	E56009*	E56018	E56026	E56034	E56042
E56001*	E56010	E56019	E56027*	E56035	E56043
E56002	E56011	E56020	E56028	E56036	E56044
E56003	E56012	E56021	E56029	E56037	E56045
E56004*	E56013	E56022	E56030	E56038	E56046
E56005*	E56014	E56023*	E56031	E56039	E56047
E56006	E56015	E56024	E56032	E56040	E56048
E56007*	E56016	E56025	E56033	E56041	E56049
E56008*	E56017				

Metropolitan-Cammell (2)
DRIVING TRAILER COMPOSITE (L) ■
Body: 57′ 0″ × 9′ 3″   **Weight:** 25 tons   **Seats:** 1st, 12; 2nd, 53

E56050	E56058	E56066	E56073	E56080	E56087
E56051	E56059	E56067	E56074	E56081	E56088
E56052	E56060	E56068	E56075	E56082	E56089
E56053	E56061	E56069	E56076	E56083	M56090
E56054	E56062	E56070	E56077	E56084	M56091
E56055	E56063	E56071	E56078	E56085	M56092
E56056	E56064	E56072	E56079	E56086	M56093
E56057	E56065				

Gloucester R. C. & W. Co. (2)
DRIVING TRAILER COMPOSITE (L) ■
Body: 57′ 6″ × 9′ 3″   **Weight:** 25 tons   **Seats:** 1st, 12; 2nd, 54

SC56094	SC56098	SC56102	M56105	M56108	M56111
SC56095	SC56099	M56103	M56106	M56109	M56112
SC56096	SC56100	M56104	M56107	M56110	M56113
SC56097	SC56101				

Cravens (2)
DRIVING TRAILER COMPOSITE (L) ■
Body: 57′ 6″ × 9′ 2″   **Weight:** 23 tons   **Seats:** 1st, 12; 2nd, 51 (54*)

E56114	E56120	E56126	E56132	E56138	E56144
E56115	E56121	E56127	E56133	E56139	M56145*
E56116	E56122	E56128	E56134	E56140	M56146*
E56117	E56123	E56129	E56135	E56141	M56147*
E56118	E56124	E56130	E56136	E56142	M56148*
E56119	E56125	E56131	E56137	E56143	M56149*

Park Royal Vehicles (2)

DRIVING TRAILER COMPOSITE (L) ■

Body: 57′ 6″ × 9′ 3″   **Weight:** 26 tons 7 cwt   **Seats:** 1st, 16; 2nd, 48

M56150	M56154	M56158	M56161	M56164	M56167
M56151	M56155	M56159	M56162	M56165	M56168
M56152	M56156	M56160	M56163	M56166	M56169
M56153	M56157				

D. Wickham & Co. (2)

DRIVING TRAILER COMPOSITE (L) ■

Body: 57′ 6″ × 9′ 3″   **Weight:** 20 tons 10 cwt   **Seats:** 1st, 16; 2nd, 50

E56171	E56172	E56173

Birmingham R. C. & W. Co. (2)

DRIVING TRAILER COMPOSITE (L) ■

Body: 57′ 6″ × 9′ 3″   **Weight:**   **Seats:** 1st, 12; 2nd, 54

M56175	M56177	M56179	M56181	M56183	M56184
M56176	M56178	M56180	M56182		

Birmingham R. C. & W. Co. (2)

DRIVING TRAILER COMPOSITE (L) ■

Body: 57′ 6″ × 9′ 3″   **Weight:** 24 tons   **Seats:** 1st, 12; 2nd, 54

E56185	E56186	E56187	E56188	E56189

Derby Works, B.R. (2)

DRIVING TRAILER COMPOSITE (L)

Body: 57′ 6″ × 9′ 2″   **Weight:** 22 tons   **Seats:** 1st, 12; 2nd, 53

E56190	E56195	E56200	E56204	E56208	M56212
E56191	E56196	E56201	E56205	E56209	M56213
E56192	E56197	E56202	E56206	E56210	M56214
E56193	E56198	E56203	E56207	M56211	M56215
E56194	E56199				

Metropolitan-Cammell (2)
DRIVING TRAILER COMPOSITE (L) ■
Body: 57′ 0″ × 9′ 3″   **Weight:** 25 tons   **Seats:** 1st, 12; 2nd, 45

| E56218 | E56219 | E56220 |

Derby Works, B.R. (2)
DRIVING TRAILER COMPOSITE (L) ■
Body: 57′ 6″ × 9′ 2″   **Weight:** 22 tons   **Seats:** 1st, 12; 2nd, 53

M56221	M56231	M56241	M56251	M56261	M56271
M56222	M56232	M56242	M56252	M56262	M56272
M56223	M56233	M56243	M56253	M56263	M56273
M56224	M56234	M56244	M56254	M56264	M56274
M56225	M56235	M56245	M56255	M56265	M56275
M56226	M56236	M56246	M56256	M56266	M56276
M56227	M56237	M56247	M56257	M56267	M56277
M56228	M56238	M56248	M56258	M56268	M56278
M56229	M56239	M56249	M56259	M56269	M56279
M56230	M56240	M56250	M56260	M56270	

Pressed Steel Co. (2)
DRIVING TRAILER SECOND ■
(For use with Single Unit cars Nos. W55000-35)
Body: 64′ 0″ × 9′ 3″. Non-gangwayed, side doors to each seating bay
Weight: **Seats:** 2nd, 95

| W56280 | W56282 | W56284 | W56286 | W56288 | W56289 |
| W56281 | W56283 | W56285 | W56287 | | |

Gloucester R. C. & W. Co. (2)
DRIVING TRAILER SECOND ■
(For use with Single Unit cars Nos. W55000-35)
Body: 64′ 0″ × 9′ 3″. Non-gangwayed, side doors to each seating bay
Weight: 29 tons   **Seats:** 2nd, 95

| W56291 | W56293 | W56295 | W56297 | W56298 | W56299 |
| W56292 | W56294 | W56296 | | | |

Above: Pressed Steel
driving trailer second
and two three-car subur-
ban units   *[G. Goza*

Right: Park Royal twin
unit   *[M. Mensing*

Below: Cravens twin
unit on a King's Cross-
Hitchin working
    [D. Percival

Gloucester R. C. & W. Co. (2)

DRIVING TRAILER COMPOSITE (L) ■

For details see SC56094-M56113

SC56300	SC56304	SC56308	SC56311	SC56314	SC56317
SC56301	SC56305	SC56309	SC56312	SC56315	SC56318
SC56302	SC56306	SC56310	SC56313	SC56316	SC56319
SC56303	SC56307				

Metropolitan-Cammell (2)

DRIVING TRAILER COMPOSITE (L) ■

Body: 57′ 0″ × 9′ 3″   **Weight:** 25 tons   **Seats:** 1st, 12; 2nd, 53

M56332	M56346	M56360	E56373	SC56386	SC56399
M56333	M56347	M56361	E56374	SC56387	SC56400
M56334	M56348	E56362	E56375	SC56388	SC56401
M56335	M56349	E56363	E56376	SC56389	SC56402
M56336	M56350	E56364	E56377	SC56390	SC56403
M56337	M56351	E56365	E56378	SC56391	SC56404
M56338	M56352	E56366	E56379	SC56392	SC56405
M56339	M56353	E56367	E56380	SC56393	SC56406
M56340	M56354	E56368	E56381	SC56394	SC56407
M56341	M56355	E56369	SC56382	SC56395	SC56408
M56342	M56356	E56370	SC56383	SC56396	SC56409
M56343	M56357	E56371	SC56384	SC56397	SC56410
M56344	M56358	E56372	SC56385	SC56398	SC56411
M56345	M56359				

Cravens (2)

DRIVING TRAILER COMPOSITE (L) ■

Body: 57′ 6″ × 9′ 2″   **Weight:** 24 tons   **Seats:** 1st, 12; 2nd, 51

E56412	E56424	E56436	E56448	E56460	SC56472
E56413	E56425	E56437	E56449	E56461	SC56473
E56414	E56426	E56438	E56450	SC56462	SC56474
E56415	E56427	E56439	E56451	SC56463	SC56475
E56416	E56428	E56440	E56452	SC56464	SC56476
E56417	E56429	E56441	E56453	SC56465	SC56477
E56418	E56430	E56442	E56454	SC56466	SC56478
E56419	E56431	E56443	E56455	SC56467	SC56479
E56420	E56432	E56444	E56456	SC56468	SC56480
E56421	E56433	E56445	E56457	SC56469	SC56481
E56422	E56434	E56446	E56458	SC56470	SC56482
E56423	E56435	E56447	E56459	SC56471	SC56483

Derby Works, B.R. (2)
DRIVING TRAILER COMPOSITE (L) ■

Body: 57′ 6″ × 9′ 2″　　　**Weight:** 22 tons　　　**Seats:** 1st, 12; 2nd, 53

M56484	M56488	M56492	M56496	M56499	M56502
M56485	M56489	M56493	M56497	M56500	M56503
M56486	M56490	M56494	M56498	M56501	M56504
M56487	M56491	M56495			

Derby Works, B.R. (3 Suburban)
TRAILER COMPOSITE ■

Body: 63′ 8¾″ × 9′ 3″. Non-gangwayed, side doors to each seating bay
Weight: 28 tons 10 cwt　　　**Seats:** 1st, 28; 2nd, 74

W59000	W59006	W59012	W59017	W59022	W59027
W59001	W59007	W59013	W59018	W59023	W59028
W59002	W59008	W59014	W59019	W59024	W59029
W59003	W59009	W59015	W59020	W59025	W59030
W59004	W59010	W59016	W59021	W59026	W59031
W59005	W59011				

Derby Works, B.R. (3 Suburban)
TRAILER SECOND ■

Body: 63′ 8¼″ × 9′ 3″. Non-gangwayed, side doors to each seating bay
Weight: 28 tons 10 cwt　　　**Seats:** 2nd, 106

W59032	W59034	W59036	W59038	W59040	W59041
W59033	W59035	W59037	W59039		

Metropolitan-Cammell (4)
TRAILER SECOND (L) ■

Body: 57′ 0″ × 9′ 3″　　　**Weight:** 25 tons　　　**Seats:** 2nd, 61

E59042	E59044	E59045	E59046	E59047	E59048
E59043					

Metropolitan-Cammell (4)
TRAILER BRAKE SECOND (L) ■

Body: 57′ 0″ × 9′ 3″　　　**Weight:** 25 tons　　　**Seats:** 2nd, 45

E59049	E59051	E59052	E59053	E59054	E59055
E59050					

Metropolitan-Cammell (4)
TRAILER SECOND (L) ■
Body: 57′ 0″ × 9′ 3″   **Weight:** 25 tons   **Seats: 2nd,** 71

E59060	E59063	E59065	E59067	E59069	E59071
E59061	E59064	E59066	E59068	E59070	E59072
E59062					

Metropolitan-Cammell (4)
TRAILER BRAKE SECOND (L) ■
Body: 57′ 0″ × 9′ 3″   **Weight:** 25 tons   **Seats: 2nd,** 53

E59073	E59076	E59078	E59080	E59082	E59084
E59074	E59077	E59079	E59081	E59083	E59085
E59075					

Metropolitan-Cammell (4)
TRAILER SECOND (L) ■
For details see E59042-8

E59086	E59087	E59088	E59089	E59090	E59091

Metropolitan-Cammell (4)
TRAILER BRAKE SECOND (L) ■
For details see E59049-55

E59092	E59093	E59094	E59095	E59096	E59097

Swindon Works, B.R. (3 or 6 Inter-City)
TRAILER BUFFET FIRST (L) ●
Body: **Weight:**   **Seats: 1st, ; Buffet**

SC59098	SC59099

Metropolitan-Cammell (3)
TRAILER SECOND (L) ■
Body: 57′ 0″ × 9′ 3″   **Weight:** 24 tons 10 cwt   **Seats: 2nd,** 71

E59100	E59102	E59104	E59106	E59108	E59109
E59101	E59103	E59105	E59107		

Metropolitan-Cammell (4)

TRAILER BRAKE SECOND (L) ■

Body: 57′ 0″ × 9′ 3″   **Weight:** 25 tons   **Seats: 2nd, 53**

E59112   E59113

Metropolitan-Cammell (3)

TRAILER COMPOSITE (L) ■

Body: 57′ 0″ × 9′ 3″   **Weight:** 25 tons   **Seats: 1st, 12; 2nd, 53**

M59114	M59117	M59120	M59123	M59126	M59129
M59115	M59118	M59121	M59124	M59127	M59130
M59116	M59119	M59122	M59125	M59128	M59131

Birmingham R. C. & W. Co. (3)

TRAILER COMPOSITE (L) ■

Body: 57′ 0″ × 9′ 3″   **Weight:** 24 tons   **Seats: 1st, 12; 2nd, 54**

M59132	M59142	M59152	M59161	M59170	M59179
M59133	M59143	M59153	M59162	M59171	M59180
M59134	M59144	M59154	M59163	M59172	M59181
M59135	M59145	M59155	M59164	M59173	M59182
M59136	M59146	M59156	M59165	M59174	M59183
M59137	M59147	M59157	M59166	M59175	M59184
M59138	M59148	M59158	M59167	M59176	M59185
M59139	M59149	M59159	M59168	M59177	M59186
M59140	M59150	M59160	M59169	M59178	M59187
M59141	M59151				

Birmingham R. C. & W. Co. (4)

TRAILER SECOND (L) ■

Body: 57′ 0″ × 9′ 3″   **Weight:** 24 tons   **Seats: 2nd, 69**

E59188	E59192	E59196	E59200	E59203	E59206
E59189	E59193	E59197	E59201	E59204	E59207
E59190	E59194	E59198	E59202	E59205	E59208
E59191	E59195	E59199			

Birmingham R. C. & W. Co. (4)

TRAILER BRAKE SECOND (L) ■

Body: 57′ 0″ × 9′ 3″   **Weight:** 25 tons   **Seats: 2nd, 51**

E59209	E59213	E59217	E59220	E59224	E59227
E59210	E59214	E59218	E59221	E59225	E59228
E59211	E59215	E59219	E59223	E59226	E59229
E59212	E59216				

Birmingham R. C. & W. Co. (4)

TRAILER SECOND (L) ■

For details see E59188-E59208

E59230	E59231	E59232	E59233	E59234

Swindon Works, B.R. (4 Inter-City)

TRAILER SECOND (L) ■

Body: 64′ 6″ × 9′ 3″   **Weight:**   **Seats:** 2nd, 64

W59235	W59236	W59237	W59238	W59239

Birmingham R. C. & W. Co. (4)

TRAILER BRAKE SECOND (L) ■

For details see E59209-29

E59240	E59241	E59242	E59243	E59244

Derby Works, B.R. (4)

TRAILER BRAKE SECOND (L) ■

Body: 57′ 6″ × 9′ 2″   **Weight:** 22 tons 10 cwt   **Seats:** 2nd, 50

E59245	E59246	E59247	E59248	E59249	E59250

Swindon Works, B.R. (3 Cross Country)

TRAILER BUFFET SECOND (L) ■

Body: 64′ 6″ × 9′ 3″ Open second with miniature buffet at one end

Weight: 31 tons   **Seats:** 2nd, 60; Buffet, 4

W59255	W59263	W59271	W59279	W59287	W59295
W59256	W59264	W59272	W59280	W59288	W59296
W59257	W59265	W59273	W59281	W59289	W59297
W59258	W59266	W59274	W59282	W59290	W59298
W59259	W59267	W59275	W59283	W59291	W59299
W59260	W59268	W59276	W59284	W59292	W59300
W59261	W59269	W59277	W59285	W59293	W59301
W59262	W59270	W59278	W59286	W59294	

Metropolitan-Cammell   (3)
TRAILER SECOND (L)   ■
Body: 57′ 0″ × 9′ 3″   **Weight:** 25 tons   **Seats: 2nd,** 71

E59302	E59303	E59304

Metropolitan-Cammell   (4)
TRAILER SECOND (L)   ■
Body: 57′ 0″ × 9′ 3″   **Weight:** 25 tons   **Seats: 2nd,** 71

E59305	E59306

Cravens   (3)
TRAILER SECOND (L)   ■
OR TRAILER COMPOSITE (L)*
Body: 57′ 6″ × 9′ 2″   **Weight:** 23 tons   **Seats: 2nd,** 69 (1st, 12; 2nd, 54*

M59307*	M59311	M59314	M59317*	M59320*	M59323
M59308	M59312	M59315	M59318*	M59321*	M59324
M59309	M59313	M59316*	M59319	M59322*	M59325
M59310*					

Derby Works, B.R.   (3 Suburban)
TRAILER COMPOSITE   ■
For details see W59000-31

W59326	W59335	W59344	W59353	W59361	W59369
W59327	W59336	W59345	W59354	W59362	W59370
W59328	W59337	W59346	W59355	W59363	W59371
W59329	W59338	W59347	W59356	W59364	W59372
W59330	W59338	W59348	W59357	W59365	W59373
W59331	W59340	W59349	W59358	W59366	W59374
W59332	W59341	W59350	W59359	W59367	W59375
W59333	W59342	W59351	W59360	W59368	W59376
W59334	W59343	W59352			

Derby Works, B.R.   (3* or 4)
TRAILER SECOND (L)   ■
Body: 57′ 6″ × 9′ 2″   **Weight:** 22 tons (22 tons 10 cwt*) **Seats: 2nd,** 68

E59380	E59382	E59384	E59386*	E59388*	E59390*
E59381	E59383	E59385	E59387*	E59389*	

Swindon Works, B.R.   (3 or 6 Inter-City)

TRAILER FIRST (K)   ●

Body: 64' 6" × 9' 3"   Weight: Seats: 1st, 42

SC59391	SC59393	SC59395	SC59397	SC59399	SC59400
SC59392	SC59394	SC59396	SC59398		

Swindon Works, B.R.   (3 or 6 Inter-City)

TRAILER COMPOSITE (L)   ●

Body: 64' 6" × 9' 3"   Weight: Seats: 1st, 18; 2nd, 32

SC59402	SC59404	SC59406	SC59408	SC59410	SC59412
SC59403	SC59405	SC59407	SC59409	SC59411	

Gloucester R. C. & W. Co.   (3 Cross Country)

TRAILER BUFFET SECOND (L)   ■

Body: 64' 6" × 9' 3". Open second with miniature buffet at one end

Weight: 31 tons 8 cwt   Seats: 2nd, 60; Buffet, 4

W59413	W59418	W59422	W59426	W59430	W59434
W59414	W59419	W59423	W59427	W59431	W59435
W59415	W59420	W59424	W59428	W59432	W59436
W59416	W59421	W59425	W59429	W59433	W69437
W59417					

Derby Works, B.R.   (3 Suburban)

TRAILER COMPOSITE   ■

For details see W59000-31

W59438	W59440	W59442	W59444	W59446	W59448
W59439	W59441	W59443	W59445	W59447	

Derby Works, B.R.   (3 Suburban)

TRAILER SECOND   ✱

Body: 63' 8¾" × 9' 3". Non-gangwayed, side doors to each seating bay

Weight: 28 tons 10 cwt   Seats: 2nd, 110

E59449	E59453	E59457	E59460	E59463	E59466
E59450	E59454	E59458	E59461	E59464	E59467
E59451	E59455	E59459	E59462	E59465	E59468
E59452	E59456				

Birmingham R. C. & W. Co.　　　　　(3 Suburban)
TRAILER COMPOSITE (L)　　　　　■
Body: 63′ 10″ × 9′ 3″. Non-gangwayed, side doors to each seating bay
Weight:　　　　　　**Seats: 1st,** 24; **2nd,** 50

W59469	W59472	W59475	W59478	W59480	W59482
W59470	W59473	W59476	W59479	W59481	W59483
W59471	W59474	W59477			

Pressed Steel Co.　　　　　(3 Suburban)
TRAILER COMPOSITE (L)　　　　　■
Body: 63′ 10″ × 9′ 3″. Non-gangwayed, side doors to each seating bay
Weight: 30 tons　　　**Seats: 1st,** 24; **2nd,** 50

W59484	W59491	W59498	W59505	W59511	W59517
W59485	W59492	W59499	W59506	W59512	W59518
W59486	W59493	W59500	W59507	W59513	W59519
W59487	W59494	W59501	W59508	W59514	W59520
W59488	W59495	W59502	W59509	W59515	W59521
W59489	W59496	W59503	W59510	W59516	W59522
W59490	W59497	W59504			

Metropolitan-Cammell　　　　　(3 or 4*)
TRAILER COMPOSITE (L)　　　　　■
Body: 57′ 0″ × 9′ 3″　　**Weight:** 25 tons　　**Seats: 1st,** 12; **2nd,** 53

E59523*	E59531*	E59539*	SC59547	SC59555	SC59563
E59524*	E59532*	E59540*	SC59548	SC59556	SC59564
E59525*	E59533*	E59541*	SC59549	SC59557	SC59565
E59526*	E59534*	E59542*	SC59550	SC59558	SC59566
E59527*	E59535*	SC59543	SC59551	SC59559	SC59567
E59528*	E59536*	SC59544	SC59552	SC59560	SC59568
E59529*	E59537*	SC59545	SC59553	SC59561	
E59530*	E59538*	SC59546	SC59554	SC59562	

Metropolitan-Cammell　　　　　(3)
TRAILER SECOND (L)　　　　　■
Body: 57′ 0″ × 9′ 3″　　**Weight:** 24 tons 10 cwt　　**Seats: 2nd,** 71

E59569	E59570	E59571	E59572

Metropolitan-Cammell (4)
TRAILER BUFFET SECOND (L) ∎
Body: 57' 0" × 9' 3" Open second with miniature buffet at one end
Weight: 26 tons 10 cwt   **Seats: 2nd,** 53; **Buffet,**

E59573	E59574	E59575	E59576	E59577	E59578

Swindon Works, B.R. (3 Cross Country)
TRAILER BUFFET SECOND (L) ∎
Body: 64' 6" × 9' 3". Open second with miniature buffet at one end
Weight: 30 tons 12 cwt   **Seats:** 60; **Buffet,** 4

W59579	W59581	W59583	W59585	W59587	W59588
W59580	W59582	W59584	W59586		

Derby Works, B.R. (4 Suburban)
TRAILER SECOND (L) ∎
Body: 63' 10" × 9' 3". Non-gangwayed, side doors to each seating bay. Intermediate lavatories on each side of central passageway
Weight: 30 tons   **Seats: 2nd,** 90

M59589	M59594	M59599	M59604	M59609	M59614
M59590	M59595	M59600	M59605	M59610	M59615
M59591	M59596	M59601	M59606	M59611	M59616
M59592	M59597	M59602	M59607	M59612	M59617
M59593	M59598	M59603	M59608	M59613	M59618

Derby Works, B.R. (4 Suburban)
TRAILER SECOND ∎
Body: 63' 8¾" × 9' 3". Non-gangwayed, side doors to each seating bay
Weight: 29 tons   **Seats: 2nd,** 106

M59619	M59627	M59635	M59643	M59650	M59657
M59620	M59628	M59636	M59644	M59651	M59658
M59621	M59629	M59637	M59645	M59652	M59659
M59622	M59630	M59638	M59646	M59653	M59660
M59623	M59631	M59639	M59647	M59654	M59661
M59624	M59632	M59640	M59648	M59655	M59662
M59625	M59633	M59641	M59649	M59656	M59663
M59626	M59634	M59642			

Derby Works, B.R. (4 Suburban)

TRAILER COMPOSITE (L) ■

Body: 63' 6" × 9' 3". Non-gangwayed, side doors to each seating bay

Weight: 30 tons   Seats: 1st, 30; 2nd, 40

M59664	M59667	M59670	M59673	M59675	M59677
M59665	M59668	M59671	M59674	M59676	M59678
M59666	M59669	M59672			

Swindon Works, B.R. (3 Cross Country)

TRAILER BUFFET SECOND (L) ■

Body: 64' 6" × 9' 3". Open second with miniature buffet at one end

Weight: 30 tons 12 cwt   Seats: 2nd, 60; Buffet, 4

SC59679	SC49681	SC59682	SC59683	SC59684	SC59685
SC59680					

Metropolitan-Cammell (3)

TRAILER COMPOSITE (L) ■

Body: 57' 0" × 9' 3"   Weight: 25 tons   Seats: 1st, 12; 2nd, 53

SC59686	SC59688	SC59689	SC59690	SC59691	SC59692
SC59687					

Birmingham R. C. & W. Co. (3)

TRAILER SECOND (L) ■

Body: 57' 6" × 9' 3"   Weight: 24 tons   Seats: 2nd, 72

E59693	E59697	E59700	E59703	E59707	E59710
E59794	E59698	E59701	E59704	E59708	E59711
E59695	E59699	E59702	E59705	E59709	E59712
E59696					

Derby Works, B.R. (4 Suburban)

TRAILER SECOND ■

Body: 63' 6" × 9' 3". Non-gangwayed, side doors to each seating bay

Weight: 28 tons   Seats: 2nd, 106

M59713	M59714	M59715	M59716	M59717	M59718

Derby Works, B.R. (4 Suburban)
TRAILER COMPOSITE (L) ∎

Body: 63′ 6″ × 9′ 3″. Non-gangwayed, side doors to each seating bay
Weight: 30 tons   **Seats:** 1st, 30; 2nd, 40

M59719	M59720	M59721	M59722	M59723	M59724

Derby Works, B.R. (4 Suburban)
TRAILER SECOND ∎

For details see M59713-8

M59725	M59729	M59733	M59736	M59739	M59742
M59726	M59730	M59734	M59737	M59740	M59743
M59727	M59731	M59735	M59738	M59741	M59744
M59728	M59732				

Derby Works, B.R. (4 Suburban)
TRAILER COMPOSITE (L) ∎

For details see M59719-24

M59745	M59749	M59753	M59756	M59759	M59762
M59746	M59750	M59754	M59757	M59760	M59763
M59747	M59751	M59755	M59758	M59761	M59764
M59748	M59752				

Swindon Works, B.R. (6 Trans-Pennine)
TRAILER SECOND (L) ∎

Body: 64′ 6″ × 9′ 3″   **Weight:**   **Seats:** 2nd, 64

E59765	E59767	E59769	E59771	E59772	E59773
E59766	E59768	E59770			

Swindon Works, B.R. (6 Trans-Pennine)
TRAILER BUFFET FIRST (L) ∎

Body: 64′ 6″ × 9′ 3″   **Weight:**   **Seats:** 1st, 18; Buffet, 8

E59774	E59776	E59778	E59779	E59780	E59781
E59775	E59777				

Derby Works, B.R. (3)

TRAILER SECOND (L) ■

Body: 58′ 1″ × 9′ 3″   **Weight:** 28 tons   **Seats:** 2nd, 71

SC59782	SC59787	SC59792	SC59796	SC59800	SC59804
SC59783	SC59788	SC59793	SC59797	SC59801	SC59805
SC59784	SC59789	SC59794	SC59798	SC59802	SC59806
SC59785	SC59790	SC59795	SC59799	SC59803	SC59807
SC59786	SC59791				

Birmingham R. C. & W. Co. (3)

TRAILER SECOND (L) ■

Body: 57′ 6″ × 9′ 3″   **Weight:**   **Seats:** 2nd,

M59808	M59810	M59812	M59814	M59816	M59817
M59809	M59811	M59813	M59815		

Swindon Works, B.R. (4 Inter-City)

TRAILER COMPOSITE (K) ■

Body: 64′ 6″ × 9′ 3″   **Weight:**   **Seats:** 1st, 24; 2nd, 24

W59818	W59820	W59822	W59824	W59826	W59827
W59819	W59821	W59823	W59825		

Swindon Works, B.R. (4 Inter-City)

TRAILER BUFFET SECOND ■

Body: 64′ 6″ × 9′ 3″   **Weight:**   **Seats:** 2nd, 32

W59828	W59829	W59830	W59831	W59832

Metropolitan-Cammell (6 Pullman Units)

MOTOR BRAKE FIRST (L)

Engine
One North British/M.A.N. 12-cyl. pressure-charged V-type L12V18/21BS of 1,000 b.h.p.

Transmission
Electric. Two 425 h.p. G.E.C. traction motors driving through Brown-Boveri spring drive

Body: 66′ 5½″ × 9′ 3″. Guard's, luggage compartment, engine room and full width driving cab at outer end of car

Weight: 67 tons 10 cwt   **Seats:** 1st, 12

M60090	M60091	M60092	M60093

Metropolitan-Cammell

MOTOR BRAKE SECOND (L)

Engine
One North British/M.A.N. 12-cyl. pressure-charged V-type L12V18/21BS of 1,000 b.h.p.

Transmission
Electric. Two 425 h.p. G.E.C. traction motors driving through Brown-Boveri spring drive

Body: 66′ 5½″ × 9′ 3″. Guard's, luggage compartment, engine room and full width driving cab at outer end of car

Weight: 67 tons 10 cwt   **Seats: 2nd,** 18

W60094   W60095   W60096   W60097   W60098   W60099

Metropolitan-Cammell

MOTOR PARLOUR SECOND (L)
(non-driving)

Transmission. Electric. Two 425 h.p. G.E.C. traction motors driving through Brown-Boveri spring drive

Body: 65′ 6″ × 9′ 3″   **Weight:** 45 tons 10 cwt   **Seats: 2nd,** 42

W60644   W60645   W60646   W60647   W60648   W60649

Metropolitan-Cammell

MOTOR KITCHEN FIRST (L)
(non-driving)

Transmission: Electric. Two 425 h.p. G.E.C. traction motors driving through Brown-Boveri spring drive

Body: 65′ 6″ × 9′ 3″   **Weight:** 49 tons   **Seats: 1st,** 18

M60730   M60731   M60732   M60733

Metropolitan-Cammell

TRAILER KITCHEN FIRST (L)

Body: 65′ 6″ × 9′ 3″   **Weight:** 36 tons   **Seats: 1st,** 18

W60734   W60735   W60736   W60737   W60738   W60739

Metropolitan-Cammell

TRAILER PARLOUR FIRST (L)

Body: 65′ 6″ × 9′ 3″   **Weight:** 33 tons   **Seats: 1st,** 36

M60740   M60742   W60744*   W60746*   W60748*   W60749*
M60741   M60743   W60745*   W60747*

Metropolitan-Cammell six-car diesel-electric Midland Pullman unit   [C. P. Boocock

Metropolitan-Cammell eight-car Pullman unit approaching Iver on the down Bristol Pullman service   [B. Stephenson

Derby twin unit. The leading car is motor second No. E79150   [P. J. Sharpe

Derby Works, B.R. (2)

MOTOR BRAKE SECOND ◆

Engines
Two B.U.T. (A.E.C.) 6-cyl. horizontal
type of 150 b.h.p.

Transmission
Mechanical. Standard

Body: 57' 6" × 9' 2"   **Weight:** 27 tons   **Seats: 2nd,** 61 (56*)

M79008	M79015	E79022*	E79028*	E79034*	E79040*
M79009	M79016	E79023*	E79029*	E79035*	E79041*
M79010	M79017	E79024*	E79030*	E79036*	E79043*
M79011	M79018	E79025*	E79031*	E79037*	E79044*
M79012	M79019	E79026*	E79032*	E79038*	E79045*
M79013	M79020	E79027*	E79033*	E79039*	E79046*
M79014	E79021*				

Metropolitan-Cammell (2)

MOTOR BRAKE SECOND ◆

Engines
Two B.U.T. (A.E.C.) 6-cyl. horizontal
type of 150 b.h.p.

Transmission
Mechanical. Standard

Body: 57' 0" × 9' 3"   **Weight:** 26 tons 10 cwt   **Seats: 2nd,** 57 (53*)

E79047	E79053	E79059	E79065	E79071	M79077*
E79048	E79054	E79060	E79066	E79072	M79078*
E79049	E79055	E79061	E79067	E79073	M79079*
E79050	E79056	E79062	E79068	E79074	M79080*
E79051	E79057	E79063	E79069	E79075	M79081*
E79052	E79058	E79064	E79070	M79076*	M79082*

Swindon Works, B.R. (3 or 6 Inter-City)

MOTOR BRAKE SECOND (L) ●

Engines
Two B.U.T. (A.E.C.) 6-cyl. horizontal
type of 150 b.h.p.

Transmission
Mechanical. Standard

Body: 64' 6" × 9' 3". Guard's and luggage compartment at outer end. Two types of car; "leading"* with full width driving compartment, gangwayed at inner end only; "intermediate"† with side driving compartment gangwayed at both ends

Weight: 38 tons   **Seats: 2nd,** 52

SC79083†	SC79088†	SC79093*	SC79098*	SC79103*	SC79108*
SC79084†	SC79089†	SC79094*	SC79099*	SC79104*	SC79109*
SC79085†	SC79090†	SC79095†	SC79100*	SC79105*	SC79110*
SC79086†	SC79091*	SC79096*	SC79101*	SC79106*	SC79111*
SC79087†	SC79092*	SC79097*	SC79102*	SC79107*	

Derby Works, B.R. (2)

MOTOR BRAKE SECOND (L) ◆

Engines
Two B.U.T. 6-cyl. horizontal type of 150 b.h.p.

Transmission
Mechanical. Standard
*Fitted with Self-Changing Gears Ltd.
automatic four-speed gearbox

Body: 57′ 6″ × 9′ 2″   **Weight:** 27 tons   **Seats: 2nd, 52**

M79118	M79124	M79129	M79134	E79140	M79145
M79119	M79125	M79130	M79135*	M79141	M79146
M79120	M79126	M79131	M79136	M79142	M79147
M79121	M79127	M79132	E79137	M79143	M79148
M79122	M79128	M79133	E79138	M79144	M79149
M79123					

Derby Works, B.R. (4)

MOTOR SECOND ◆

Engines
Two B.U.T. (A.E.C.) 6-cyl. horizontal type of 150 b.h.p.

Transmission
Mechanical. Standard

Body: 57′ 6″ × 9′ 2″   **Weight:** 26 tons   **Seats: 2nd, 64**

E79150	E79151	E79152	E79153	E79154

Swindon Works, B.R. (6 Inter-City)

MOTOR SECOND (L) ●

Engines
Two B.U.T. (A.E.C.) 6-cyl. horizontal type of 150 b.h.p.

Transmission
Mechanical. Standard

Body: 64′ 6″ × 9′ 3″. Gangwayed both ends. Side driving compartment at one end

Weight: 39 tons 3 cwt   **Seats: 2nd, 64**

SC79155	SC79158	SC79161	SC79163	SC79165	SC79167
SC79156	SC79159	SC79162	SC79164	SC79166	SC79168
SC79157	SC79160				

Derby Works, B.R. (2)

MOTOR BRAKE SECOND ◆

For details see M79118-49

M79169	M79172	M79174	M79176	M79178	M79180
M79171	M79173	M79175	M79177	M79179	M79181

Derby Works, B.R. (2)

MOTOR BRAKE SECOND ◆

For details see M79008-20

M79184	M79185	M79186	M79187	M79188

Derby Works, B.R. (2)

MOTOR COMPOSITE (L) ◆

Engines
Two B.U.T. (A.E.C.) 6-cyl. horizontal type of 150 b.h.p.

Transmission
Mechanical. Standard

Body: 57′ 6″ × 9′ 2″   **Weight:** 27 tons   **Seats:** 1st, 12; 2nd, 53

M79189	M79190	M79192

Derby Works, B.R. (2)

DRIVING TRAILER COMPOSITE (L) ◆

Body: 57′ 6″ × 9′ 2″   **Weight:** 20 tons   **Seats:** 1st, 16; 2nd, 53

E79250	E79253	E79255	E79257	E79259	E79261
E79251	E79254	E79256	E79258	E79260	E79262
E79252					

Metropolitan-Cammell (2)
DRIVING TRAILER SECOND (L) ◆
Body: 57′ 0″ × 9′ 3″   **Weight:** 25 tons   **Seats:** 2nd, 71

E79263	E79268	E79273	E79278	E79283	E79288
E79264	E79269	E79274	E79279	E79284	E79289
E79265	E79270	E79275	E79280	E79285	E79290
E79266	E79271	E79276	E79281	E79286	E79291
E79267	E79272	E79277	E79282	E79287	

Derby Works, B.R. (4)
TRAILER BRAKE SECOND (L) ◆
Body: 57′ 6″ × 9′ 2″   **Weight:** 20 tons 10 cwt   **Seats:** 2nd, 45

E79325	E79326	E79327	E79328	E79329

Derby Works, B.R. (4)
TRAILER SECOND (L) ◆
Body: 57′ 6″ × 9′ 2″   **Weight:** 20 tons 10 cwt   **Seats:** 2nd, 61

E79400	E79401	E79402	E79403	E79404

Swindon Works, B.R. (3 or 6 Inter-City)
TRAILER BUFFET FIRST (K) ●
Body: 64′ 6″ × 9′ 3″. Side corridor with three first class compartments. Buffet with kitchen, bar and saloon
Weight: 34 tons   **Seats:** 1st, 18; **Buffet,** 12

SC79440	SC79442	SC79444	SC79445	SC79446	SC79447
SC79441	SC79443				

Swindon Works, B.R. (3 or 6 Inter-City)
TRAILER FIRST (K) ●
Body: 64′ 6″ × 9′ 3″. Side corridor with seven first class compartments and end doors
Weight: 33 tons 9 cwt   **Seats:** 1st, 42

SC79470	SC79473	SC79475	SC79477	SC79479	SC79481
SC79471	SC79474	SC79476	SC79478	SC79480	SC79482
SC79472					

Derby Works, B.R. (4)
MOTOR COMPOSITE ◆

Engines
Two B.U.T. (A.E.C.) 6-cyl. horizontal
type of 150 b.h.p.

Transmission
Mechanical. Standard

Body: 57′ 6″ × 9′ 2″   **Weight:** 26 tons 10 cwt   **Seats:** 1st, 20; 2nd, 36

E79508	E79509	E79510	E79511	E79512

Derby Works, B.R. (2)
DRIVING TRAILER COMPOSITE (L) ◆

Body: 57′ 6″ × 9′ 2″   **Weight:** 21 tons   **Seats:** 1st, 9 (16*); 2nd, 53

M79600	M79605	M79609	E79613*	E79618*	E79622*
M79601	M79606	M79610	E79614*	E79619*	E79623*
M79602	M79607	M79611	E79615*	E79620*	E79624*
M79603	M79608	M79612	E79617*	E79621*	E79625*
M79604					

Metropolitan-Cammell (2)
DRIVING TRAILER COMPOSITE (L) ◆

Body: 57′ 0″ × 9′ 3″   **Weight:** 25 tons   **Seats:** 1st, 12; 2nd, 53

M79626	M79628	M79629	M79630	M79631	M79632
M79627					

Derby Works, B.R. (2)
DRIVING TRAILER COMPOSITE (L) ◆

Body: 57′ 6″ × 9′ 2″   **Weight:** 20 tons   **Seats:** 1st, 12; 2nd, 53

M79633	M79635

Metro-Cammell two-car unit at Leamington Spa Avenue   [M. Mensing

Derby single-unit motor brake second No. M79900   [M. Mensing

Bristol/E.C.W. four-wheel railbus No. SC79959   [B. Roberts

Waggon und Maschinenbau four-wheel railbus No. E79961   [P. J. Sharpe

Derby Works, B.R. (2)

DRIVING TRAILER COMPOSITE (L) ◆

For details see M79600-E79625

M79639	M79647	M79655	M79664	M79671	M79678
M79640	M79648	M79656	M79665	M79672	M79679
M79641	M79649†	M79657	M79666	M79673	M79680
M79642	M79650	E79658*	M79667	M79674	M79681
M79643	M79651	E79660*	M79668	M79675	M79682
M79644	M79652	E79661*	M79669	M79676	M79683
M79645	M79653	M79662	M79670	M79677	M79684
M79646	M79654	M79663			

† This vehicle has been fitted internally for use as an inspection saloon including a pantry, and is not in public service. It has been rewired to work with "Blue Square" type motor-coaches

Derby Works, B.R. (1)

MOTOR BRAKE SECOND ◆

Engines
Two B.U.T. (A.E.C.) 6-cyl. horizontal type of 150 b.h.p.

Transmission
Mechanical. Standard

Body: 57′ 6″ × 9′ 2″. Non-gangwayed. Driving compartments at each end

Weight: 27 tons

Seats: 2nd, 52

M79900   M79901

Bristol/E.C.W.

FOUR-WHEEL RAILBUS

Engine
Gardner 6.H.L.W. 6-cyl. type of 112 b.h.p. at 1,700 r.p.m.

Transmission
Mechanical. Standard. Fitted with Self-Changing Gears Ltd. five-speed epicyclic gearbox

Body: 42′ 4″ × 9′ 3″. Non-gangwayed

Weight: 13 tons 10 cwt   **Seats:** 2nd, 56

SC79958   SC79959

Waggon und Maschinenbau

FOUR-WHEEL RAILBUS

Engine
Buessing 150 b.h.p. at 1,900 r.p.m.
*A.E.C. A220X type

Transmission
Mechanical. Cardan shaft to ZF electro-magnetic six-speed gearbox

Body: 41′ 10″ × 8′ 8$\frac{5}{16}$″. Non-gangwayed

Weight: 15 tons   **Seats:** 2nd, 56

E79960   E79961*   E79962   E79963*   E79964

Park Royal four-wheel railbus No. SC79974 at Prestwick   [*P. J. Sharpe*

A.C. Cars four-wheel railbus No. W79978 approaching Cirencester   [*M. Mensing*

D. Wickham & Co.
FOUR-WHEEL RAILBUS

Engine
Meadows 6-cyl. type 6HDT500 of 105 b.h.p. at 1,800 r.p.m.

Body: 38' 0" × 9' 0". Non-gangwayed

Weight: 11 tons 5 cwt

Transmission
Mechanical. Freeborn-Wickham disc-and-ring coupling driving Self-Changing Gears Ltd. four-speed epicyclic gearbox and cardan shaft to final drive

Seats 2nd, 44

SC79965	SC79966	SC79967	SC79968

Park Royal Vehicles
FOUR-WHEEL RAILBUS

Engine
B.U.T. (A.E.C.) 6-cyl. horizontal type of 150 b.h.p.

Body: 42' 0" × 9' 3". Non-gangwayed

Weight: 15 tons

Transmission
Mechanical. Standard. Fitted with Self-Changing Gears Ltd. four-speed epicyclic gearbox

Seats, 2nd, 50

SC79970	SC79971	SC79972	SC79973	SC79974

A.C. Cars
FOUR-WHEEL RAILBUS

Engine
B.U.T. (A.E.C.) 6-cyl. horizontal type of 150 b.h.p.

Body: 36' 0" × 8' 11". Non-gangwayed

Weight: 11 tons

Transmission
Mechanical. Standard

Seats: 2nd, 46

W79975	W79976	W79977	W79978	SC79979

Derby/Cowlairs Works, B.R.   (2)
BATTERY ELECTRIC RAILCAR
MOTOR BRAKE SECOND

Electrical Equipment: Two 100 kW Siemens-Schuckert nose-suspended traction motors powered by 216 lead-acid cell batteries of 1070 amp/hour capacity

Body: 57' 6" × 9' 2"   **Weight:** 37 tons 10 cwt   **Seats: 2nd,** 52

SC79998

Derby/Cowlairs Works, B.R.   (2)
BATTERY ELECTRIC RAILCAR
DRIVING TRAILER COMPOSITE

Body: 57' 6" × 9' 2"   **Weight:** 32 tons 10 cwt   **Seats: 1st,** 12; **2nd,** 53

SC79999

TRAILER COMPOSITE (K) ∎

(Ex-G.W. vehicles converted for use with diesel units)

W7254W   W7804W   W7813W

SOUTHERN REGION DIESEL-ELECTRIC MULTIPLE-UNITS

Eastleigh Works, B.R.   **(6 or 4¶)**

HASTINGS

(Gangwayed within set)

MOTOR BRAKE SECOND

Engine
English Electric 4-cyl. type 4SRKT Mark II of 500 b.h.p. at 850 r.p.m.

Transmission
Electric. Two nose-suspended axle-hung traction motors

Body: 58′ 0″ (64′ 6″*†) × 8′ 2½″ & 9′ 0″. Guard's, luggage compartment, engine room and full width driving compartment at outer end of car

Weight: 54 tons 2 cwt (55 tons*†)   **Seats: 2nd,** 22 (30*†)

TRAILER FIRST (K)

Body: 58′ 0″ (64′ 6″*†) × 8′ 2½″ & 9′ 0″. Side corridor with seven (eight*†) first class compartments with side door to each compartment

Weight: 30 tons (31 tons*†)   **Seats: 1st,** 42 (48*†)

TRAILER SECOND (L)

Body: 58′ 0″ (64′ 6″*†) × 8′ 2½″ & 9′ 0″

Weight: 29 tons (30 tons*†)   **Seats: 2nd,** 52 (60*†)

TRAILER SECOND (L)¶

Body: 58′ 0″ (64′ 6″*, 58′ 0″†) × 8′ 2½ & 9′ 0″

Weight: 29 tons (30 tons*, 29 tons†)   **Seats: 2nd,** 52 (60* 52†)

TRAILER SECOND (L)¶

Body: 58′ 0″ (64′ 6″*, 58′ 0″†) × 8′ 2½″ & 9′ 0″

Weight: 29 tons (30 tons*, 29 tons†)   **Seats: 2nd,** 52 (60*, 52†)

MOTOR BRAKE SECOND

(as above)

1001	1004	1007¶	1013*	1016*	1019*
1002	1005	1011*	1014*	1017*	1031*
1003	1006	1012*	1015*	1018*	1032†

¶Two Trailer Seconds removed from unit 1007

Hastings line six-car diesel-electric unit No. 1002   [*P. J. Sharpe*

Trailer second of six-car long-underframe Hastings unit No. 1032   [*P. J. Sharpe*

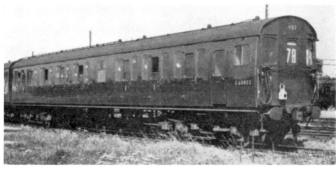

Driving trailer composite of Hampshire three-car unit No. 1103   [*P. J. Sharpe*

HASTINGS
(Gangwayed within set)

MOTOR BRAKE SECOND

Engine
English Electric 4-cyl. type 4SRKT Mark II of 500 b.h.p. at 850 r.p.m.

Transmission
Electric. Two nose-suspended axle-hung traction motors

Body: 64' 6" × 8' 2½" & 9' 0". Guard's, luggage compartment, engine room and full-width driving compartment at outer end of car

Weight: 55 tons   **Seats:** 2nd, 30

TRAILER SECOND (L)

Body: 64' 6" × 8' 2½" & 9' 0"   **Weight:** 30 tons   **Seats:** 2nd, 60

TRAILER BUFFET

Body: 64' 6" × 8' 2½" & 9' 0". Buffet with kitchen and bar; self-contained seating saloon

Weight: 35 tons   **Seats:** Buffet, 21

TRAILER FIRST (K)

Body: 64' 6" × 8' 2½" & 9' 0". Side corridor with eight first class compartments with side door to each compartment

Weight: 31 tons   **Seats:** 1st, 48

TRAILER SECOND (L)

(as above)

MOTOR BRAKE SECOND

(as above)

      1033   1034   1035   1036   1037

HAMPSHIRE
HASTINGS*
BERKSHIRE†

MOTOR BRAKE SECOND

Engine
English Electric 4-cyl. type 4SRKT Mark II of 600 b.h.p. at 850 r.p.m.
¶Dorman type 12QTCW V-12 of 725 b.h.p.

Transmission
Electric. Two nose-suspended axle-hung traction motors

Body: 64' 0" × 9' 3". Guard's, luggage compartment, engine room and full-width driving compartment at outer end of car. Non-gangwayed, side doors to each seating bay

Weight: 56 tons   **Seats:** 2nd, 52 (42†)

Eastleigh-built three-car Hampshire unit No. 1129   [C. *Symes*

East Sussex area three-car unit No. 1303 at Ham Street and Orlestone   [D. C. *Ovenden*

TRAILER SEMI-SALOON SECOND

(three-car units only)

Body: 63′ 6″ × 9′ 3″. Non-gangwayed, side doors to each seating bay
Weight: **Seats: 2nd, 104**

DRIVING TRAILER COMPOSITE (L)

Body: 64′ 0″ × 9′ 3″. Non-gangwayed, side doors to each seating bay or compartment. 5-bay 2nd class saloon and 2 1st class compartments with intermediate lavatories, also a 2nd class compartment next to driving compartment. A luggage compartment has been fitted in place of the 2nd class compartment in the Hampshire units

Weight: 32 tons   **Seats: 1st, 13: 2nd, 50 (62*†)**

1101	1107	1113	1119*	1124	1129†¶
1102	1108	1114	1120*	1125	1130†
1103	1109	1115	1121*	1126	1131†
1104	1110	1116	1122*	1127†	1132†
1105	1111	1117	1123	1128†	1133†
1106	1112	1118			

Eastleigh Works, B.R.   (3)

EAST SUSSEX
MOTOR BRAKE SECOND

Engine
English Electric 4-cyl. type 4SRKT Mark II of 600 b.h.p. at 850 r.p.m.

Transmission
Electric. Two nose-suspended axle-hung traction motors

Body: 64′ 0″ × 8′ 6″ & 9′ 0″. Guard's, luggage compartment, engine room and full-width driving compartment at outer end of car. Non-gangwayed, side doors to each seating bay

Weight: 56 tons   **Seats: 2nd, 42**

TRAILER COMPOSITE

Body: 63′ 6″ × 8′ 6″ & 9′ 0″. Non-gangwayed side doors to each seating bay or compartment. 3-bay 2nd class saloon, 4 1st class compartments, side lavatory and further 2-bay 2nd class saloon connected by side corridor.

Weight: 31 tons   **Seats: 1st, 24: 2nd, 42**

DRIVING TRAILER SEMI-SALOON SECOND

Body: 64′ 0″ × 9′ 6″ & 9′ 0″. Non-gangwayed, side doors to each seating bay

Weight: 32 tons   **Seats: 2nd, 76**

1301	1305	1308	1311	1314	1317
1302	1306	1309	1312	1315	1318
1303	1307	1310	1313	1316	1319
1304					

B.R. ELECTRIC LOCOMOTIVES AND MULTIPLE-UNITS

ELECTRIC locomotives on British Railways are numbered in two series. Those built by British Railways as part of the modernisation programme carry the prefix "E" in a series ranging from E1000 for a.c. units and from E5000 for d.c. units. The first figure of the a.c. series, in addition to indentifying the locomotive, also gives an indication of its horsepower—for example, E2001 for a unit in the 2,000, h.p. range and E3001 for a locomotive in the 3,000 h.p. range. Earlier locomotives built to S.R. or L.N.E.R. designs are numbered in the 20000 series.

The headings to each class show the type designation or class, principal manufacturer and wheel arrangement. Originally the type designation A or B was intended to be used to identify locomotives suited for passenger and freight haulage respectively, but subsequent experience has shown that locomotives need not be specially geared for freight working and the designation B has disappeared.

Wheel arrangements of electric (and diesel) locomotives are described by a development of the Continental notation. This calculates by axles and not by wheels, and uses letters instead of numerals to denote driving axles ("A" = 1, "B" = 2, "C" = 3, etc.) and numerals only for non-powered axles. An indication of the grouping of axles is given, but powered and non-powered axles may be found in the same group. Thus, diesel-electric locomotive No. D5500 is described as an A1A-A1A, indicating that it is mounted on two six-wheel bogies, each of which has a non-powered axle in the centre and a motored axle at either end. Groups of axles are separated by a hyphen if they are quite independant of each other, but by a "plus" sign in cases where powered bogies are linked by an articulated joint to take certain stresses.

If all axles on a bogie or frame unit are individually powered, a suffix letter "o" is added to the descriptive letter. Thus B.R. electric locomotive No. E5001 is shown as a Bo-Bo, indicating that it has two four-wheel bogies, each axle of which has an individual traction motor.

Electric multiple-unit trains are listed Region by Region and sub-divided into areas or lines or, in the case of the S.R., into types of stock. Details of all coaches in a particular set are listed together. The dimensions are shown length and width over body and width overall. The letter (L) in the headings indicates an open vehicle fitted with toilet facilities; (K) indicates a side corridor vehicle with toilet. Unit numbers, which are painted on the front and rear of each set, are listed where used by British Railways; otherwise individual coach numbers are shown.

ELECTRIC LOCOMOTIVES

Metropolitan Vickers   AIA-AIA

Introduced
1958

Equipment
Four 625 h.p. Metropolitan-Vickers
nose-suspended traction motors

Driving wheel diameter
3′ 8″

System
25 kV. a.c. overhead
(Rebuilt from former Gas Turbine
Locomotive No. 18100)

Total h.p.
2,500

Weight
109 tons 0 cwt

Maximum tractive effort
40,000 lb

E2001

Type A   A.E.I.   Bo-Bo
(British Thomson-Houston)

Introduced
1959

Equipment
Four A.E.I. (B.T.H.) spring-borne
d.c. traction motors of 847 h.p. (continuous) driving through Alsthom
quill drive

Driving wheel diameter
4′ 0″

System
25 kV. a.c. overhead

Total h.p.
3,300

Weight
79 tons 12 cwt

Maximum tractive effort
48,000 lb

E3001	E3005	E3009	E3012	E3015	E3018	E3021
E3002	E3006	E3010	E3013	E3016	E3019	E3022
E3003	E3007	E3011	E3014	E3017	E3020	E3023
E3004	E3008					

Type A   English Electric   Bo-Bo

Introduced
1960

Equipment
Four English Electric spring-borne
d.c. traction motors of 740 h.p. (continuous) driving through S.L.M.
resilient drives

Driving wheel diameter
4′ 0″

System
25 kV a.c. overhead

Total h.p.
3,300

Weight
73 tons 0 cwt

Maximum tractive effort
40,000 lb

E3024	E3026	E3028	E3030	E3032	E3034	E3035
E3025	E3027	E3029	E3031	E3033		

A.E.I. Type A 3,300 h.p. 25kV a.c. Bo-Bo No. E3007   [N. E. Preedy

English Electric Type A 3,300 h.p. 25kV a.c. Bo-Bo No. E3032   [C. P. Boocock

General Electric Type A 3,300 h.p. 25kV a.c. Bo-Bo No. E3038   [B. Walker

Type A General Electric Bo-Bo

Introduced
1960

Total h.p.
3,300

Equipment
Four G.E.C. spring-borne d.c. traction motors of 750 h.p. (continuous), driving through Brown-Boveri spring drives

Weight
76 tons 10 cwt

Driving wheel diameter
4' 0"

Maximum tractive effort
50,000 lb

System
25 kV. a.c. overhead

E3036	E3038	E3040	E3042	E3043	E3044	E3045
E3037	E3039	E3041				

Type A A.E.I. Bo-Bo
(Metropolitan-Vickers)

Introduced
1960

Total h.p.
3,300

Equipment
Four A.E.I. (M.V.) d.c. traction motors of 847 h.p. (continuous) driving through Alsthom quill drive

Weight
78 tons 8 cwt

Driving wheel diameter
4' 0"

Maximum tractive effort
48,000 lb

System
25 kV. a.c. overhead

E3046	E3048	E3050	E3052	E3053	E3054	E3055
E3047	E3049	E3051				

Type A British Railways Bo-Bo

Introduced
1960

Total h.p.
3,300

Equipment
Four A.E.I. (B.T.H.) d.c. traction motors of 847 h.p. (continuous) driving through Alsthom quill drive

Weight
79 tons 0 cwt

Driving wheel diameter
4' 0"

Maximum tractive effort
48,000 lb

System
25 kV. a.c. overhead

E3056	E3059	E3062	E3065	E3068	E3071	E3074
E3057	E3060	E3063	E3066	E3069	E3072	E3075
E3058	E3061	E3064	E3067	E3070	E3073	

Type A   British Railways   Bo-Bo

Introduced
1962

Equipment
B.T.H.

Driving wheel diameter
4′ 0″

System
25 kV a.c. overhead

Total h.p.
3,300

Weight
80 tons 0 cwt

Maximum tractive effort
48,000 lb

E3076	E3079	E3082	E3085	E3088	E3091	E3094
E3077	E3080	E3083	E3086	E3089	E3092	E3095
E3078	E3081	E3084	E3087	E3090	E3093	

Type A   A.E.I.   Bo-Bo
(British Thomson-Houston)

Introduced
1963

Equipment
Four A.E.I. (B.T.H.) spring-borne d.c. traction motors of 847 h.p. (continuous) driving through Alsthom quill drive

Driving wheel diameter
4′ 0″

System
25 kV. a.c. overhead

Total h.p.
3,300

Weight
80 tons 0 cwt

Maximum tractive effort
60,000 lb

E3096 E3097

Type A   English Electric   Bo-Bo

Introduced
1961

Equipment
Four English Electric springborne d.c. traction motors of 740 h.p. (continuous) driving through S.L.M. resilient drives

Driving wheel diameter
4′ 0″

System
25 kV a.c. overhead

Total h.p.
3,300

Weight
73 tons 0 cwt

Maximum tractive effort

E3098 E3099

English Electric Type A 3,300 h.p. 25kV a.c. Bo-Bo No. E3099   [C. P. Boocock

British Railways 2,552 h.p. 750V d.c. Bo-Bo No. E5005   [R. A. Panting

British Railways 1,600/600 h.p. electro-diesel Bo-Bo No. E6001   [Alan Williams

Type A   English Electric   Bo-Bo

Introduced
1962

Equipment
As E3024. Adopted as the test loco-motive for a stepless form of supply voltage control to the traction motors, using semi-conductor recti-fiers. Equipped with rheostatic braking

Driving wheel diameter
4′ 0″

System
25 kV. a.c. overhead

Total h.p.
3,300

Weight

Maximum tractive effort

  E3100

British Railways   Bo-Bo

Introduced
1958

Equipment
Motor generator booster set and four 638 h.p. English Electric spring-borne traction motors driving through S.L.M. flexible drive

Driving wheel diameter
4′ 0″

System
750 V. d.c. 3rd rail and overhead

Total h.p.
2,552

Weight
77 tons 0 cwt

Maximum tractive effort
43,000 lb

E5001	E5005	E5009	E5013	E5016	E5019	E5022
E5002	E5006	E5010	E5014	E5017	E5020	E5023
E5003	E5007	E5011	E5015	E5018	E5021	E5024
E5004	E5008	E5012				

Electro-Diesel   British Railways   Bo-Bo

Introduced
1962

Equipment
English Electric 4-cyl type 4 SRKT mark II 600 b.h.p. diesel engine; four English Electric 400 h.p. traction motors. These locomotives can work either direct from a 750 V. d.c. third rail supply or, when this is not avail-able, with the diesel generator power-ing the traction motors, though at reduced horsepower

Driving wheel diameter
3′ 4″

System
750 V. d.c. 3rd rail or diesel

Total h.p.
Electric 1,600
Diesel 600

Weight
73 tons 0 cwt

Maximum tractive effort
42,000 lb

| E6001 | E6002 | E6003 | E6004 | E6005 | E6006 |

Note: 100 more a.c. electric locomotives for the L.M.R. and 30 electro-diesel locomotives for the S.R. have been ordered, but details were not available as this edition closed for press.

CC   S.R.   Co-Co

Introduced
1941
1948*

Equipment
Motor generator booster set and six
245 h.p. English Electric nose-suspended traction motors.

Driving wheel diameter
3′ 6″

System
750 V. d.c. 3rd rail and overhead

Total h.p.
1,470

Weight
99 tons 14 cwt
104 tons 14 cwt*

Maximum tractive effort
40,000 lb
45,000 lb*

20001	20002	20003*

EMI   L.N.E.R. & British Railways   Bo-Bo

Introduced
1941*
1950

Equipment
Four 467 h.p. Metropolitan-Vickers
nose-suspended traction motors

Driving wheel diameter
4′ 2″

System
1,500 V. d.c. overhead

Total h.p.
1,868

Weight
87 tons 18 cwt

Maximum tractive effort
45,000 lb

26000*   Tommy

26001	26008	25015	26022	26028	26034	26040
26002	26009	26016	26023	26029	26035	26041
26003	26010	26017	26024	26030	26036	26042
26004	26011	26018	26025	26031	26037	26043
26005	26012	26019	26026	26032	26038	26044
26006	26013	26020	26027	26033	26039	26045
26007	26014	26021				

26046	Archimedes	26052	Nestor
26047	Diomedes	26053	Perseus
26048	Hector	26054	Pluto
26049	Jason	26055	Prometheus
26050	Stentor	26056	Triton
26051	Mentor	26057	Ulysses

Southern Railway 1,470 h.p. 750V d.c. Co-Co No. 20003 *[G. W. Morrison*

.N.E.R. Class EM1 1,868 h.p. 1,500V d.c. Bo-Bo No. 26000 *Tommy* *[K. R. Pirt*

British Railways Class EM2 2,490 h.p. 1,500V d.c. Co-Co No. 27004 *Juno [P. J. Sharpe*

ES1　　　　　Brush　　　　　Bo-Bo

Introduced
1902

Equipment
Four B.T.H. nose-suspended traction motors

Driving wheel diameter

System
630 V. d.c. overhead and 3rd rail

Total h.p.

Weight
46 tons 0 cwt

Maximum tractive effort
25,000 lb

26500　　26501

EM2　　　British Railways　　　Co-Co

Introduced
1954

Equipment
Six 415 h.p. Metropolitan-Vickers nose-suspended traction motors

Driving wheel diameter
4' 2"

System
1,500 V. d.c. overhead

Total h.p.
2,490

Weight
102 tons 0 cwt

Maximum tractive effort
45,000 lb

27000	*Electra*	27004	*Juno*
27001	*Ariadne*	27005	*Minerva*
27002	*Aurora*	27006	*Pandora*
27003	*Diana*		

DEPARTMENTAL LOCOMOTIVES
SOUTHERN REGION

Bo-Bo DS74　　　　　　**Bo**　　DS75

LONDON MIDLAND REGION

Battery Electric L.M.S.　　　　　　　　　　Bo

Introduced
1914*
1917†

Equipment
*Two Dick Kerr traction motors
†Two B.T.H. traction motors

Driving wheel diameter
3' 1"

Total h.p.
44*
82†

Weight
18 tons*
17 tons†

Maximum tractive effort

BEL　1*　　　　　　　　　BEL　2†

ELECTRIC MULTIPLE-UNITS
London Midland Region

SYSTEM: 630 VOLTS D.C. 3rd AND 4th RAIL

London District Three-Car Sets
B.R. Standard design

MOTOR OPEN BRAKE SECOND
Body: 57′ 5″ × 9′ 0″ & 9′ 6″   **Weight:** 47 tons   **Seats:** 2nd, 74
Equipment: Four 185 h.p. G.E.C. traction motors

M61133	M61143	M61153	M61163	M61172	M61181
M61134	M61144	M61154	M61164	M61173	M61182
M61135	M61145	M61155	M61165	M61174	M61183
M61136	M61146	M61156	M61166	M61175	M61184
M61137	M61147	M61157	M61167	M61176	M61185
M61138	M61148	M61158	M61168	M61177	M61186
M61139	M61149	M61159	M61169	M61178	M61187
M61140	M61150	M61160	M61170	M61179	M61188
M61141	M61151	M61161	M61171	M61180	M61189
M61142	M61152	M61162			

TRAILER SECOND
Body: 57′ 1″ × 9′ 0″ & 9′ 6″   **Weight:** 29 tons   **Seats:** 2nd, 108

M70133	M70143	M70153	M70163	M70172	M70181
M70134	M70144	M70154	M70164	M70173	M70182
M70135	M70145	M70155	M70165	M70174	M70183
M70136	M70146	M70156	M70166	M70175	M70184
M70137	M70147	M70157	M70167	M70176	M70185
M70138	M70148	M70158	M70168	M70177	M70186
M70139	M70149	M70159	M70169	M70178	M70187
M70140	M70150	M70160	M70170	M70179	M70188
M70141	M70151	M70161	M70171	M70180	M70189
M70142	M70152	M70162			

DRIVING TRAILER OPEN BRAKE SECOND
Body: 57′ 5″ × 9′ 0″ & 9′ 6″   **Weight:** 30 tons   **Seats:** 2nd, 74

M75133	M75143	M75153	M75163	M75172	M75181
M75134	M75144	M75154	M75164	M75173	M75182
M75135	M75145	M75155	M75165	M75174	M75183
M75136	M75146	M75156	M75166	M75175	M75184
M75137	M75147	M75157	M75167	M75176	M75185
M75138	M75148	M75158	M75168	M75177	M75186
M75139	M75149	M75159	M75169	M75178	M75187
M75140	M75150	M75160	M75170	M75179	M75188
M75141	M75151	M75161	M75171	M75180	M75189
M75142	M75152	M75162			

Two L.M.R. London district B.R. standard three-car sets   [G. M. Kichenside

Motor open brake second No. M28343M of a Liverpool-Southport set   [P. J. Sharpe

Former South Tyneside motor parcels car No. E68000 now running on the Liverpool-Southport line   [P. J. Sharpe

Three-Car Compartment Set

This set has been retained for shunting at Stonebridge Park Carriage Depot

MOTOR BRAKE SECOND

Body: 59′ 0″ × 8′ 11″ & 9′ 6″   **Weight:** 56 tons   **Seats:** 2nd, 84
Equipment: Four 280 h.p. traction motors
M28024M

TRAILER SECOND

Body: 57′ 0″ × 8′ 11″ & 9′ 6″   **Weight:** 28 tons   **Seats:** 2nd, 108
M29622M

DRIVING TRAILER BRAKE SECOND

Body: 57′ 0″ × 8′ 11″ & 9′ 6″   **Weight:** 30 tons   **Seats:** 2nd, 96
M28824M

SYSTEM: 630 VOLTS D.C. 3rd RAIL

Liverpool-Southport
Two- and Three-Car Open Sets

MOTOR OPEN BRAKE SECOND

Body: 66′ 6″ × 9′ 3″ & 9′ 5″   **Weight:** 41 tons   **Seats:** 2nd, 88
Equipment: Four 235 h.p. English traction motors

M28311M	M28322M	M28332M	M28342M	M28352M	M28361M
M28312M	M28323M	M28333M	M28343M	M28353M	M28362M
M28313M	M28324M	M28334M	M28344M	M28354M	M28363M
M28314M	M28325M	M28335M	M28345M	M28355M	M28364M
M28315M	M28326M	M28336M	M28347M	M28356M	M28365M
M28316M	M28327M	M28337M	M28348M	M28357M	M28366M
M28317M	M28328M	M28338M	M28349M	M28358M	M28367M
M28318M	M28329M	M28339M	M28350M	M28359M	M28368M
M28319M	M28330M	M28340M	M28351M	M28360M	M28369M
M28321M	M28331M	M28341M			

TRAILER OPEN SECOND

Body: 66′ 6″ × 9′ 3″ & 9′ 5″   **Weight:** 24 tons   **Seats:** 2nd, 102

M29545M	M29554M	M29563M	M29571M	M29579M	M29587M
M29546M	M29555M	M29564M	M29572M	M29580M	M29588M
M29547M	M29556M	M29565M	M29573M	M29581M	M29589M
M29548M	M29557M	M29566M	M29574M	M29582M	M29590M
M29549M	M29558M	M29567M	M29575M	M29583M	M29591M
M29550M	M29559M	M29568M	M29576M	M29584M	M29592M
M29551M	M29560M	M29569M	M29577M	M29585M	M29593M
M29552M	M29561M	M29570M	M29578M	M29586M	M29594M
M29553M	M29562M				

TRAILER OPEN SECOND

(Built as Composite)

Body: 66′ 6″ × 9′ 3″ & 9′ 5″   **Weight:** 24 tons   **Seats: 2nd, 82**

M29812M	M29814M	M29816M	M29818M	M29819M	M29820M
M29813M	M29815M	M29817M			

DRIVING TRAILER OPEN COMPOSITE

Body: 66′ 6″ × 9′ 3″ & 9′ 5″   **Weight:** 25 tons **Seats:** 1st, 53; **2nd, 25**

M29866M	M29872M	M29878M	M29884M	M29890M	M29895M
M29867M	M29873M	M29879M	M29885M	M29891M	M29896M
M29868M	M29874M	M29880M	M29886M	M29892M	M29897M
M29869M	M29875M	M29881M	M29887M	M29893M	M29898M
M29870M	M29876M	M29882M	M29888M	M29894M	M29899M
M29871M	M29877M	M29883M	M29889M		

Liverpool-Southport Single Unit

B.R. Standard design

MOTOR PARCELS VAN

Body: 64′ 5″ × 9′ 0″ & 9′ 3″   **Weight:** 49 tons
Equipment: Four 250 h.p. English Electric traction motors

M68000

Wirral & Mersey
Three-Car Open Sets

MOTOR OPEN BRAKE SECOND

Body: 58′ 0″ × 8′ 8″ & 9′ 11″ **Weight:** 36 tons **Seats:** 2nd, 58
Equipment: Four 135 h.p. B.T.H. traction motors

M28371M	M28379M	M28387M	M28394M	M28677M	M28684M
M28372M	M28380M	M28388M		M28678M	M28685M
M28373M	M28381M	M28389M	M28672M	M28679M	M28686M
M28374M	M28382M	M28390M	M28673M	M28680M	M28687M
M28375M	M28383M	M28391M	M28674M	M28681M	M28688M
M28376M	M28384M	M28392M	M28675M	M28682M	M28689M
M28377M	M28385M	M28393M	M28676M	M28683M	M28690M
M28378M	M28386M				

TRAILER OPEN COMPOSITE

Body: 56′ 0″ × 8′ 8″ & 9′ 11″ **Weight:** 20 tons **Seats:** 1st, 40; 2nd, 15

M29702M	M29710M	M29718M	M29825M	M29833M	M29840M
M29703M	M29711M	M29719M	M29826M	M29834M	M29841M
M29704M	M29712M	M29720M	M29827M	M29835M	M29842M
M29705M	M29713M		M29828M	M29836M	M29843M
M29706M	M29714M	M29821M	M29829M	M29837M	M29844M
M29707M	M29715M	M29822M	M29830M	M29838M	M29845M
M29708M	M29716M	M29823M	M29831M	M29839M	M29846M
M29709M	M29717M	M29824M	M29832M		

DRIVING TRAILER OPEN SECOND

Body: 58′ 0″ × 8′ 8″ & 8′ 11″ **Weight:** 21 tons **Seats:** 2nd, 68

M29131M	M29139M	M29147M	M29155M	M29276M	M29283M
M29132M	M29140M	M29148M	M29156M	M29277M	M29284M
M29133M	M29141M	M29149M		M29278M	M29285M
M29134M	M29142M	M29150M	M29271M	M29279M	M29286M
M29135M	M29143M	M29151M	M29272M	M29280M	M29287M
M29136M	M29144M	M29152M	M29273M	M29281M	M29288M
M29137M	M29145M	M29153M	M29274M	M29282M	M29289M
M29138M	M29146M	M29154M	M29275M		

Manchester-Bury Two-Car B.R. Sets

B.R. Standard design

Two L.M.R. Wirral & Mersey sets at Birkenhead with motor open brake second
No. M28688M leading   [P. J. Sharpe

Motor open brake second No. M65461 of a Manchester–Bury two-car set [P. J. Sharpe

Two L.M.R. Manchester–Bury two-car sets   [P. J. Sharpe

MOTOR OPEN BRAKE SECOND

Body: 63′ 11½″ × 9′ 0″ & 9′ 3″   **Weight:**   **Seats: 2nd,** 84
Equipment: Two 141 h.p. English Electric traction motors

M65436	M65441	M65446	M65450	M65454	M65458
M65437	M65442	M65447	M65451	M65455	M65459
M65438	M65443	M65448	M65452	M65456	M65460
M65439	M65444	M65449	M65453	M65457	M65461
M65440	M65445				

DRIVING TRAILER SECOND

Body: 63′ 11½″ × 9′ 0″ & 9′ 3″   **Weight:**   **Seats: 2nd,** 102

M77157	M77162	M77167	M77171	M77175	M77179
M77158	M77163	M77168	M77172	M77176	M77180
M77159	M77164	M77169	M77173	M77177	M77181
M77160	M77165	M77170	M77174	M77178	M77182
M77161	M77166				

SYSTEM: 1,500 VOLTS D.C. OVERHEAD

Manchester-Altrincham

Three-Car Sets

MOTOR BRAKE SECOND

Body: 58′ 1″ × 8′ 11″ & 9′ 3″   **Weight:** 57 tons   **Seats: 2nd,** 72
Equipment: Four 330 h.p. traction motors

M28571M	M28576M	M28580M	M28584M	M28588M	M28592M
M28572M	M28577M	M28581M	M28585M	M28589M	M28593M
M28573M	M28578M	M28582M	M28586M	M28590M	M28594M
M28574M	M28579M	M28583M	M28587M	M28591M	

TRAILER COMPOSITE

Body: 57′ 1″ × 8′ 11″ & 9′ 3″   **Weight:** 30 tons   **Seats:** 1st, 24; 2nd, 72

M29396M	M29652M	M29656M	M29660M	M29665M	M29669M
	M29653M	M29657M	M29661M	M29666M	M29670M
M29650M	M29654M	M29658M	M29662M	M29667M	M29671M
M29651M	M29655M	M29659M	M29663M	M29668M	

DRIVING TRAILER SECOND

Body: 58′ 1″ × 8′ 11″ & 9′ 3″   **Weight:** 31 tons   **Seats: 2nd,** 108

M29231M	M29235M	M29239M	M29243M	M29247M	M29250M
M29232M	M29236M	M29240M	M29244M	M29248M	M29251M
M29233M	M29237M	M29241M	M29245M	M29249M	M29252M
M29234M	M29238M	M29242M	M29246M		

[G. M. Kichenside

Motor brake second No. M28577M leading two Manchester–Altrincham three-car sets

Lancaster-Morecambe-Heysham
Three-Car Open Sets

MOTOR OPEN BRAKE SECOND

Body: 57′ 0″ × 8′ 11″ & 9′ 6″   **Weight:** 57 tons   **Seats: 2nd,** 28 (38*)

Equipment: Four 215 h.p. English Electric traction motors. (*Four 215 h.p. Metropolitan-Vickers traction motors)

M28219M   M28220M   M28221M   M28222M*

TRAILER OPEN SECOND

Body: 57′ 0″ × 8′ 11″ & 9′ 6″   **Weight:** 26 tons   **Seats: 2nd,** 62

M29721M   M29722M   M29723M   M29724M

DRIVING TRAILER OPEN SECOND

Body: 57′ 0″ × 8′ 11″ & 9′ 6″   **Weight:**   **Seats: 2nd,** 56

M29021M   M29022M   M29023M   M29024M

Manchester-Glossop-Hadfield
Three-car Open Sets

MOTOR OPEN BRAKE SECOND

Body: 60′ 4½″ × 9′ 0″ & 9′ 3″   **Weight:** 50 tons 12 cwt   **Seats: 2nd,** 52

Equipment: Four 185 h.p. G.E.C. traction motors

M59401   M59403   M59405   M59406   M59407   M59408
M59402   M59404

TRAILER OPEN SECOND

Body: 55′ 0½″ × 9′ 0″ & 9′ 3″   **Weight:** 26 tons 8 cwt   **Seats: 2nd,**

M59501   M59503   M59505   M59506   M59507   M59508
M59502   M59504

DRIVING TRAILER OPEN SECOND

Body: 55′ 4½″ × 9′ 0″ & 9′ 3″   **Weight:** 27 tons 9 cwt   **Seats: 2nd,** 60

M59601   M59603   M59605   M59606   M59607   M59608
M59602   M59604

Lancaster–Morecambe–Heysham three-car open set [*British Railways*

Three-car Manchester–Glossop–Hadfield set with motor open brake second No. M59408 leading [*G. M. Kichenside*

Western Lines Four-Car Units

Manchester, Liverpool, Crewe and Stafford (some units are temporarily running on G.E. line services from Liverpool Street)

B.R. Standard design

DRIVING TRAILER OPEN BRAKE SECOND

Body: 64′ 0⅞″ × 9′ 0″ & 9′ 3″   **Weight:** 31 tons 8 cwt   **Seats: 2nd,** 82

TRAILER COMPOSITE (L)

Body: 63′ 6⅛″ × 9′ 0″ & 9′ 3″   **Weight:** 31 tons 5 cwt

Seats: 1st, 19; **2nd,** 60

NON-DRIVING MOTOR BRAKE SECOND (OPEN*)

Body: 63′ 6⅛″ × 9′ 0″ & 9′ 3″ **Weight:** 53 tons 12 cwt   **Seats: 2nd,** 96 (72*)

Equipment: Four A.E.I. 207 h.p. axle-hung nose-suspended d.c. traction motors

DRIVING TRAILER OPEN SECOND (L)

Body: 64′ 0⅞″ × 9′ 0″ & 9′ 3″   **Weight:** 35 tons 12 cwt   **Seats: 2nd,** 80

UNIT Nos.

001	007	013	019*	025*	031*	036*	041*
002	008	014	020*	026*	032*	037*	042*
003	009	015	021*	027*	033*	038*	043*
004	010	016*	022*	028*	034*	039*	044*
005	011	017*	023*	029*	035*	040*	045*
006	012	018*	024*	030*			

Eastern Region

(All Eastern Region 25 kV. multiple-units are interchangeable, and may be used on all G.E. and L.T. & S. a.c. electric lines.)

Liverpool St.-Shenfield
Three-Car Open Units

These units were converted for working on 25,000 volts a.c. from 1,500 volts d.c. The centre trailers were altered to include the guard's compartment and pantograph, and part of the passenger saloon thus displaced transferred to the existing motor coach. The centre trailer now carries the transformer and rectifier to feed the existing d.c. control equipment and traction motors on the original motor coach.

Top: L.M.R. Western Lines four-car unit No. 024 with driving trailer open second leading
[M. Mensing

Centre: Driving trailer open brake second of L.M.R. Western Lines unit No. 028
[B. A. Haresnape

Left: E.R. Liverpool Street–Shenfield three-car unit No. 001
[P. J. Sharpe

MOTOR OPEN SECOND

Body: 60′ 4½″ × 9′ 0″ & 9′ 6″   **Weight:** 50 tons 17 cwt   **Seats: 2nd, 62**

Equipment: Four 157 h.p. nose-suspended d.c. traction motors

TRAILER OPEN BRAKE SECOND
(with transformer and rectifier)

Body: 55′ 0½″ × 9′ 0″ & 9′ 6″   **Weight:** 26 tons   **Seats: 2nd, 46**

DRIVING TRAILER OPEN SECOND

Body: 55′ 4″ × 9′ 0″ & 9′ 6″   **Weight:** 27 tons 10 cwt   **Seats: 2nd, 60**

UNIT Nos.

001	013	025	037	049	060	071	082
002	014	026	038	050	061	072	083
003	015	027	039	051	062	073	084
004	016	028	040	052	063	074	085
005	017	029	041	053	064	075	086
006	018	030	042	054	065	076	087
007	019	031	043	055	066	077	088
008	020	032	044	056	067	078	089
009	021	033	045	057	068	079	090
010	022	034	046	058	069	080	091
011	023	035	047	059	070	081	092
012	024	036	048				

G.E. Outer Suburban Four-Car Units

These units have been converted for working on 25,000 volts a.c. from 1,500 volts d.c. A new pantograph, transformer and rectifier mounted on one of the original driving trailers feeds the existing d.c. control and traction equipment on the motor coach. The original guard's compartment has been rebuilt in the driving trailer now carrying the pantograph and the compartments thus displaced transferred to the motor coach.

B.R. Standard design

DRIVING TRAILER BRAKE SECOND
(with transformer and rectifier)

Body: 63′ 11½″ × 9′ 0″ & 9′ 3″   **Weight:**   **Seats: 2nd, 84**

NON-DRIVING MOTOR SECOND

Body: 63′ 6″ × 9′ 0″ & 9′ 3″   **Weight:**   **Seats: 2nd, 120**

Equipment: Four G.E.C. 174 h.p. axle-hung nose-suspended d.c traction motors

TRAILER COMPOSITE (L)

Body: 63′ 6″ × 9′ 0″ & 9′ 3″   **Weight:** 30 tons   **Seats: 1st, 19; 2nd, 60**

DRIVING TRAILER OPEN SECOND (L)

Body: 63′ 11½″ × 9′ 0″ & 9′ 3″   **Weight:**   **Seats: 2nd, 80**

101	105	109	113	117	121	125	129
102	106	110	114	118	122	126	130
103	107	111	115	119	123	127	131
104	108	112	116	120	124	128	132

G.E. Outer Suburban Four-Car Units

B.R. Standard design

DRIVING TRAILER SECOND

Body: 64′ 0½″ × 9′ 0″ & 9′ 3″   **Weight:** 32 tons   **Seats: 2nd,** 108

TRAILER COMPOSITE (L)

Body: 63′ 6″ × 9′ 0″ & 9′ 3″   **Weight:** 31 tons   **Seats: 1st,** 19; **2nd,** 60

NON-DRIVING MOTOR BRAKE SECOND

Body: 63′ 6″ × 9′ 0″ & 9′ 3″   **Weight:** 54 tons   **Seats: 2nd,** 96

Equipment: Four English Electric 200 h.p. axle-hung nose-suspended d.c. traction motors

DRIVING TRAILER OPEN SECOND (L)

Body: 64′ 0½″ × 9′ 0″ & 9′ 3″   **Weight:** 36 tons   **Seats: 2nd,** 80

UNIT Nos.

133	138	142	146	150	154	158	162
134	139	143	147	151	155	159	163
135	140	144	148	152	156	160	164
136	141	145	149	153	157	161	165
137							

Fenchurch St.-Shoeburyness Four-Car Units

B.R. Standard design

DRIVING TRAILER SECOND

Body: 63′ 11½″ × 9′ 0″ & 9′ 3″   **Weight:** 32 tons   **Seats: 2nd,** 108

TRAILER COMPOSITE (L)

Body: 63′ 6″ × 9′ 0″ & 9′ 3″   **Weight:** 31 tons   **Seats: 1st,** 19; **2nd,** 60

NON-DRIVING MOTOR BRAKE SECOND

Body: 63′ 6″ × 9′ 0″ & 9′ 3″   **Weight:** 56 tons 10 cwt   **Seats: 2nd,** 96
Equipment: Four 192 h.p. English Electric nose-suspended traction motors

Trailer open brake second of E.R. Liverpool Street–Shenfield unit No. 025

[P. J. Sharpe

E.R. Great Eastern outer suburban four-car unit No. 108 *[P. J. Sharpe*

Trailer composite of E.R. Great Eastern outer suburban unit No. 109 *[P. J. Sharpe*

E.R. Great Eastern outer suburban four-car unit No. 149   *[P. J. Sharpe*

E.R. Fenchurch Street–Shoeburyness four-car unit No. 292   *[G. M. Kichenside*

Driving trailer open second of E.R. Liverpool Street–Enfield and Chingford three-car unit No. 422   *[R. K. Evans*

DRIVING TRAILER OPEN SECOND (L)

Body: 63′ 11½″ × 9′ 0″ & 9′ 3″   **Weight:** 36 tons   **Seats:** 2nd, 80

UNIT Nos.

201	215	229	243	257	271	285	299
202	216	230	244	258	272	286	300
203	217	231	245	259	273	287	301
204	218	232	246	260	274	288	302
205	219	233	247	261	275	289	303
206	220	234	248	262	276	290	304
207	221	235	249	263	277	291	305
208	222	236	250	264	278	292	306
209	223	237	251	265	279	293	307
210	224	238	252	266	280	294	308
211	225	239	253	267	281	295	309
212	226	240	254	268	282	296	310
213	227	241	255	269	283	297	311
214	228	242	256	270	284	298	312

Fenchurch St.-Shoeburyness
Four-Car Units

B.R. Standard design

DRIVING TRAILER SECOND

Body: 63′ 11½″ × 9′ 0″ & 9′ 3″   **Weight:** 32 tons   **Seats:** 2nd, 108

TRAILER COMPOSITE (L)

Body: 63′ 6″ × 9′ 0″ & 9′ 3″   **Weight:** 31 tons   **Seats:** 1st, 19; **2nd, 60**

NON-DRIVING MOTOR LUGGAGE VAN

Body: 63′ 6″ × 9′ 0″ & 9′ 3″   **Weight:** 51 tons 12 cwt

Equipment: Four 192 h.p. English Electric nose-suspended traction motors

DRIVING TRAILER OPEN
SECOND (L)

Body: 63′ 11½″ × 9′ 0″ & 9′ 3″   **Weight:** 36 tons   **Seats:** 2nd, 80

UNIT Nos.

313	315	316	317	318	319	320	321
314							

Liverpool St.-Enfield and Chingford
Three-Car Units

B.R. Standard design

DRIVING TRAILER OPEN SECOND

Body: 63′ 11½″ × 9′ 0″ & 9′ 3″   **Weight:**   **Seats: 2nd,** 94

NON-DRIVING MOTOR OPEN BRAKE SECOND

Body: 63′ 6″ × 9′ 0″ & 9′ 3″   **Weight:**   **Seats: 2nd,** 84
Equipment: Four G.E.C. 200 h.p. axle-hung nose-suspended d.c. traction motors

DRIVING TRAILER OPEN SECOND

Body: 63′ 11½″ × 9′ 0″ & 9′ 3″   **Weight:**   **Seats: 2nd,** 94

UNIT Nos.

401	408	415	422	429	436	443	450
402	409	416	423	430	437	444	451
403	410	417	424	431	438	445	452
404	411	418	425	432	439	446	453
405	412	419	426	433	440	447	454
406	413	420	427	434	441	448	455
407	414	421	428	435	442	449	

G.E. Outer Suburban Four-Car Units

B.R. Standard design

DRIVING TRAILER SECOND

Body: 64′ 0½″ × 9′ 0″ & 9′ 3″   **Weight:** 32 tons   **Seats: 2nd,** 108

TRAILER COMPOSITE (L)

Body: 63′ 6″ × 9′ 0″ & 9′ 3″   **Weight:** 31 tons   **Seats: 1st,** 19; **2nd,** 60

NON-DRIVING MOTOR BRAKE SECOND

Body: 63′ 6″ × 9′ 0″ & 9′ 3″   **Weight:** 54 tons   **Seats: 2nd,** 96
Equipment: Four G.E.C. 200 h.p. axle-hung nose-suspended d.c. traction motors

DRIVING TRAILER OPEN SECOND (L)

Body: 64′ 0½″ × 9′ 0″ & 9′3″   **Weight:** 36 tons   **Seats: 2nd,** 80

501	504	507	510	512	514	516	518
502	505	508	511	513	615	517	519
503	506	509

Liverpool St.-Clacton and Walton
Two-Car Units

B.R. Standard design

Gangwayed throughout

MOTOR BRAKE SECOND (L)
Body: 64′ 9¾″ × 9′ 0″ & 9′ 3″   **Weight:** 59 tons 6 cwt   **Seats, 2nd,** 48
Equipment: Four 282 h.p G.E.C. traction motors

DRIVING TRAILER OPEN SECOND (L)
Body: 64′ 9¾″ × 9′ 0″ & 9′ 3″   **Weight:** 39 tons 11 cwt   **Seats: 2nd,** 60

UNIT Nos.

| 601 | 602 | 603 | 604 | 605 | 606 | 607 | 608 |

Liverpool St.-Clacton and Walton
Four-Car Buffet Units

B.R. Standard design

Gangwayed throughout

DRIVING TRAILER SEMI-OPEN
COMPOSITE (L)
Body: 64′ 9¾″ × 9′ 0″ & 9′ 3″ **Weight:** 39 tons 7 cwt **Seats: 1st,** 18: **2nd,** 32

NON-DRIVING MOTOR BRAKE
SECOND (L)
Body: 64′ 6″ × 9′ 0″ & 9′ 3″   **Weight:** 56 tons 16 cwt **Seats: 2nd,** 48
Equipment: Four 282 h.p. G.E.C. traction motors

TRAILER GRIDDLE/BUFFET CAR
Body: 64′ 6″ × 9′ 0″ & 9′ 3″ **Weight:** 35 tons 16 cwt   **Seats: Buffet,** 32

DRIVING TRAILER OPEN
COMPOSITE (L)
Body: 64′ 9¾″ × 9′ 0″ & 9′ 3″ **Weight:** 36 tons 1 cwt **Seats: 1st,** 18; **2nd,** 32

UNIT Nos.

| 611 | 612 | 613 | 614 | 615 | 616 | 617 | 618 |

Liverpool St.-Clacton and Walton
Four-Car Units

B.R. Standard design
Gangwayed throughout

DRIVING TRAILER SEMI-OPEN COMPOSITE (L)

Body: 64′ 9¾″ × 9′ 0″ & 9′ 3″ **Weight:** 39 tons 7 cwt **Seats: 1st,** 18; **2nd,** 32

NON-DRIVING MOTOR BRAKE SECOND (L)

Body: 64′ 6″ × 9′ 0″ & 9′ 3″ **Weight:** 56 tons 16 cwt **Seats: 2nd,** 48
Equipment: Four 282 h.p. G.E.C. traction motors

TRAILER OPEN SECOND (L)

Body: 64′ 6″ × 9′ 0″ & 9′ 3″ **Weight:** 34 tons 8 cwt **Seats: 2nd,** 64

DRIVING TRAILER SEMI-OPEN COMPOSITE (L)

Body: 64′ 9¾″ × 9′ 0″ & 9′ 3″ **Weight:** 36 tons 15 cwt **Seats: 1st,** 18; **2nd,** 32

UNIT Nos.

621	622	623	624	625	626	627

North Eastern Region

SYSTEM: 600 VOLTS D.C. 3rd RAIL

North Tyneside Articulated Twin Units
MOTOR OPEN BRAKE SECOND

Body: 55′ 0″ × 9′ 0½″ & 9′ 3″ **Combined weight with trailer:** 54 tons 19 cwt
Seats: 2nd, 52
Equipment: Two 154 h.p. Crompton Parkinson traction motors

DRIVING TRAILER OPEN SECOND

Body: 55′ 0″ × 9′ 0½″ & 9′ 3″ **Seats: 2nd,** 76

Motor Coaches			*Driving Trailers*		
E29101E	E29105E	E29109E	E29301E	E29305E	E29309E
E29102E	E29106E	E29110E	E29302E	E29306E	E29310E
E29103E	E29107E	E29111E	E29303E	E39207E	E29311E
E29104E	E29108E		E29304E	E29308E	

MOTOR OPEN BRAKE SECOND

Body: 55′ 0″ × 9′ 0½″ & 9′ 3″ **Combined weight with trailer:** 55 tons 7 cwt

Seats: 2nd, 52

Equipment: Two 154 h.p. Crompton Parkinson traction motors

DRIVING TRAILER OPEN SECOND

Body: 55′ 0″ × 9′ 0½″ & 9′ 3″   **Seats: 2nd,** 60

Motor Coaches			Driving Trailers		
E29113E	E29119E	E29124E	E29313E	E29319E	E29324E
E29114E	E29120E	E29125E	E29314E	E29320E	E29325E
E29115E	E29121E	E29126E	E29315E	E29321E	E29326E
E29116E	E29122E	E29127E	E29316E	E29322E	E29327E
E29117E	E29123E	E29128E	E29317E	E29323E	E29328E
E29118E			E29318E		

MOTOR OPEN BRAKE SECOND

Body: 55′ 0″ × 9′ 0½″ & 9′ 3″ **Combined weight with trailer:** 53 tons 12 cwt

Seats: 2nd, 52

Equipment: Two 154 h.p. Crompton Parkinson traction motors

TRAILER OPEN SECOND

Body: 55′ 0″ × 9′ 0½″ & 9′ 3″   **Seats: 2nd,** 80

Motor Coaches			Trailers		
E29129E	E29135E	E29141E	E29229E	E29235E	E29241E
E29130E	E29136E	E29142E	E29230E	E29236E	E29242E
E29131E	E29137E	E29144E	E29231E	E29237E	E29244E
E29132E	E29138E	E29145E	E29232E	E29238E	E29245E
E29133E	E29139E	E29146E	E29233E	E29239E	E29246E
E29134E	E29140E		E29234E	E29240E	

MOTOR OPEN BRAKE SECOND

Body: 55′ 0″ × 9′ 0½″ & 9′ 3″ **Combined weight with trailer:** 54 tons 6 cwt

Seats: 2nd, 52

Equipment: Two 154 h.p. Crompton Parkinson traction motors

TRAILER OPEN SECOND

Body: 55′ 0″ × 9′ 0″ & 9′ 3″   **Seats: 2nd,** 64

E.R. Liverpool Street–Clacton and Walton four-car buffet unit No. 616 *[B. A. Haresnape*

North Tyneside two-car articulated unit

Scottish Region three-car suburban unit No. 028   *[P. J. Sharpe*

	Motor Coaches			Trailers	
E29147E	E29153E	E29159E	E29247E	E29253E	E29259E
E29148E	E29154E	E29160E	E29248E	E29254E	E29260E
E29149E	E29155E	E29161E	E29249E	E29255E	E29261E
E29150E	E29156E	E29162E	E29250E	E29256E	E29262E
E29151E	E29157E	E29163E	E29251E	E29257E	E29263E
E29152E	E29158E	E29164E	E29252E	E29248E	E29264E

North Tyneside Single Units

MOTOR OPEN BRAKE SECOND

Body: 59' 0" × 9' 0½" & 9' 3"   **Weight:** 47 tons 5 cwt   **Seats: 2nd, 52**

Equipment: Two 154 h.p. Crompton Parkinson traction motors

E29165E   E29166E

DRIVING TRAILER OPEN SECOND

Body: 56' 6" × 9' 0¾" & 9' 3"   **Weight:** 26 tons 10 cwt   **Seats: 2nd, 68**

E29376E   E29387E   E29388E   E29390E

MOTOR PARCELS VAN

Body: 59' 0" × 9' 0½" & 9' 3"   **Weight:** 38 tons 15 cwt

Equipment: Four 154 h.p. Crompton Parkinson traction motors

E29467E   E29468E

Scottish Region

SYSTEM: 25 kV. A.C. 50 CYCLES OVERHEAD

Glasgow Suburban Three-Car Units

B.R. Standard design

DRIVING TRAILER OPEN SECOND

Body: 63' 11⅝" × 9' 3" & 9' 3"   **Weight:** 34 tons   **Seats: 2nd, 83**

NON-DRIVING MOTOR OPEN BRAKE SECOND

Body: 63' 6½" × 9' 3" & 9' 3"   **Weight:** 56 tons   **Seats: 2nd, 70**

Equipment: Four A.E.I. (MV) 207 h.p. axle-hung nose-suspended d.c. traction motors

DRIVING TRAILER OPEN SECOND

Body: 63' 11⅝" × 9' 3" & 9' 3"   **Weight:** 38 tons   **Seats: 2nd, 83**

001	013	025	037	048	059	070	081
002	014	026	038	049	060	071	082
003	015	027	039	050	061	072	083
004	016	028	040	051	062	073	084
005	017	029	041	052	063	074	085
006	018	030	042	053	064	075	086
007	019	031	043	054	065	076	087
008	020	032	044	055	066	077	088
009	021	033	045	056	067	078	089
010	022	034	046	057	068	079	090
011	023	035	047	058	069	080	091
012	024	036					

Southern Region

The numbers of Southern Electric units have been checked to March 3, 1963

SYSTEM: 750 VOLTS D.C. 3rd RAIL

Two-Car Units (2-BIL)
MOTOR BRAKE SECOND (K)
Body: 62′ 6″ × 9′ 0″ × 9′ 3″ **Weight:** 43 tons 10 cwt **Seats: 2nd,** 52 (56*
Equipment: Two 275 h.p. English Electric traction motors

DRIVING TRAILER COMPOSITE (K)
Body: 62′ 6″ × 9′ 0″ & 9′ 3″   **Weight:** 31 tons 5 cwt
Seats: 1st, 24; 2nd, 32

2001*	2022	2041	2059	2077	2096	2115	2135
2002*	2023	2042	2060	2078	2097	2116	2136
2003*	2024	2043	2061	2079	2098	2117	2137
2004*	2025	2044	2062	2080	2099	2118	2138
2005*	2026	2045	2063	2081	2100‡	2120	2139
2007*	2027	2046	2064	2082	2101	2121	2140
2008*	2028	2047	2065	2083	2103	2122	2141
2009*	2029	2048	2066	2084	2104	2123	2142
2010*	2030	2049	2067	2085	2105	2124	2143
2011	2031	2050	2068	2086	2106	2125	2144
2012	2032	2051	2069‡	2087	2107	2126	2145
2013	2033	2052	2070	2089	2108	2127	2146
2015	2034	2053	2071	2090	2109	2128	2147
2016	2035	2054	2072	2091	2110	2129	2148
2017	2036	2055	2073	2092	2111	2130	2149
2018	2037	2056†	2074	2093	2112	2132	2150
2019	2038	2057	2075	2094	2113	2133‡	2151
2020	2039	2058	2076	2095	2114	2134	2152
2021	2040						

‡ Unit 2056 has a BIL motor coach and a 1939-type HAL trailer.
† Units 2069, 2100 and 2133 have BIL motor coaches and post-war all-steel
   HAL trailers.

Southern Region 2-BIL unit No. 2010 [P. J. Sharpe

Southern Region 2-BIL unit No. 2121 [J. Scrace

Southern Region 2-HAL unit No. 2608 [Alan Williams

Two-Car Units (2-HAL) 1939-type

MOTOR BRAKE SECOND

Body: 62′ 6″ × 9′ 0″ & 9′ 3″   **Weight:** 44 tons   **Seats: 2nd,** 70

Equipment: Two 275 h.p. English Electric nose-suspended traction motors

DRIVING TRAILER COMPOSITE (K)

Body: 62′ 6″ × 9′ 0″ & 9′ 3″   **Weight:** 32 tons

Seats: 1st, 18 or 24; **2nd,** 40 or 32

2601	2613	2625	2636	2648	2659	2670	2682
2602	2614	2626	2637	2649	2660	2671	2683
2603	2615	2627	2638	2650	2661	2672	2684
2604	2616	2628	2639	2651	2662	2673	2685
2605	2617	2629	2640	2652	2663	2674	2686
2606	2618	2630	2641	2653*	2664	2675	2687
2607	2619	2631	2642	2654	2665	2676	2688
2608	2620	2632	2643	2655	2666	2677	2689
2609	2621	2633	2644	2656	2667	2678	2690
2610	2622	2634	2645	2657	2668	2679	2691
2611	2623	2635	2647	2658	2669	2681	2692
2612	2624						

* Unit 2653 has a post-war all-steel HAL trailer

Two-Car Units (2-HAL) Post-war all-steel type

MOTOR BRAKE SECOND

Body: 62′ 6″ × 9′ 0″ & 9′ 3″   **Weight:** 42 tons   **Seats: 2nd,** 84

Equipment: Two 275 h.p. English Electric nose-suspended traction motors

DRIVING TRAILER COMPOSITE (K)

Body: 62′ 6″ × 9′ 0″ & 9′ 3″   **Weight:** 31 tons   **Seats: 1st,** 18; **2nd,** 40

2693	2694	2695	2696	2697	2698	2699

Two-Car Unit (2-HAL) Post-war all-steel type

MOTOR BRAKE SALOON SECOND

Body: 62′ 6″ × 9′ 0″ & 9′ 3″   **Weight:** 39 tons   **Seats: 2nd,** 82

Equipment: Two 275 h.p. English Electric nose-suspended traction motors

DRIVING TRAILER COMPOSITE (K)

Body: 62′ 6″ × 9′ 0″ & 9′ 3″   **Weight:** 31 tons   **Seats: 1st,** 24; **2nd,** 32

2700

Driving trailer composite of Southern Region 2-HAL unit No. 2639   [*Alan Williams*

Motor brake second of Southern Region 4-LAV unit No. 2927   [*P. J. Sharpe*

Trailer composite of Southern Region 4-LAV unit No. 2953   [*P. J. Sharpe*

Southern Region 6-PUL unit No. 3011 near Merstham on a Victoria–Ore working

[J. Scrace]

Four-Car Units (4-LAV)

MOTOR BRAKE SECOND

Body: 62′ 6″ × 9′ 0″ & 9′ 3″ **Weight:** 41 tons (*†44 tons) **Seats:** 2nd, 70
Equipment: Two 275 h.p. Metropolitan-Vickers traction motors. (*†Two 275 h.p. English Electric traction motors)

TRAILER COMPOSITE

Body: 62′ 0″ × 9′ 0″ & 9′ 3″   **Weight:** 28 tons
Seats: 1st, 16; 2nd, 70   *29 tons

TRAILER COMPOSITE (K) (†SECOND)

Body: 62′ 0″ × 9′ 0″ & 9′ 3″   **Weight:** 29 tons
Seats: 1st, 30; 2nd, 24   *30 tons
         †2nd, 120   †26 tons

MOTOR BRAKE SECOND

(As above)

2921	2926†	2931	2936	2940	2944	2948	2952
2922	2927	2932	2937	2941	2945	2949	2953
2923	2928	2933	2938	2942	2946	2950	2954*
2924	2929	2934	2939	2943	2947	2951	2955*
2925	2930	2935					

* 1939 Bulleid units.
† Unit 2926 has one 1939-type HAL motor coach and one all-steel SUB trailer compartment second.

Six-Car Units (6-PUL)

Gangwayed within set

MOTOR SALOON BRAKE SECOND

Body: 63′ 6″ × 9′ 0″ & 9′ 5″   **Weight:** 59 tons   **Seats:** 2nd, 52
Equipment: Four 225 h.p. B.T.H. traction motors

TRAILER SECOND (K)

Body: 63′ 6″ × 9′ 0″ & 9′ 3″   **Weight:** 35 tons   **Seats:** 2nd, 68

TRAILER COMPOSITE (K)

Body: 63′ 6″ × 9′ 0″ & 9′ 3″   **Weight:** 35 tons   **Seats:** 1st, 30; 2nd, 24

TRAILER COMPOSITE PULLMAN (L)

Body: 66′ 0″ × 8′ 11½″ & 8′ 11½″   **Weight:** 43 tons   **Seats:** 1st, 12; 2nd, 16

TRAILER COMPOSITE (K)

(As above)

MOTOR SALOON BRAKE SECOND

(As above)

3001	3005	3007	3009	3011	3013	3016
3002	3006	3008	3010	3012	3015	3019
3003*

* Unit 3003 has one PAN motor coach.

Six-Car Units (6-PAN)

Gangwayed within set

MOTOR SALOON BRAKE SECOND

Body: 63′ 6″ × 9′ 0″ & 9′ 5″ **Weight:** 59 tons **Seats: 2nd, 52**
Equipment: Four 225 h.p. English Electric traction motors

TRAILER SECOND (K)

Body: 63′ 6″ × 9′ 0″ & 9′ 3″ **Weight:** 31 tons 10 cwt **Seats: 2nd, 68**

TRAILER FIRST (K)

Body: 59′ 0″ × 9′ 0″ & 9′ 3″ **Weight:** 31 tons **Seats: 1st, 42**

TRAILER PANTRY FIRST (K)

Body: 63′ 6″ × 9′ 0″ & 9′ 3″ **Weight:** 32 tons **Seats: 1st, 30**

TRAILER SECOND (K)

(As above)

MOTOR SALOON BRAKE SECOND

(As above)

3021	3023	3025	3028	3030	3035	3036	3037
3022	3024	3026†	3029	3034

† Unit 3026 has one PUL motor coach.

Six-Car Units (6-PUL)

Gangwayed within set

MOTOR SALOON BRAKE SECOND

Body: 63′ 6″ × 9′ 0″ & 9′ 5″ **Weight:** 57 tons (59 tons*) **Seats: 2nd, 56 (52*)**
Equipment: Four 225 h.p. B.T.H. traction motors

TRAILER SECOND (K)

Body: 59′ 0″ × 9′ 0″ & 9′ 3″ **Weight:** 34 tons **Seats: 2nd, 56**

Southern Region 6-PAN unit No. 3033 *[P. J. Sharpe*

Southern Region 5-BEL unit No. 3051 *[J. Scrace*

Southern Region 4-BUF unit No. 3083 *[J. Scrace*

TRAILER COMPOSITE (K)

Body: 59′ 0″ × 9′ 0″ & 9′ 3″   **Weight:** 34 tons   **Seats:** 1st, 30; 2nd, 16

TRAILER COMPOSITE PULLMAN (L)

Body: 66′ 0″ × 8′ 11½″ & 8′ 11½″   **Weight:** 43 tons   **Seats:** 1st, 12; 2nd, 16

TRAILER COMPOSITE (K)

(As Above)

MOTOR SALOON BRAKE SECOND

Body: 63′ 6″ × 9′ 0″ & 9′ 5″   **Weight:** 59 tons   **Seats:** 2nd, 52
Equipment: Four 225 h.p. B.T.H. traction motors

  3041   3042   3043*

Five-Car Pullman Units (5-BEL)

All-Pullman: Gangwayed within set

MOTOR BRAKE SECOND PULLMAN (L)

Body: 66′ 0″ × 8′ 11½″ & 8′ 11½″   **Weight:** 62 tons   **Seats:** 2nd, 48
Equipment: Four 225 h.p. B.T.H. traction motors

TRAILER SECOND PULLMAN (L)

Body: 66′ 0″ × 8′ 11½″ & 8′ 11½″   **Weight:** 39 tons   **Seats:** 2nd, 56

TRAILER KITCHEN FIRST PULLMAN (L)

Body: 66′ 0″ × 8′ 11½″ & 8′ 11½″   **Weight:** 43 tons   **Seats:** 1st, 20

TRAILER KITCHEN FIRST PULLMAN (L)

(As Above)

MOTOR BRAKE SECOND PULLMAN (L)

(As Above)

  3051   3052   3053

Four-Car Units (4-PUL)
Gangwayed throughout

MOTOR SALOON BRAKE SECOND

Body: 63′ 6″ × 9′ 0″ & 9′ 4½″   **Weight:** 46 tons 10 cwt   **Seats: 2nd,** 52

Equipment: Two 225 h.p. English Electric traction motors

TRAILER FIRST (K)

Body: 63′ 6″ × 9′ 0″ & 9′ 3″   **Weight:** 33 tons

Seats: 1st, 30; **1st Dining.** 12

TRAILER COMPOSITE PULLMAN (L)

Body: 66′ 0″ × 8′ 11½″ & 8′ 11½″   **Weight:** 43 tons   **Seats: 1st,** 12; **2nd,** 16

MOTOR SALOON BRAKE SECOND
(As Above)

3054   3055   3056   3057   3059

Four-Car Units (4-COR N)
Gangwayed throughout

MOTOR SALOON BRAKE SECOND

Body: 63′ 6″ × 9′ 0″ & 9″ 4½″   **Weight:** 46 tons 10 cwt   **Seats: 2nd,** 52

Equipment: Two 225 h.p. English Electric traction motors

TRAILER SECOND (K)

Body: 63′ 6″ × 9′ 0″ & 9′ 3″   **Weight:** 31 tons 10 cwt   **Seats: 2nd,** 68

TRAILER FIRST (K)

Body: 63′ 6″ × 9′ 0″ & 9′ 3″   **Weight:** 33 tons   **Seats: 1st,** 42

MOTOR SALOON BRAKE SECOND
(As Above)

3065   3066   3067   3068   3069   3070   3071

Four-Car Units (4-BUF)

Gangwayed throughout

MOTOR SALOON BRAKE SECOND
Body: 63′ 6″ × 9′ 0″ & 9′ 4½″   **Weight:** 46 tons 10 cwt   **Seats: 2nd,** 52
Equipment: Two 225 h.p. English Electric traction motors

TRAILER COMPOSITE (K)
Body: 63′ 6″ × 9′ 0″ & 9′ 3″   **Weight:** 32 tons 12 cwt
Seats: 1st, 30; **2nd,** 24

TRAILER BUFFET (L)
Body: 63′ 6″ × 9′ 0″ & 9′ 3″   **Weight:** 37 tons   **Seats: Buffet,** 26
                                    *35 tons   *36

MOTOR SALOON BRAKE SECOND
(As Above)

3072*	3074	3076	3078	3081	3083	3084	3085
3073	3075	3077	3080	3082			

Four-Car Units (4-GRI)

Gangwayed throughout

MOTOR SALOON BRAKE SECOND
Body: 63′ 6″ × 9′ 0″ & 9′ 4½″   **Weight:** 46 tons 10 cwt   **Seats: 2nd,** 52
Equipment: Two 225 h.p. English Electric traction motors

TRAILER FIRST (K)
Body: 63′ 6″ × 9′ 0″ & 9′ 3″   **Weight:** 33 tons
Seats 1st, 30 ; **1st Dining.** 12

TRAILER GRIDDLE CAR
Body: 63′ 6″ × 9′ 0″ & 9′ 4½″   **Weight:** 34 tons   **Seats:** 26

MOTOR SALOON BRAKE SECOND
(As Above)

3086   3087   3088

Four-Car Units (4-COR)

Gangwayed throughout

MOTOR SALOON BRAKE SECOND

Body: 63' 6" × 9' 0" & 9' 4½"　　**Weight:** 46 tons 10 cwt　**Seats: 2nd,** 52
　　*63' 6" × 9' 0" & 9' 5"　　　　*59 tons

Equipment: Two 225 h.p. English Electric traction motors
　　*Four 225 h.p. B.T.H. traction motors

TRAILER SECOND (K)

Body: 63' 6" × 9' 0" & 9' 3"　　　**Weight:** 32 tons 13 cwt　**Seats: 2nd,** 68

TRAILER COMPOSITE (K)

Body: 63' 6" × 9' 0" & 9' 3"　　　**Weight:** 32 tons 12 cwt
Seats: 1st, 30; **2nd,** 24

MOTOR SALOON BRAKE SECOND

(As Above)

3101	3109	3117	3124*	3131	3138	3145	3152
3102	3110	3118	3125	3132	3139	3146	3153
3103	3111	3119	3126	3133	3140	3147	3154
3104	3112	3120	3127	3134	3141	3148*	3155
3105	3113	3121	3128	3135	3142	3149	3156
3106	3114	3122	3129	3136	3143	3150	3157
3107	3115	3123	3130	3137	3144	3151	3158
3108	3116						

　* Units 3124/48 have one 6-PUL motor coach.

Four-Car Double Deck Suburban Units (4-DD)

MOTOR BRAKE SECOND

Body: 62' 6" × 9' 0" & 9' 3"　　**Weight:** 39 tons
Seats: 2nd, Lower deck 55; Upper deck 55 (*plus* 10 tip-up)
Equipment: Two 250 h.p. English Electric traction motors

TRAILER SECOND

Body: 62' 0" × 9' 0" & 9' 3"　　**Weight:** 28 tons
Seats: 2nd, Lower deck 78; Upper deck 66 (*plus* 12 tip-up)

TRAILER SECOND

(As Above)

MOTOR BRAKE SECOND

(As above)

　4001　　4002

Trailer Griddle Car of Southern Region 4-GRI unit No. 3088   [*Alan Williams*

Southern Region 4-SUB unit No. 4101   [*Alan Williams*

Motor brake second of Southern Region 4-SUB unit No. 4114   [*P. J. Sharpe*

Four-Car Suburban Units (4-SUB)

MOTOR BRAKE SECOND

Seats: 62′ 6″ × 9′ 0″ & 9′ 3″   **Weight:** 43 tons   **Seats: 2nd,** 102
Equipment: Two 275 h.p. English Electric traction motors

TRAILER SECOND

Body: 62′ 0″ × 9′ 0″ & 9′ 3″   **Weight:** 29 tons   **Seats: 2nd,** 132

TRAILER SECOND

Body: 62′ 0″ × 9′ 0″ & 9′ 3″   **Weight:** 29 tons   **Seats: 2nd,** 120

MOTOR BRAKE SECOND

(As Above)

4101	4103	4105	4106	4107	4108	4109	4110
4102	4104						

Four-Car Suburban Units (4-SUB)

MOTOR BRAKE SECOND

Body: 62′ 6″ × 9′ 0″ & 9′ 3″   **Weight:** 43 tons   **Seats: 2nd,** 96
Equipment: Two 275 h.p. English Electric traction motors

TRAILER SECOND

Body: 62′ 0″ × 9′ 0″ & 9′ 3″   **Weight:** 28 tons   **Seats: 2nd,** 108

TRAILER SECOND

Body: 62′ 0″ × 9′ 0″ & 9′ 3″   **Weight:** 28 tons   **Seats: 2nd,** 120

MOTOR BRAKE SECOND

(As Above)

4111	4113	4114	4115	4116	4117	4118	4119
4112							

Four-Car Suburban Unit (4-SUB)

MOTOR BRAKE SECOND

Body: 62′ 6″ × 9′ 0″ & 9′ 3″   **Weight:** 43 tons   **Seats: 2nd,** 96
Equipment: Two 275 h.p. English Electric traction motors

TRAILER SECOND

Body: 62′ 0″ × 9′ 0″ & 9′ 3″   **Weight:** 28 tons   **Seats: 2nd,** 108

TRAILER SECOND
Body: 62′ 0″ × 9′ 0″ & 9′ 3″ **Weight:** 28 tons **Seats:** 2nd, 120

MOTOR SALOON BRAKE SECOND
Body: 62′ 6″ × 9′ 0″ & 9′ 3″ **Weight:** 39 tons **Seats:** 2nd, 82
Equipment: Two 250 h.p. English Electric traction motors

4120

Four-Car Suburban Units (4-SUB)

MOTOR BRAKE SECOND (SEMI-SALOON)
Body: 62′ 6″ × 9′ 0″ & 9′ 3″ **Weight:** 43 tons **Seats:** 2nd, 84
Equipment: Two 275 h.p. English Electric traction motors

TRAILER SECOND
Body: 62′ 0″ × 9′ 0″ & 9′ 3″ **Weight:** 28 tons **Seats:** 2nd, 108

TRAILER SECOND (SEMI-SALOON)
Body: 62′ 0″ × 9′ 0″ & 9′ 3″ **Weight:** 28 tons **Seats:** 2nd, 106

MOTOR BRAKE SECOND (SEMI-SALOON)
(As Above)

4121	4123	4125	4126	4127	4128	4129	4130
4122	4124						

Four-Car Suburban Units (4-SUB)

MOTOR SALOON BRAKE SECOND
Body: 62′ 6″ × 9′ 0″ & 9′ 3″ **Weight:** 39 tons **Seats:** 2nd, 82
Equipment: Two 250 h.p. English Electric traction motors

TRAILER SECOND
Body: 62′ 0″ × 9′ 0″ & 9′ 3″ **Weight:** 28 tons **Seats:** 2nd, 120

TRAILER SALOON SECOND
Body: 62′ 0″ × 9′ 0″ & 9′ 3″ **Weight:** 28 tons **Seats:** 2nd, 102

MOTOR SALOON BRAKE SECOND
(As Above)

4277	4280	4283	4286	4289	4292	4295	4298
4278	4281	4284	4287	4290	4293	4296	4299
4279	4282	4285	4288	4291	4294	4297	

Four-Car Suburban Units (4-SUB)

MOTOR BRAKE SECOND

Body: 62′ 6″ × 9′ 0″ & 9′ 3″   **Weight:** 43 tons   **Seats: 2nd, 96**

Equipment: Two 275 English Electric traction motors

TRAILER SECOND

Body: 62′ 0″ × 9′ 0″ & 9′ 3″   **Weight:** 28 tons   **Seats: 2nd, 120**

TRAILER SECOND

(As Above)

MOTOR BRAKE SECOND

As Above)

4355	4357	4358	4359	4360	4361	4362	4363
4356							

Four-Car Suburban Units (4-SUB)

MOTOR BRAKE SECOND

Body: 62′ 6″ × 9′ 0″ & 9′ 3″   **Weight:** 43 tons   **Seats: 2nd, 96**

Equipment: Two 275 h.p. English Electric traction motors

TRAILER SECOND

Body: 62′ 0″ × 9′ 0″ & 9′ 3″   **Weight:** 28 tons   **Seats: 2nd, 108**

TRAILER SECOND

Body: 62′ 0″ × 9′ 0″ & 9′ 3″   **Weight:** 28 tons   **Seats: 2nd, 120**

MOTOR BRAKE SECOND

(As Above)

4364	4366	4368	4370	4372	4374	4375	4376
4365	4367	4369	4371	4373			

Four-Car Suburban Unit (4-SUB)

MOTOR BRAKE SECOND

Body: 62′ 6″ × 9′ 0″ & 9′ 3″   **Weight:**   **Seats: 2nd, 96**

Equipment: Two 275 h.p. English Electric traction motors

TRAILER SECOND

Body: 62′ 0″ × 9′ 0″ & 9′ 3″   **Weight:** 28 tons   **Seats: 2nd, 108**

TRAILER SALOON SECOND

Body: 62′ 0″ × 9′ 0″ & 9′ 3″   **Weight:** 28 tons   **Seats: 2nd, 102**

MOTOR BRAKE SECOND

(As Above)
  4377

Four-Car Suburban Units (4-SUB)
MOTOR SALOON BRAKE SECOND
Body: 62′ 6″ × 9′ 0″ & 9′ 3″   **Weight:** 42 tons   **Seats:** 2nd, 82
Equipment: Two 275 h.p. English Electric traction motors

TRAILER SECOND
Body: 62′ 0″ × 9′ 0″ & 9′ 3″   **Weight:** 28 tons   **Seats:** 2nd, 120

TRAILER SALOON SECOND
Body: 62′ 0″ × 9′ 0″ & 9′ 3″   **Weight:** 28 tons   **Seats:** 2nd, 102

MOTOR SALOON BRAKE SECOND
(As Above)
  4378   4380   4382   4383   4384   4385   4386   4387
  4379   4381

Four-Car Suburban Units (4-SUB)
MOTOR SALOON BRAKE SECOND
Body: 62′ 6″ × 9′ 0″ & 9′ 3″   **Weight:** 39 tons   **Seats:** 2nd, 82
Equipment: Two 250 h.p. English Electric traction motors

TRAILER SECOND
Body: 62′ 0″ × 9′ 0″ & 9′ 3″   **Weight:** 28 tons   **Seats:** 2nd, 120

TRAILER SECOND
(As Above)

MOTOR SALOON BRAKE SECOND
(As Above)
  4601   4602   4603   4604   4605   4606   4607

Four-Car Suburban Units (4-SUB)
MOTOR SALOON BRAKE SECOND
Body: 62′ 6″ × 9′ 0″ & 9′ 3″   **Weight:** 39 tons   **Seats:** 2nd, 82
Equipment: Two 250 h.p. English Electric traction motors

TRAILER SECOND

Body: 62′ 0″ × 9′ 0″ & 9′ 3″   **Weight:** 28 tons (27 tons*)
Seats: 2nd, 120 (108*)

TRAILER SALOON SECOND

Body: 62′ 0″ × 9′ 0″ & 9′ 3″   **Weight:** 26 tons (28 tons)   **Seats:** 2nd, 102

MOTOR SALOON BRAKE SECOND

(As Above)

4621	4638	4656	4673	4690	4707	4723*	4739*
4622	4639	4657	4674	4691	4708	4724	4740
4623	4640	4658	4675	4692	4709	4725	4741
4624	4641	4659	4676	4693	4710	4726	4742
4625	4642	4660	4677	4694	4711	4727	4743
4626	4643	4661	4678	4695	4712	4728*	4744
4627	4644	4662	4679	4696*	4713	4729	4745
4628	4645	4663	4680	4697	4714	4730	4746
4629	4646	4664	4681	4698	4715	4731	4747
4630	4647	4665	4682	4699	4716	4732	4748
4631	4648	4666	4683	4700	4717	4733*	4749
4632	4649	4667	4684	4701	4718	4734	4750
4633	4650	4668	4685	4702	4719	4735	4751
4634	4651	4669	4686	4703	4720	4736	4752
4635	4653	4670	4687	4704	4721	4737	4753
4636	4654	4671	4688*	4705	4722	4738	4754
4637	4655	4672	4689	4706			

Four-Car Suburban Units (4-EPB)

MOTOR SALOON BRAKE SECOND

Body: 62′ 6″ × 9′ 0″ & 9′ 3″   **Weight:** 40 tons   **Seats:** 2nd, 82
Equipment: Two 250 h.p. English Electric traction motors

TRAILER SECOND

Body: 62′ 0″ × 9′ 0″ & 9′ 3″   **Weight:** 28 tons   **Seats:** 2nd, 120 (108*)

TRAILER SALOON SECOND

Body: 62′ 0″ × 9′ 0″ & 9′ 3″   **Weight:** 27 tons   **Seats:** 2nd, 102

Southern Region 4-SUB unit No. 4378   [P. J. Sharpe

Southern Region 4-SUB unit No. 4676   [P. J. Sharpe

Southern Region 4-EPB unit   [Alan Williams

MOTOR SALOON BRAKE SECOND

(As Above)

5001	5029	5103	5129	5156	5182	5209	5235
5002	5030	5104	5130	5157	5183	5210	5236
5003	5031	5105	5131	5158	5184	5211	5237
5004	5032	5106	5132	5159	5185	5212	5238
5005*	5033	5107	5133	5160	5186	5213	5239
5006	5034	5108	5134	5161	5187	5214	5240
5007	5035	5109	5135	5162	5188	5215	5241
5008	5036	5110	5136	5163	5189	5216	5242
5009	5037	5111	5137	5164	5190	5217	5243
5010	5038	5112	5138	5165	5191	5218	5244
5011	5039	5113	5139	5166	5192	5219	5245†
5012	5040	5114	5140	5167	5193	5220*	5246
5013	5041	5115	5142	5168	5194	5221	5247
5014	5042	5116	5143	5169	5195	5222	5248
5015	5043	5117	5144	5170	5196	5223	5249
5016	5044	5118	5145	5171	5197	5224	5250
5017	5045	5119	5146	5172	5198	5225	5251
5018	5046	5120	5147	5173	5199	5226	5252
5019	5047	5121	5148	5174	5200	5227	5253
5020	5048	5122	5149	5175	5201	5228	5254
5021	5049	5123	5150	5176	5202	5229	5255
5022	5050	5124	5151	5177	5203	5230	5256
5024	5051	5125	5152	5178	5205	5231	5257
5025	5052	5126	5153	5179	5206	5232	5258
5026	5053	5127	5154	5180	5207	5233	5259
5027	5101	5128	5155	5181	5208	5234	5260
5028	5102						

†Unit 5245 has two trailer compartment seconds

Four-Car Suburban Units (4-EPB)

B.R. Standard design

MOTOR SALOON BRAKE SECOND

Body: 63′ 11½″ × 9′ 0″ & 9′ 3″   **Weight:** 39 tons or 40 tons

Seats: 2nd, 82

Equipment: Two 250 h.p. English Electric traction motors

TRAILER SECOND (SEMI-COMPARTMENT)

Body: 63′ 6″ × 9′ 0″ & 9′ 3″   **Weight:** 29 tons   **Seats:** 2nd, 112

TRAILER SECOND (SEMI-COMPARTMENT)

(As Above)

MOTOR SALOON BRAKE SECOND

(As Above)

5301*	5310	5319	5328	5337	5346	5355	5363
5302*	5311	5320	5329	5338	5347	5356	5364
5303	5312	5321	5330	5339	5348	5357	5365
5304	5313	5322	5331	5340	5349	5358	5366
5305	5314	5323	5332	5341	5350	5359	5367
5306	5315	5324	5333	5342	5351	5360	5368
5307	5316	5325	5334	5343	5352	5361	5369
5308	5317	5326	5335	5344	5353	5362	5370
5309	5318	5327	5336	5345	5354		

*Both trailer seconds in units 5301/2 are S.R. type vehicles on 62′ 0″ underframes, weights as 5001-5260.

Two-Car Units (2-HAP)

MOTOR BRAKE SECOND (SEMI-SALOON)

Body: 62′ 6″ × 9′ 0″ & 9′ 3″   **Weight:** 40 tons   **Seats:** 2nd, 84

Equipment: Two 250 h.p. English Electric traction motors

DRIVING TRAILER COMPOSITE (K)

Body: 62′ 6″ × 9′ 0″ & 9′ 3″   **Weight:** 32 tons   **Seats:** 1st, 18; 2nd, 36

5601	5606	5611	5616	5621	5625	5629	5633
5602	5607	5612	5617	5622	5626	5630	5634
5603	5608	5613	5618	5623	5627	5631	5635
5604	5609	5614	5619	5624	5628	5632	5636
5605	5610	5615	5620				

Two-Car Suburban Units (2-EPB)

MOTOR BRAKE SECOND (SEMI-SALOON)

Body: 62′ 6″ × 9′ 0″ & 9′ 3″   **Weight:** 40 tons   **Seats:** 2nd, 84

Equipment: Two 250 h.p. English Electric traction motors

DRIVING TRAILER SECOND (SEMI-SALOON)

Body: 62′ 6″ × 9′ 0″ & 9′ 3″   **Weight:** 30 tons   **Seats:** 2nd, 94

5651	5656	5661	5665	5669	5673	5677	5681
5652	5657	5662	5666	5670	5674	5678	5682
5653	5658	5663	5667	5671	5675	5679	5683
5654	5659	5664	5668	5672	5676	5680	5684
5655	5660						

Southern Region B.R. standard 4-EPB unit No. 5328   *[P. J. Sharpe*

Southern Region 2-EPB unit No. 5669   *[P. J. Sharpe*

Southern Region B.R. standard 2-EPB unit No. 5779   *[J. Scrace*

Two-Car Suburban Units (2-EPB)

B.R. Standard design

MOTOR BRAKE SECOND (SEMI-SALOON)

Body: 63′ 11½″ × 9′ 0″ & 9′ 3″   **Weight:** 40 tons   **Seats:** 2nd, 84

Equipment: Two 250 h.p. English Electric traction motors

DRIVING TRAILER SECOND (SEMI-COMPARTMENT)

Body: 63′ 11½″″ × 9′ 0″ & 9′ 3″   **Weight:** 30 tons (31 tons*)   **Seats:** 2nd, 102

5701	5711	5721	5731	5741	5751	5761	5772
5702	5712	5722	5732	5742	5752	5762	5773
5703	5713	5723	5733	5743	5753	5763	5774
5704	5714	5724	5734	5744	5754	5764	5775
5705	5715	5725	5735	5745	5755	5765	5776
5706	5716	5726	5736	5746	5756	5767	5777
5707	5717	5727	5737	5747	5757	5768	5778
5708	5718	5728	5738	5748	5758	5769	5779
5709	5719	5729	5739	5749	5759	5770	
5710	5720	5730	5740	5750	5760	5771	

Two-Car Suburban Units (2-EPB)

B.R. Standard design

MOTOR OPEN BRAKE SECOND

Body: 63′ 11½″ × 9′ 0″ & 9′ 3″   **Weight:** 40 tons   **Seats:** 2nd, 74

Equipment: Two 250 h.p. English Electric traction motors

DRIVING TRAILER SECOND

Body: 63′ 11½″ × 9′ 0″ & 9′ 3″   **Weight:** 30 tons   **Seats:** 2nd,

5781	5783	5785	5787	5789	5791	5793	5795
5782	5784	5786	5788	5790	5792	5794	

Two-Car Units (2-HAP)

B.R. Standard design

MOTOR BRAKE SECOND (SEMI-SALOON)

Body: 63′ 11½″ × 9′ 0″ & 9′ 3″   **Weight:** 40 tons   **Seats:** 2nd, 84

Equipment: Two 250 h.p. English Electric traction motors

DRIVING TRAILER COMPOSITE (L)

Body: 63′ 11½″ × 9′ 0″ & 9′ 3″   **Weight:** 30 tons   **Seats:** 1st, 19; 2nd, 50

6001	6023	6045	6067	6089	6111	6132	6153
6002	6024	6046	6068	6090	6112	6133	6154
6003	6025	6047	6069	6091	6113	6134	6155
6004	6026	6048	6070	6092	6114	6135	6156
6005	6027	6049	6071	6093	6115	6136	6157
6006	6028	6050	6072	6094	6116	6137	6158
6007	6029	6051	6073	6095	6117	6138	6159
6008	6030	6052	6074	6096	6118	6139	6160
6009	6031	6053	6075	6097	6119	6140	6161
6010	6032	6054	6076	6098	6120	6141	6162
6011	6033	6055	6077	6099	6121	6142	6163
6012	6034	6056	6078	6100	6122	6143	6164
6013	6035	6057	6079	6101	6123	6144	6165
6014	6036	6058	6080	6102	6124	6145	6166
6015	6037	6059	6081	6103	6125	6146	6167
6016	6038	6060	6082	6104	6126	6147	6168
6017	6039	6061	6083	6105	6127	6148	6169
6018	6040	6062	6084	6106	6128	6149	6170
6019	6041	6063	6085	6107	6129	6150	6171
6020	6042	6064	6086	6108	6130	6151	6172
6021	6043	6065	6087	6109	6131	6152	6173
6022	6044	6066	6088	6110			

Four-Car Units (4-BEP)

B.R. Standard design

Gangwayed throughout

MOTOR SALOON BRAKE SECOND

Body: 64′ 6″ × 9′ 0″ & 9′ 3″   **Weight:** 41 tons (40 tons*)   **Seats:** 2nd, 56
Equipment: Two 250 h.p. English Electric traction motors

TRAILER COMPOSITE (K)

Body: 64′ 6″ × 9′ 0″ & 9′ 3″   **Weight:** 33 tons (31 tons*)
Seats: 1st, 24; 2nd, 24

TRAILER BUFFET

Body: 64′ 6″ × 9′ 0″ & 9′ 3″   **Weight:** 36 tons (35 tons*)   **Seats:** Buffet, 21

MOTOR SALOON BRAKE SECOND

(As Above)

7001*	7004	7007	7010	7013	7016	7019	7021
7002*	7005	7008	7011	7014	7017	7020	7022
7003	7006	7009	7012	7015	7018		

Four-Car Units (4-BIG)

B.R. Standard design
Gangwayed throughout

DRIVING TRAILER COMPOSITE (L)
Body: 64′ 6″ × 9′ 0″ & 9′ 3″ **Weight:** **Seats: 1st,** 24; **2nd,** 28

TRAILER MINIATURE BUFFET
Body: 64′ 6″ × 9′ 0″ & 9′ 3″ **Weight:** **Seats: 2nd,** 40

NON-DRIVING MOTOR BRAKE SECOND
Body: 64′ 6″ × 9′ 0″ & 9′ 3″ **Weight:** **Seats: 2nd,** 56
Equipment:

DRIVING TRAILER COMPOSITE (L)
Body: 64′ 6″ × 9′ 0″ & 9′ 8″ **Weight:** **Seats: 1st,** 18; **2nd,** 36

7031	7034	7037	7039	7041	7043	7045	7047
7032	7035	7038	7040	7042	7044	7046	7048
7033	7036						

Four-Car Units (4-CEP)

B.R. Standard design
Gangwayed throughout

MOTOR SALOON BRAKE SECOND
Body: 64′ 6″ × 9′ 0″ & 9′ 3″ **Weight:** 41 tons (40 tons*) **Seats: 2nd,** 56
Equipment: Two 250 h.p. English Electric traction motors

TRAILER COMPOSITE (K)
Body: 64′ 6″ × 9′ 0″ & 9′ 3″ **Weight:** 33 tons (31 tons*)
Seats: 1st, 24; **2nd,** 24

TRAILER SECOND (K)
Body: 64′ 6″ × 9′ 0″ & 9′ 3″ **Weight:** 32 tons (31 tons*) **Seats: 2nd,** 64

MOTOR SALOON BRAKE SECOND
(As Above)

7101*	7115	7129	7143	7157	7171	7185	7199
7102*	7116	7130	7144	7158	7172	7186	7200
7103*	7117	7131	7145	7159	7173	7187	7201
7104*	7118	7132	7146	7160	7174	7188	7202
7105	7119	7133	7147	7161	7175	7189	7203
7106	7120	7134	7148	7162	7176	7190	7204
7107	7121	7135	7149	7163	7177	7191	7205
7108	7122	7136	7150	7164	7178	7192	7206
7109	7123	7137	7151	7165	7179	7193	7207
7110	7124	7138	7152	7166	7180	7194	7208
7111	7125	7139	7153	7167	7181	7195	7209
7112	7126	7140	7154	7168	7182	7196	7210
7113	7127	7141	7155	7169	7183	7197	7211
7114	7128	7142	7156	7170	7184	7198	

Four-Car Units (4-CIG)

B.R. Standard design

Gangwayed throughout

DRIVING TRAILER COMPOSITE (L)

Body: 64′ 6″ × 9′ 0″ & 9′ 3″   **Weight:**   **Seats:** 1st, 24; 2nd, 28

TRAILER OPEN SECOND

Body: 64′ 6″ × 9′ 0″ & 9′ 3″   **Weight:**   **Seats: 2nd, 72**

NON-DRIVING MOTOR BRAKE SECOND

Body: 64′ 6″ × 9′ 0″ & 9′ 3″   **Weight:**   **Seats: 2nd, 56**
Equipment:

DRIVING TRAILER COMPOSITE (L)

Body: 64′ 6″ × 9′ 0″ & 9′ 3″   **Weight:**   **Seats: 1st,** 18; **2nd, 36**

7301	7306	7311	7316	7321	7325	7329	7333
7302	7307	7312	7317	7322	7326	7330	7334
7303	7308	7313	7318	7323	7327	7331	7335
7304	7309	7314	7319	7324	7328	7332	7336
7305	7310	7315	7320				

Single Units

MOTOR LUGGAGE VAN

Body: 64′ 6″ × 9′ 0″ & 9′ 3″   **Weight:** 45 tons
Equipment: Two 250 h.p. English Electric traction motors

Southern Region B.R. standard 2-HAP unit No. 6087   *[Alan Williams*

Southern Region B.R. standard 4-CEP unit No. 7209   *[D. L. Percival*

Southern Region two-car departmental motor de-icing unit No. 93   *[C. Symes*

Note: These vehicles can work singly, hauling a limited load, or in multiple with EP-type stock. They are equipped with traction batteries for working on non-electrified quay lines at Dover and Folkestone

COACH Nos.

S68001	S68003	S68005	S68007	S68009	S68010
S68002	S68004	S68006	S68008		

Waterloo & City One- or Five-Car Units

(Tube size vehicles with air-operated sliding doors. Trains are formed of a single motor car or up to five-car units comprising two motor cars and three trailers)

MOTOR SALOON BRAKE SECOND

Body: 47′ 0″ × 8′ 7¾″   **Weight:**   **Seats: 2nd, 40**

Equipment: Two 190 h.p. English Electric traction motors

51	53	55	57	59	61
52	54	56	58	60	62

TRAILER SALOON SECOND

Body: 47′ 0″ × 8′ 7¾″   **Weight:** 18 tons 14 cwt   **Seats: 2nd, 52**

71	74	77	80	83	85
72	75	78	81	84	86
73	76	79	82		

Two-Car Departmental Motor De-Icing Units

Gangwayed within set

(Formed of the motor coaches from withdrawn Eastern Section 1925 4-SUB units; fitted with conductor rail scraping and spraying equipment)

MOTOR BRAKE

Body: 62′ 6″ × 8′ 6″ & 9′ 0″   **Weight:**

Equipment: Two 275 h.p. English Electric traction motors

MOTOR BRAKE

(As Above)

92	94	96	98	100	101
93	95	97	99		

LOCOMOTIVES PRESERVED

Date built	Previous owner	Type	Locomotive	Place of preservation
1822	Hetton Colliery	0-4-0		York Railway Museum
1825	Stockton & Darlington	0-4-0	Locomotion	Darlington Bank Top Station
1837	G.W.R.	2-2-2	North Star	Swindon Museum
	Grand Junction	2-2-2	No. 45 Columbine	York Railway Museum
1845	Stockton & Darlington	0-6-0	No. 25 Derwent	Darlington Bank Top Station
1846	Furness	0-4-0	No. 3 Coppernob	Horwich Works
1847	L.N.W.R.	2-2-2	No. 173 Cornwall	Crewe Works
1857	Wantage Tramway	0-4-0WT	No. 5 Shannon	Wantage Road Station
1865	L.N.W.R.	18" gauge 0-4-0T	Pet	Crewe Works
1865	L.N.W.R.	0-4-0ST	No. 1439	Crewe Works
1866	M.R.	2-4-0 Class 1	No. 158A	Derby Works
1866	Metropolitan	4-4-0T Class A	No. 23	Clapham Museum
1868	South Devon	Broad gauge 0-4-0T	Tiny	Newton Abbot Station
1869	N.E.R.	2-2-4T	No. 66 Aerolite	York Railway Museum
1870	G.N.R.	4-2-2	No. 1	York Railway Museum
1872	Metropolitan	0-4-0 Tram Locomotive	No. 807	Clapham Museum
1874	N.E.R.	0-6-0	No. 1275	York Railway Museum
1875	N.E.R.	2-4-0 901 Class	No. 910	York Railway Museum
1880	L.B.S.C.R.	0-6-0T Class A	No. 82 Boxhill	Clapham Museum
1882	L.B.S.C.R.	0-4-2 Class B1	No. 214 Gladstone	York Railway Museum
1885	Mersey Railway	0-6-4T	No. 5 Cecil Raikes	Derby Works
1885	N.E.R.	2-4-0 1463 Class	No. 1463	York Railway Museum
1886	C.R.	4-2-2	No. 123	
1889	L.Y.R.	2-4-2T Class K2	No. 1008	Horwich Works

Date built	Previous owner	Type	Locomotive	Place of preservation
1892	L.N.W.R.	2-4-0 'Precedent' Class	No. 790 *Hardwicke*	Crewe Works
1893	N.E.R.	4-4-0 Class M1	No. 1621	York Railway Museum
1893	L.S.W.R.	4-4-0 Class T3	No. 563	Clapham Museum
1893	Shropshire & Montgomeryshire	0-4-0WT	*Gazelle*	Longmoor
1894	H.R.	4-6-0	No. 103	
1895	G.E.R.	2-4-0 Class T26	No. 490	Clapham Museum
1897	G.W.R.	0-6-0 2301 Class	No. 2516	Swindon Museum
1898	G.N.R.	4-4-2	No. 990 *Henry Oakley*	York Railway Museum
1899	M.R.	4-2-2 115 Class	No. 118	Derby Works
1899	L.S.W.R.	4-4-0 Class T9	No. 120	
1901	S.E.C.R.	4-4-0 Class D	No. 737	Clapham Museum
1902	M R.	4-4-0 Class 4	No. 1000	Derby Works
1902	G.N.R.	4-4-2 Class C1	No. 251	York Railway Museum
1903	G.W.R.	4-4-0 'City' Class	No. 3717 *City of Truro*	Swindon Museum
1904	G.E.R	0-6-0T Class S56	No. 87	Clapham Museum
1907	G.W.R.	4-6-0 'Star' Class	No. 4003 *Lode Star*	Swindon Museum
1909	L.T.S.R.	4-4-2T 79 Class	No. 80 *Thundersley*	Derby Works
1913	N.B.R.	4-4-0 'Glen' Class	No. 256 *Glen Douglas*	
1920	G.N.S.R.	4-4-0 Class F	No. 49 *Gordon Highlander*	
1920	G.C.R.	4-4-0 Class 11F	No. 506 *Butler-Henderson*	Clapham Museum
1923	G.W.R.	4-6-0 'Castle' Class	No. 4073 *Caerphilly Castle*	Science Museum, London
1938	L.N.E.R.	4-6-2 Class A4	No. 4468 *Mallard*	Clapham Museum
1947	G.W.R.	0-6-0PT 94XX Class	No. 9400	Swindon Museum

L.S.W.R. Class T3 4-4-0 No. 563 (now preserved in L.S.W.R. livery)
[Locomotive Publishing Co.

M.R. 115 Class 4-2-2 No. 118
[R. J. Buckley

G.W.R. 4073 Class 4-6-0 No. 4073 *Caerphilly Castle*
[Locomotive Publishing Co.

LOCOMOTIVES SCHEDULED FOR PRESERVATION

Date built	Previous owner	Type	Locomotive
1874	L.S.W.R.	2-4-0WT 0298 Class	
1891	N.E.R.	0-6-0 Class C	No. 1576 (*65099)
1897	L.S.W.R.	0-4-4T Class M7	
1898	H.R.	4-4-0 'Small Ben' Class	No. 2 *Ben Alder* (*54398)
1903	G.W.R.	2-8-0 28XX Class	
1911	G.C.R.	2-8-0 Class O4	*No. 63601
1919	N.E.R.	0-8-0 Class T3	*No. 63460
1921	L.N.W.R.	0-8-0 Class G2	
1924	L.M.S.	0-6-0 Class 4F	
1925	S.R.	4-6-0 'King Arthur' Class	*No. 30777 *Sir Lamiel*
1926	S.R.	4-6-0 'Lord Nelson' Class	*No. 30850 *Lord Nelson*
1926	L.M.S.	2-6-0 Class 5	
1927	G.W.R.	4-6-0 'King' Class	No. 6000 *King George V*
1930	S.R.	4-4-0 'Schools' Class	*No. 30925 *Cheltenham*
1934	L.M.S.	4-6-0 Class 5	
1935	L.M.S.	2-6-4T Class 4 (3-cyl.)	No. 2500
1936	L.N.E.R.	2-6-2 Class V2	No. 4771 *Green Arrow*
1937	L.M.S.	4-6-2 Class 7P	No. 6235 *City of Birmingham*
1942	S.R.	0-6-0 Class Q1	
1945	S.R.	4-6-2 'West Country' Class	
1951	B.R.	4-6-2 Class 7	No. 70000 *Britannia*
1954	B.R.	4-6-2 Class 8	No. 71000 *Duke of Gloucester*
1956	B.R.	4-6-0 Class 5 (with Caprotti valve gear)	
1960	B.R.	2-10-0 Class 9	No. 92220 *Evening Star*

*B.R. number. Withdrawn from service but not yet restored for preservation.

L.N.E.R. Class Q7 (N.E.R. Class T3) 0-8-0 No. 63460 *[R. Puntis*

S.R. Class LN 4-6-0 No. 30850 *Lord Nelson* *[P. J. Hughes*

B.R. Standard Class 8P 4-6-2 No. 71000 *Duke of Gloucester* *[British Railways*

PULLMAN CARS RUNNING ON BRITISH RAILWAYS

K—Kitchen Car
B—Brake
P—Parlour Car

LOCOMOTIVE HAULED CARS
First Class

ADRIAN	(K)	HERON	(K)	PERSEUS	(P)
AMBER	(P)	IBIS	(K)	PHOENIX	(P)
AMETHYST	(P)	IONE	(K)	PHYLLIS	(K)
AQUILA	(K)	ISLE OF THANET	(B)	PLATO	(K)
ARIES	(K)	JOAN	(P)	RAVEN	(K)
BELINDA	(K)	LORAINE	(K)	ROBIN	(K)
CARINA	(K)	LUCILLE	(P)	RUBY	(P)
CYGNUS	(P)	LYDIA	(K)	SHEILA	(P)
DIAMOND BAR	(K)	MAGPIE	(K)	SNIPE	(K)
EAGLE	(K)	MINERVA	(B)	STORK	(K)
EMERALD	(P)	NILAR	(K)	SWIFT	(K)
EUNICE	(P)	OCTAVIA	(K)	THELMA	(K)
EVADNE	(K)	OPAL	(P)	THRUSH	(K)
FALCON	(K)	ORION	(K)	TOPAZ	(P)
FINCH	(K)	PEARL	(P)	URSULA	(P)
GARNET	(P)	PEGASUS BAR		WREN	(K)
HAWK	(K)	PENELOPE	(K)	ZENA	(P)
HERCULES	(P)				

Second Class

Car No. 27	(B)	Car No. 76	(P)	Car No. 337	(K)
,, ,, 33	(K)	,, ,, 77	(B)	,, ,, 338	(K)
,, ,, 34	(P)	,, ,, 78	(B)	,, ,, 339	(K)
,, ,, 36	(B)	,, ,, 79	(B)	,, ,, 340	(K)
,, ,, 54	(B)	,, ,, 80	(B)	,, ,, 341	(K)
,, ,, 55	(B)	,, ,, 81	(B)	,, ,, 342	(K)
,, ,, 60	(K)	,, ,, 82	(B)	,, ,, 343	(K)
,, ,, 61	(K)	,, ,, 83	(P)	,, ,, 344	(K)
,, ,, 62	(B)	,, ,, 84	(P)	,, ,, 345	(K)
,, ,, 63	(B)	,, ,, 105	(K)	,, ,, 346	(K)
,, ,, 64	(P)	,, ,, 106	(K)	,, ,, 347	(P)
,, ,, 65	(B)	,, ,, 107	(K)	,, ,, 348	(P)
,, ,, 67	(B)	,, ,, 208	(B)	,, ,, 349	(P)
,, ,, 68	(B)	,, ,, 303	(K)	,, ,, 350	(P)
,, ,, 69	(B)	,, ,, 332	(K)	,, ,, 351	(P)
,, ,, 70	(B)	,, ,, 333	(K)	,, ,, 352	(P)
,, ,, 71	(B)	,, ,, 334	(K)	,, ,, 353	(P)
,, ,, 72	(B)	,, ,, 335	(K)	,, ,, 354 *Hadrian Bar*	
,, ,, 75	(P)	,, ,, 336	(K)		

First Class Pullman Car *Falcon*   [*P. J. Sharpe*

Brake second Pullman Car No. 80   [*D. L. Percival*

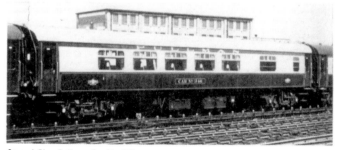

Second Class Pullman Car No. 346   [*P. J. Sharpe*

ELECTRIC MULTIPLE-UNIT CARS

First Class

AUDREY	(K)	GWEN	(K)	MONA	(K)
DORIS	(K)	HAZEL	(K)	VERA	(K)

Second Class

Car No. 85	(P)	Car No. 88	(B)	Car No. 91	(B)
,, ,, 86	(P)	,, ,, 89	(B)	,, ,, 92	(B)
,, ,, 87	(P)	,, ,, 90	(B)	,, ,, 93	(B)

Composite First and Second Class

ALICE	(K)	ETHEL	(K)	NAOMI	(K)
ANNE	(K)	GRACE	(K)	OLIVE	(K)
BERTHA	(K)	GWLADYS	(K)	PEGGY	(K)
BRENDA	(K)	IDA	(K)	RITA	(K)
CLARA	(K)	IRIS	(K)	ROSE	(K)
DAISY	(K)	JOYCE	(K)	RUTH	(K)
ELINOR	(K)	LORNA	(K)	VIOLET	(K)
ENID	(K)	MAY	(K)		

First published 1964
Reprinted 2008

ISBN (10) 0 7110 3315 3
ISBN (19) 978 0 7110 3315 3

Published by Ian Allan Publishing

an imprint of Ian Allan Publishing Ltd, Hersham, Surrey, KT12 4RG.

Printed by Ian Allan Printing Ltd, Hersham, Surrey, KT12 4RG.

Code: 0801/B

Visit the Ian Allan Publishing Website at
www.ianallanpublishing.com
Cover images reproduced courtesy of Colour-Rail